Design is the process of adding valu
Design is a fundamental shared exp
Design is everywhere.

Explore human-centric design frameworks
independent of exclusive institutions and
industry categories.

Ask what design can do for communities
by creating conversations that are
transdisciplinary and intergenerational.

Seek to uncover meaningful narratives,
connections, and patterns that might help
us better understand our histories and
imagine our futures.

Deem Journal

"Space is quantifiable. It can be measured,
manufactured, and manipulated. Place is qualitative.
It is harder to measure a shared experience or feeling.
Place exists in and through relationships, values,
and culture and is facilitated via human exchange."

—Nu Goteh, Co-Founder/Creative Director

"In a perfect world, space and place work together
to make sure that people not only belong, but
belong together."

—Marquise Stillwell, Co-Founder/Contributor

Issue Four

CONTENTS

"We are born and have our being in a place of memory. We chart our lives by everything we remember from the mundane moment to the majestic. We know ourselves through the art and act of remembering."

—bell hooks, *Belonging: A Culture of Place* (1990)

We wish to start this letter with an expression of gratitude for the life and work of the late bell hooks, who passed away shortly after the release of our last issue. The intellectual place that she created and cultivated has been a refuge for us, and will undoubtedly remain so for all those who continue to discover her ideas.

Place, which is the guiding concept of this issue of *Deem*, is so fundamental to human culture and society that the practice and philosophy of making it is as ancient and varied as history.

So, rather than beginning with a statement or belief, this time we will pose a question. How do people make place from spatial experiences? In other words, how does space come to contain meaning, significance, sentiment, feeling?

As a design journal, thinking about the words "place" and "making" together brought up the popular term *placemaking*, which, though not the crux of our investigation, did offer some points of departure.

Nearly 60 years ago, Jane Jacobs and William H. Whyte developed a framework for an emerging set of priorities around urban planning: intentional building and design practices that would help to enculturate community by using public space to connect people through the experience of sharing it. This movement became known as placemaking, and offered a new approach to thinking about the social dimensions of a built environment.

Placemaking also reflected a much longer tradition of European and Marxist philosophy, notably distilled in French scholar Henri Lefebvre's books *The Production of Space* (1974) and *The Critique of Everyday Life* (1947, 1961, 1981), in which he argued that space is produced through human interaction and, under capitalism, is measured by the use values of time and productivity.

Of course, the relationship between space and place cannot be defined, contained, or accredited to any particular canon, but we wanted to acknowledge one pathway for how these ideas have been historicized in ways that remain relevant for architects, urban planners, and designers today.

In the decades since Jacobs and Whyte's foundational work, the word "placemaking," and the historical and ethical concerns it implies, have been increasingly appropriated as marketing terminology to appease a variety of corporate interests under the pretense of community wellbeing. Much has been thought and written about this shift, and it is hardly surprising within the incentive structures of our late capitalist world.

Our intent with our fourth issue is to extend an investigation of place beyond the scope of design, architecture, and planning altogether, while acknowledging the potential power of language both to liberate and to commodify.

We wonder if place—and its making—do not need to be theorized here, but rather explored as an open-ended and highly subjective set of social relations, while also considering new types of place that are emerging from newly recognized needs, as well as from the new types of space enabled by the internet, the digital, and the virtual.

We are honored to have visionary artist Theaster Gates on our cover, who shared a very special conversation with two of our founders around place as the connecting thread in his practice.

We also welcomed points of view from a range of contributors, just a few of whom include: Doreen Chan, who shared her study of dreams; Cara Page and Sasha Constanza-Chock, who brought with them the lenses of care, access, and disability justice; Valencia Gunder, who explained her approach to education and empowerment work around the crisis of climate gentrification; Ramsay Taum, a cultural steward of native Hawaiian values who articulated a powerful framework for understanding what place is and who we are within it; and the children of the Bay Area's Mycelium Youth Network, who poignantly visualized what place means to them. These are but a few of the perspectives shared here, among them personal essays, reflections, and interventions from a number of artists and thinkers we admire.

A recurring sentiment that arose from these contributors—who, as always, represent many life experiences, professions, interests, and identities—is that place is not made for or on behalf of someone else. Place is the product of experience, and is deeply personal in its significance and interpretation.

Another feeling that emerged in these pages is grief. Place offers a sense of stability, belonging, and oneness with our environment and the other beings that inhabit it. To think about place at this moment in time is also to contend with the circumstances and challenges we are living through—climate change, ecological disaster, geopolitical strife, gentrification. It is to face unprecedented uncertainty and process immeasurable longing and loss. Dis*plac*ement is but one of the consequences we will face as we collectively reckon with how to bring our communities, neighborhoods, cities, and planet into the future. We hope the words and pictures in this issue will make this felt, and we thank you, as always, for being here with us.

Alice Grandoit-Šutka
Editor-in-chief

Isabel Flower
Executive Editor

Alexis Aceves Garcia
Managing Editor

SACRA
LIZED
SPACE

Theaster Gates on
the Practice of Placemaking

A portrait of Theaster Gates.
The photographs that accompany this story
were taken at the St. Laurence Elementary
School on Chicago's South Side.

06

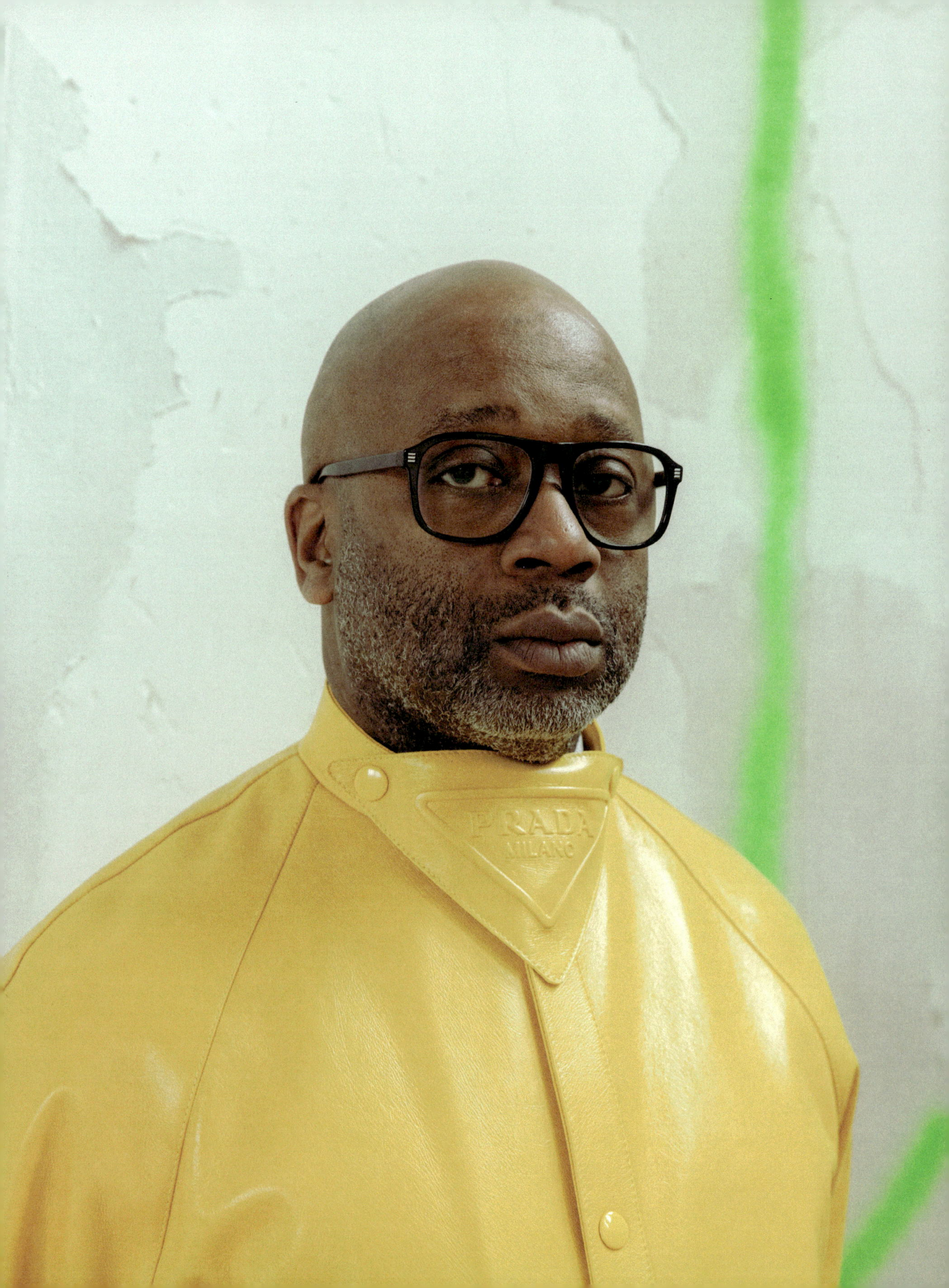

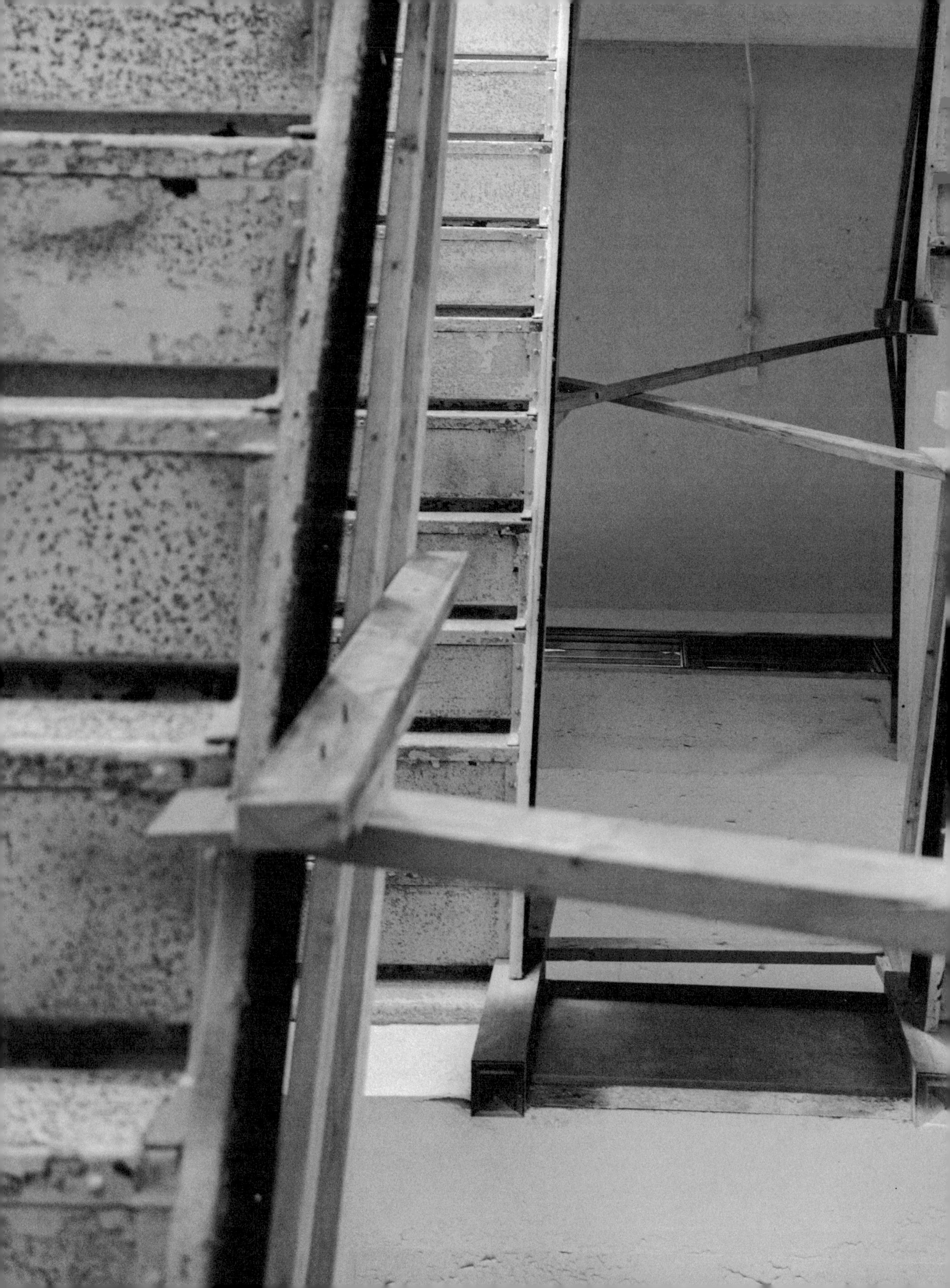

Moderated by
Alice Grandoit-Šutka
& Nu Goteh

Photography by
Nolis Anderson

ALICE GRANDOIT-ŠUTKA   Our fourth issue of *Deem* is centered around the theme and concept of place. What does place mean to you? How do you consider space differently from place?

THEASTER GATES   Place. It's the ability to locate oneself where one belongs. Place is the manifestation of care. With location alone, you've got space. With location and familiarity, intention and love, you've got place. I think that the work that I'm involved in is constantly trying to bring intention, beauty, and love back to location.

AGS   How might one sense the differentiation between the two?

TG   When I was studying at the University of Cape Town, I worked with a gentleman named David Chidester. He taught a kind of psychology of space, as well as theories on religious space. We were thinking about traditional African religious space in particular.

The question was, within a community, how do you sacralize a space or, in other words, how do you convert it from a space to a place? His theory revolved around a leader. The person says that they believe the space in question is sacred or could become sacred in the future. Then, a community of people gather around that person and say, "We believe with you that the space that you've identified could become sacred." The first thing they do is clean the space. Then they designate the space by drawing a circle or forming some kind of edge, so that sacred things can happen inside the perimeter, and non-sacred things can happen adjacent to and outside of the perimeter. Once this process is complete, they begin to do sacred work. They sing, they dance, they move, they make sounds, they express themselves in the space, and then they wait for something sacred to happen. They wait on God to show up. They wait on the spirits to descend. But they action, they labor, until God becomes present.

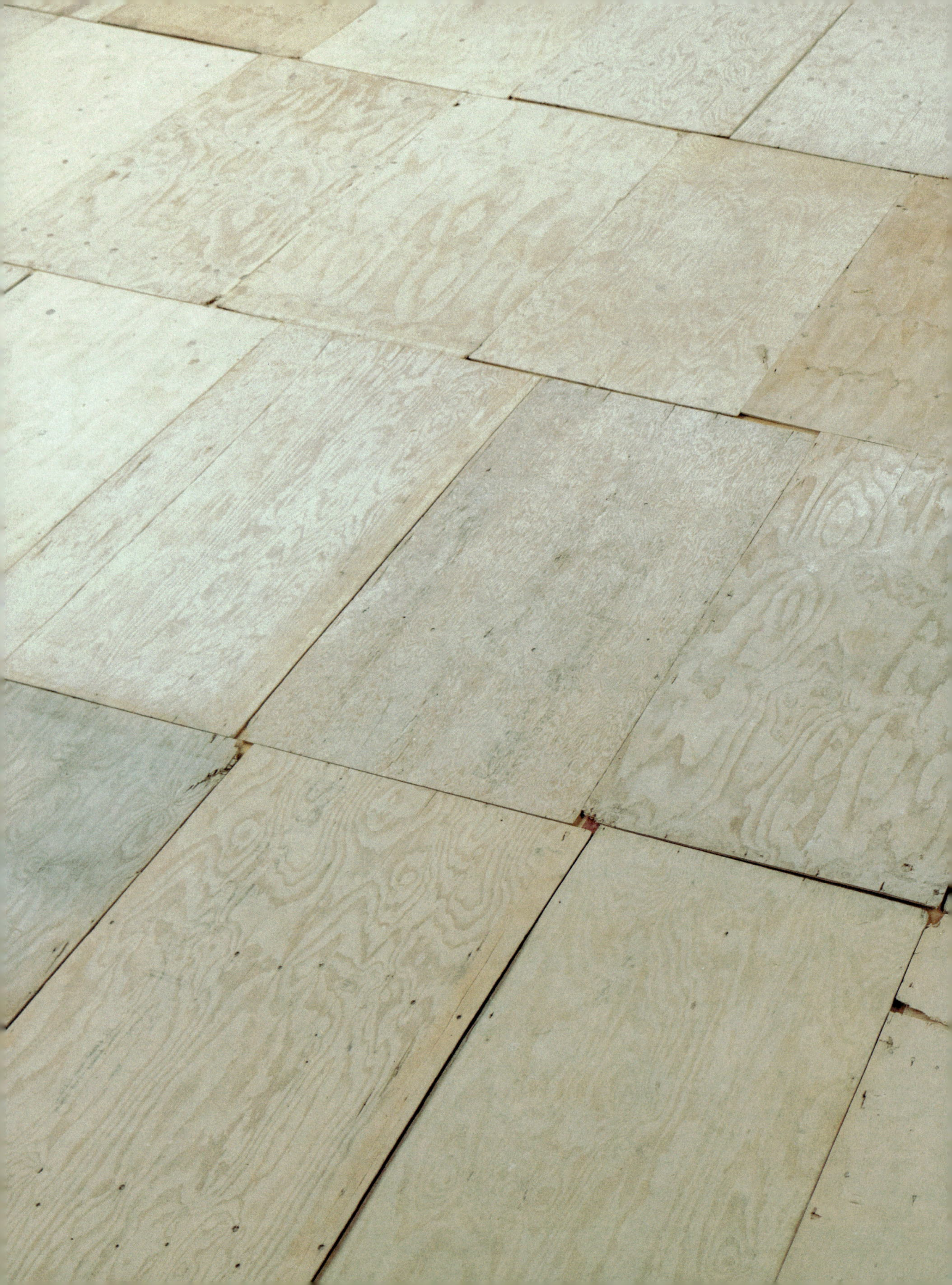

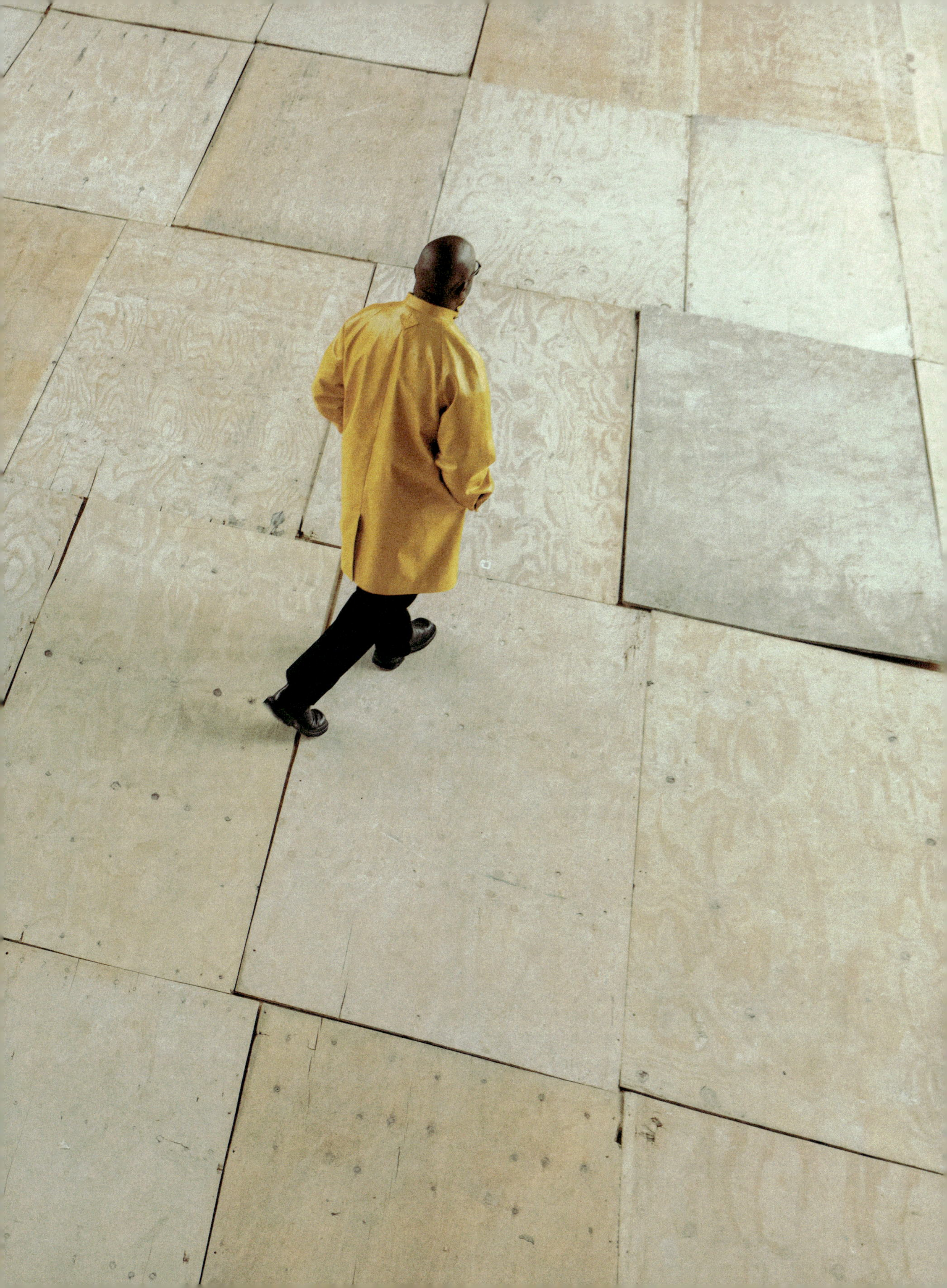

I think when I came back to the South Side of Chicago, I was entering a place that I could tell had been sacred but was no longer deemed as such. Then I said, "I believe that this space could be sacred," and the people around me agreed, "We believe with you." Then I started cleaning. Then we stepped into the perimeter and started laboring. And when God showed up, it seemed like others showed up, then institutions showed up, then resources showed up. And when those institutions and resources showed up, those things also conferred that the space had become sacred.

NU GOTEH   You've been described as a "social practice installation artist," meaning that you work directly with people and communities rather than only depicting, imaging, or speaking about them. This is quite unconventional within the art world and industry that you are also a part of and, unlike the tradition of "relational aesthetics"—which contained these interactions within art world contexts and places—the social networks you work within are based in the real world. Why is it so important that social practice be the crux of your work? Did any particular experiences or inspirations push you in this direction?

First and foremost, I feel like an artist who makes things. Then, I feel like an artist who believes in people. What's interesting about this moment— or this last decade—is that art history has started to *exhume* the social aspects of artists from their actual practices. I think artists have always been engaged in social practices and relational aesthetics. There was just no name for it. But just because there was no name or taxonomy doesn't mean this didn't exist. I think art history has done a trick, so that now we seem to believe that just by being social, we're being artful, which is reasonable, I suppose.

I feel like Black artists especially have the burden of "cousins," and I've had this conversation with other artists of color. Would we be greater if we were selfish? Would we be ostracized for our autonomous influence if we weren't spreading the love? Or is the guilt more an internal conundrum where the Black artist feels that he or she must bring along the entire South Side of the city of Chicago on their boots, on their coattails—that there is no me without *we*?

TG   The crux of my work is a hunger and thirst for meaning and the capacity to make meaning. And that capacity to make meaning splits itself, if you will—splits itself between things that happen in the studio and things that happen outside of the studio. I had never imagined myself as an artist of or within relational aesthetics, but I know that Black people are relational. I've got a good relationship with my family. I got homies and, in a way, I have a sufferable disease that deals with the desire to be connected, to be loved, and to love. And so, rather than bifurcate my life between object-making and seemingly more social activities, I ball it all up together. In some ways, it's the success of my object-based practice that has allowed my sociability to become so evident in the world. That is, I would not have a bank if it was not for my Tar Paintings. I would not have a cafe if it wasn't for my Civil Tapestries. There would be less free, cultural activity if I wasn't deeply engaged in the creation of beauty through objects. Let's say that.

The truth is I've benefited greatly from the social aspects of my work. The Stony Island Arts Bank is the love of my life. The activity that happens in the Arts Bank, the Retreat at Currency Exchange Café, and the Black Artists Retreat—these moments—they've defined who I am, in a way. And I'm talking about what I do in a day. I feel fortunate that I get to wake up in the morning with a love for object-making and a love for people, while also having strategies and platforms whereby those things play out. But when I try to remember where I started, it had something to do with the desire for meaningfulness. And that meaningfulness needed pathways.

AGS   According to architectural theories that arose in the 1960s, "placemaking" involves intentional building and design practices that enculturate community by using space to connect people through the experience of sharing it. You are involved in a variety of public projects that engage such priorities, such as the Dorchester Projects and, the aforementioned love of your life, the Stony Island Arts

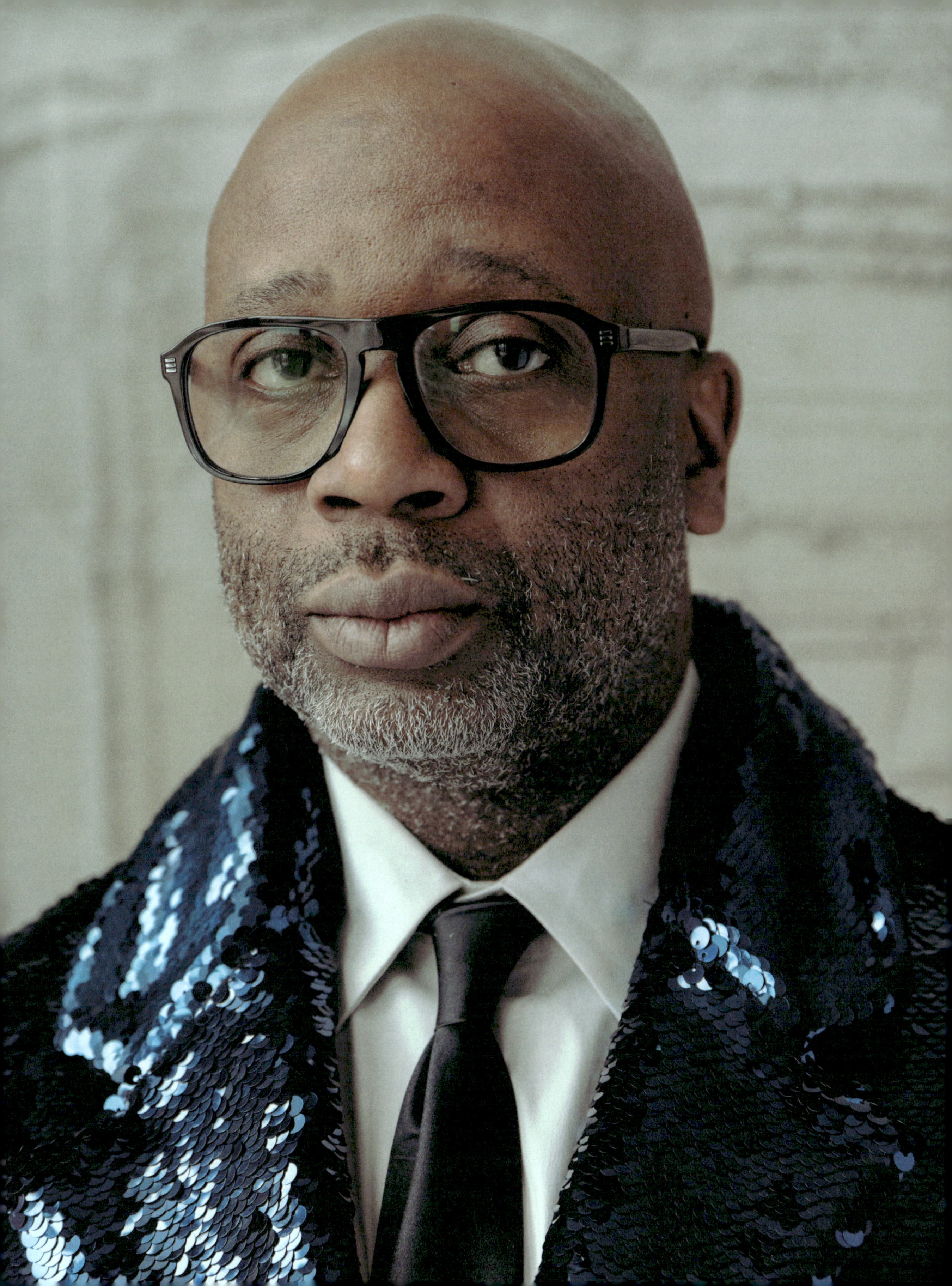

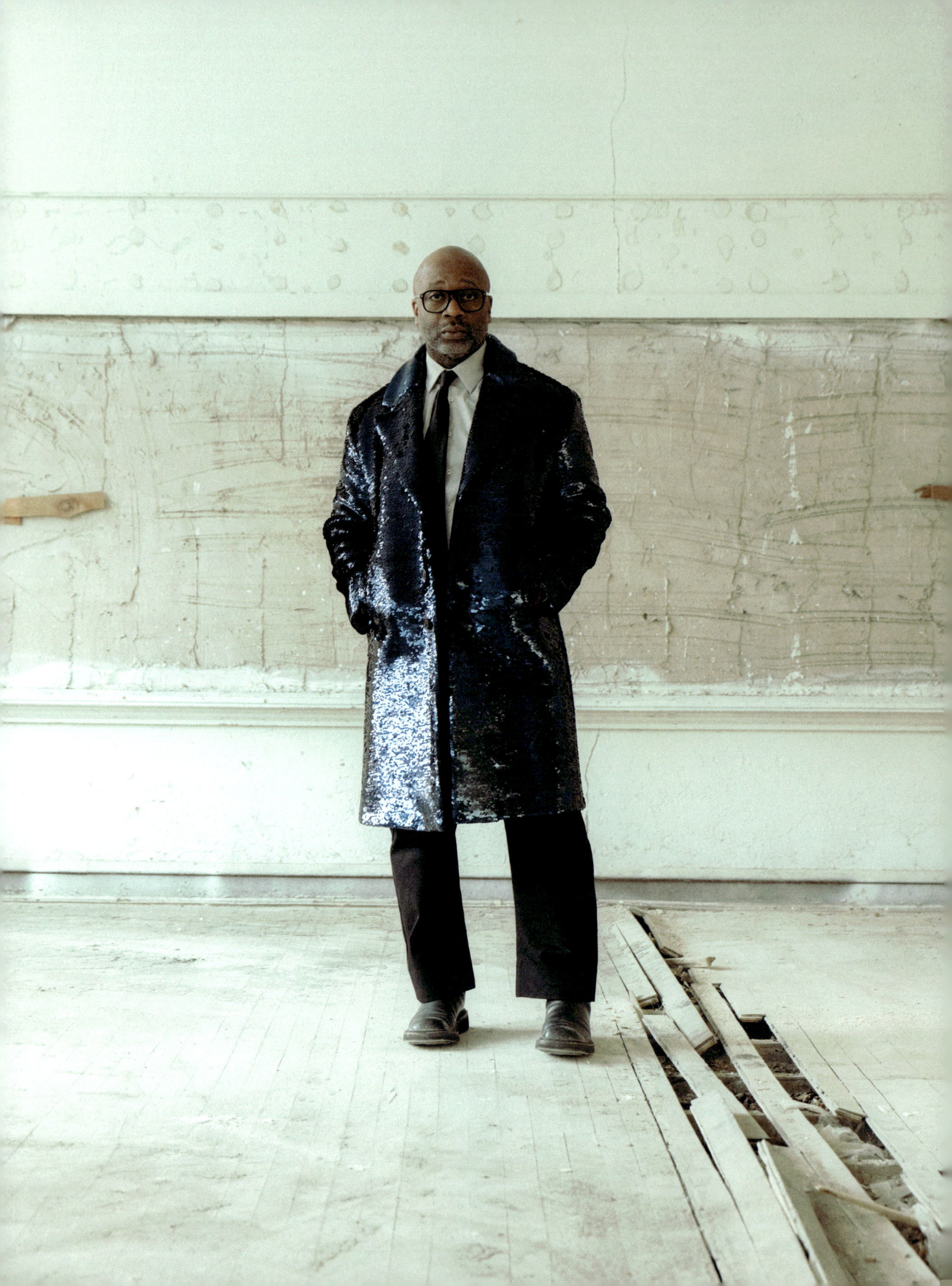

Bank. We'd love to take the Rebuild Foundation, your community development model, as a starting point. What are some strategies that you apply in this kind of work? What have you learned in this process?

TG   Alice, what's so great about this conversation is that I haven't really had to take a whole lot of time to think about how to build community. Theories around being together are already acknowledging a kind of dysfunction in the social order. But does one need theories around how to be with each other? There's a part of me that feels like some of these things, as profound as they might seem, are actually an extension of our nature, and I feel strange about giving strategy to something extremely natural.

Let's talk about Dorchester. I was broke. I was not professionally engaged in the contemporary art community, so I would host events at my house. My events are probably one iota of fun in comparison to the rent parties my brothers-in-law and my sisters hosted in the '80s. A rent party was the equivalent of the Taste of Chicago. A block

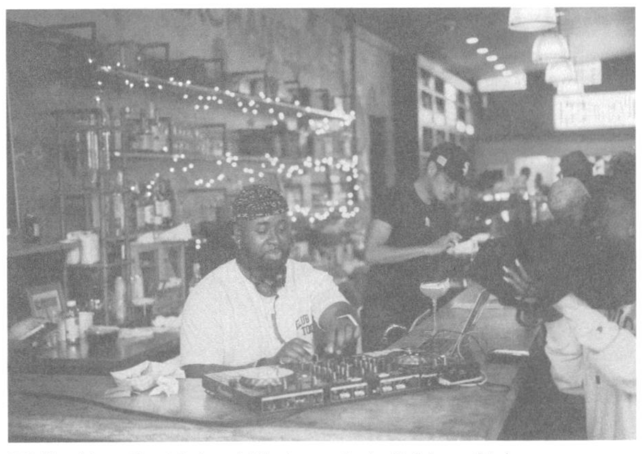

DJ Mike Abrantie at Retreat. Photography by Sulyiman Stokes.

> ## "THEORIES AROUND BEING TOGETHER ARE ALREADY ACKNOWLEDGING A KIND OF DYSFUNCTION IN THE SOCIAL ORDER. BUT DOES ONE NEED THEORIES AROUND HOW TO BE WITH EACH OTHER?"

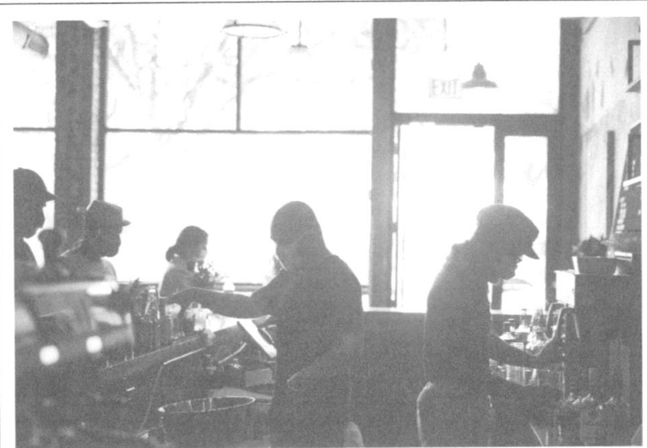

Photography by Chris Strong.

party was like Mardi Gras. When you think about Black sociability—whether it's the mosque, the church, the club, the 4th of July picnic, or the family reunion—Black people know how to get together. The challenge is that we don't always own the space. We don't always own the location of our conviviality. The only thing that I flipped was the incessant need to own the ground beneath us, because it allowed for other kinds of rights. It gave me a certain protection.

I remember, there was an empty lot to the south of my house on Dorchester. I invited a young artist, Devon Mays, to host an event. They erected some teepees, and there was music and a healing activity happening on a lot that was owned by the city. The police came by and they tried to shut me down. I said, "Officer, this is the best thing that's happened on Dorchester in the last 35 years. We are actively keeping bullshit away. The kids are having a great time. They've never seen a teepee before. Please do not shut this down." The officer said, "Sir, do you own this parcel of land?" It was that day that I was like, "Oh, let me buy that. Let me buy that lot."

THEASTER GATES

So I bought that lot. I bought that lot because I didn't want a cop telling me what the fuck I could and couldn't do on my block. Then I bought another lot. Then I bought the house next door and every indication of negative deviance happening in my space. I bought that house and made it a place.

What is placemaking? It is the continual renewal of desacralized Black space into newly sacralized Black space through love and attention and community. Am I a placemaker? I don't need no theories. I like kicking it with people. I like being in love. I like to be loved in my community. I want the people around me to feel like we built a garden together, and that it's as much theirs as it is mine. And I'm also talking about leadership, the impetus of the thing, who gets the party started. I'm the first one on the dance floor. Placemaking is about being willing to be the first one on the dance floor until the whole floor is full.

AGS   Well, I think both Nu and I can relate to this framework, as well as to the types of knowledge one generates within the context of a party or a celebration. That's a big part of how we came together in our early twenties and is a metaphor that we try to bring into our design practices as well.

NG   Let's talk about archiving. Your work also involves the possession and stewardship of several archives that are housed in the Arts Bank, including books that once belonged to *Ebony* and *Jet* founder John H. Johnson, and legendary House DJ Frankie Knuckles's record collection. A part of this issue will also focus on examining how place is created and preserved outside present time. How do you want your archives to function and what do you hope that they can convey?

TG   Most of my things are Black things. I collect these things because I am, again, trying to demonstrate that Black things are important, and that if one practices caring for things, one practices nation-building. If we could build nations, then we could also actively resist and remember the collateral damage that has happened to us over generations. We could remember our whole selves. If we don't retain the objects of our past, if we don't develop a muscle for caring, we'll find ourselves left with the things we're constantly being encouraged to buy. The only semblances we'll have of ourselves will be the semblances that others have made for us.

What an album represents, especially when it's an album that belonged to Frankie Knuckles or Jesse Owens, is evidence that there was a Black person present at the inception of a musical movement—in this case, among the progenitors of House. A collection of objects gives us a material glimpse at someone's brain, and offers us a corpus of their life's activity. It drives me wild to be a curious ally to the

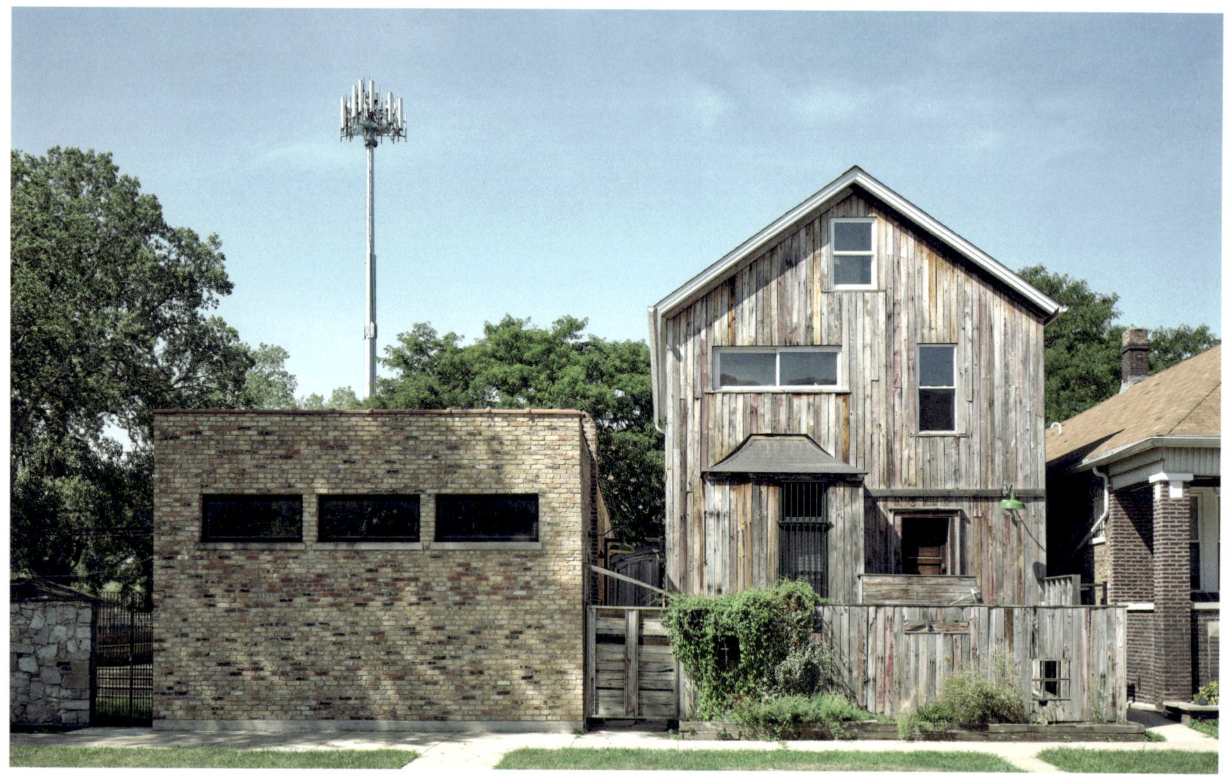

Listening House and Archive House. Photography by Sara Pooley.

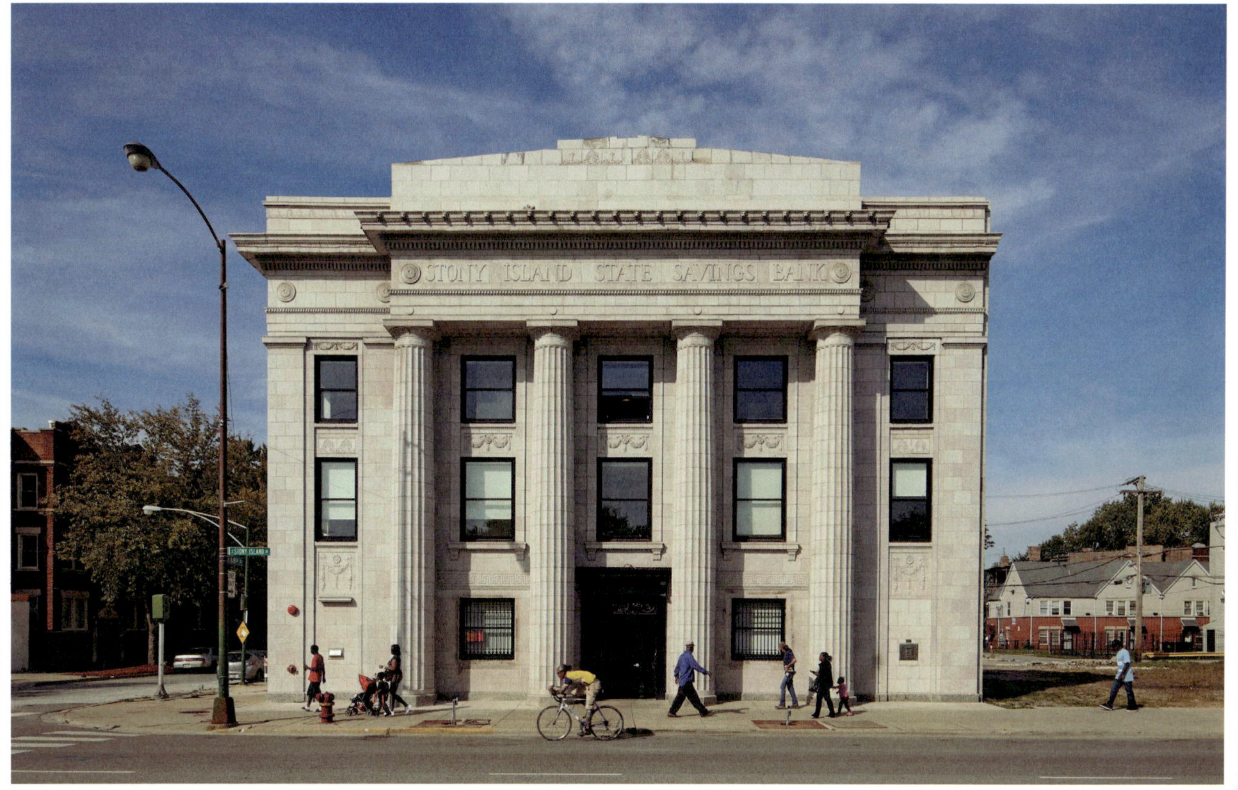

Stony Island Arts Bank. Photograph by Tom Harris. Copyright Hedrich Blessing.

past, and to use these objects to create base knowledge for the future intelligences of people, Black and otherwise. The archive at the Arts Bank also creates a reason, a seductive reason, for people to gather. The only way one can experience the archive is by visiting in person, and coming there brings new energy to and resacralizes the space.

AGS   You are also a trained ceramicist, and much of your early work addresses Japanese ceramic tradition and its intersection with ceramics in Black American culture. You even invented a character—potter and Mississippi resident Shoji Yamaguchi—as a parafictional way to express this synchronicity. Could you tell us more about how Japan has influenced your work, and perhaps also your imagination around place?

TG   All my life I've looked for markers of excellence and I've found them everywhere. I visited Japan and was immediately humbled and moved by the intelligence of hand I saw all around me.

I remember one day going to the ceramic workshop where I studied to make what I thought to be a beautiful Japanese tea bowl. The teacher came over to me and said, "What are you doing?" I was like, "I'm making a Japanese tea bowl." And he was like, "Why are you doing that?" And I said, "Because I'm in Japan." Then he was like, "But there are great potters in Mississippi." He was talking about a guy named William (Wild Bill) Ohr. They called him the Mad Potter of Biloxi. He asked me, "Why are you not making Mississippi pots? Why don't you make a Mississippi bowl?" And I was like, I'll be damned! I had to go all the way to Japan to be told I should be making the pots of my people. That's when you know that it's philosophical. It's bigger than the object. For the rest of that trip and long after, I thought to myself, "What kind of bowl do I need for the foods of Black people?" It totally changed my sensibility. I started making a plate with a lip because I needed to get up against something. I can't eat no collard greens on a flat plate—where's the juice going to go?

The idea of Yamaguchi was a way of reconciling a new binary, which is a life ungoverned by the preoccupation with whiteness. In fact, I'm preoccupied with excellence. This framework was another way of working out my Blackness through othering, and specifically self-othering. How do I know myself to be myself?

NG   You have spoken extensively about your ideas around the expanded role of the artist within society, while also making it clear that artists should not be burdened with the responsibility of alleviating injustices in their communities. One thing that affects the artist-community relationship is many artists' perceived need to move away from where

THEASTER GATES

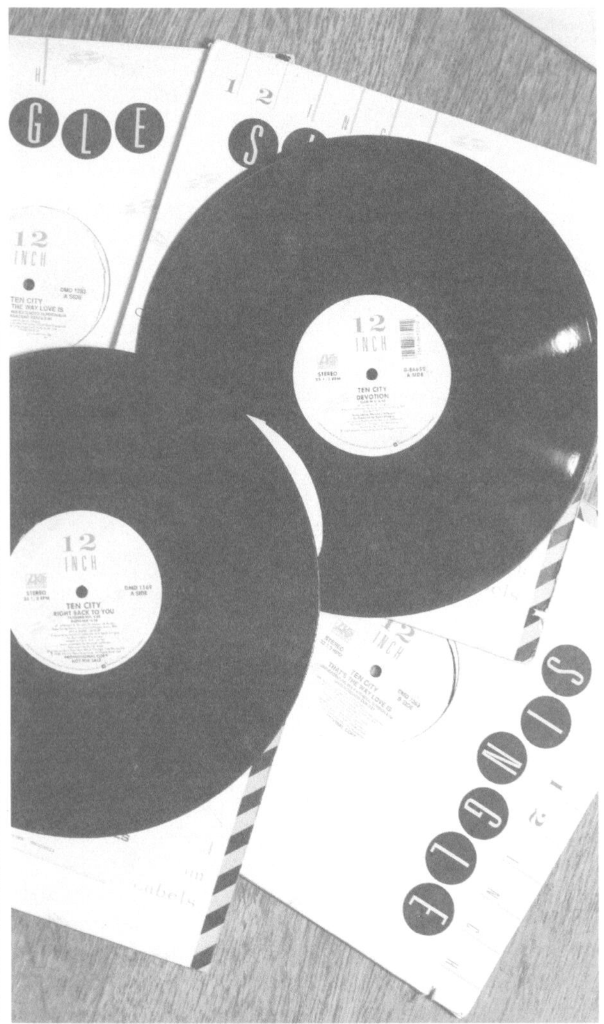

Vinyl from the Frankie Knuckles Vinyl Collection at the Stony Island Arts Bank. Courtesy of Rebuild Foundation.

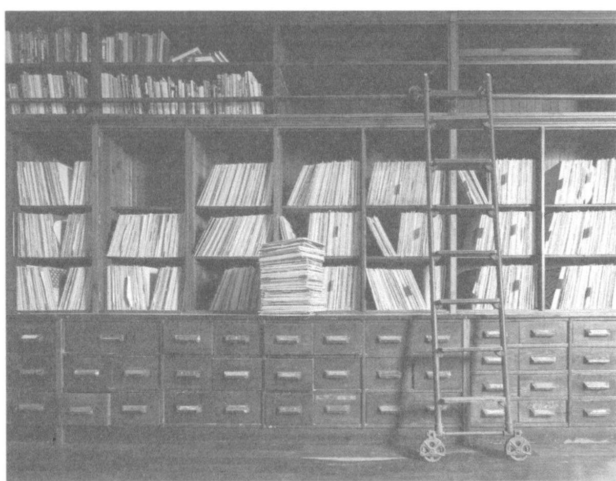

Frankie Knuckles Vinyl Collection at the Stony Island Arts Bank. Courtesy of Rebuild Foundation.

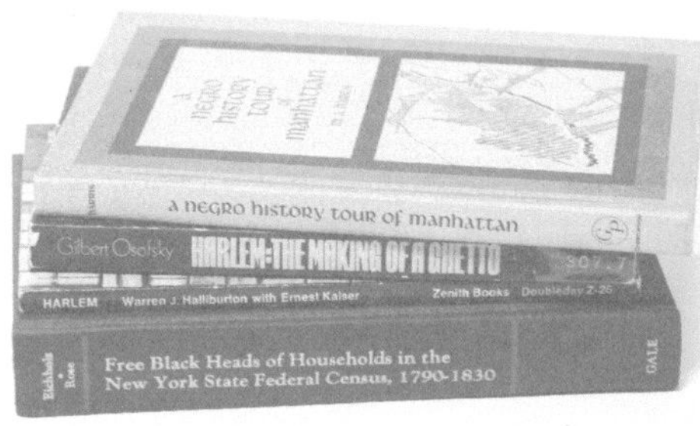

Books from the Ed J. Williams Collection of "Negrobilia" housed at the Stony Island Arts Bank. Courtesy of Rebuild Foundation.

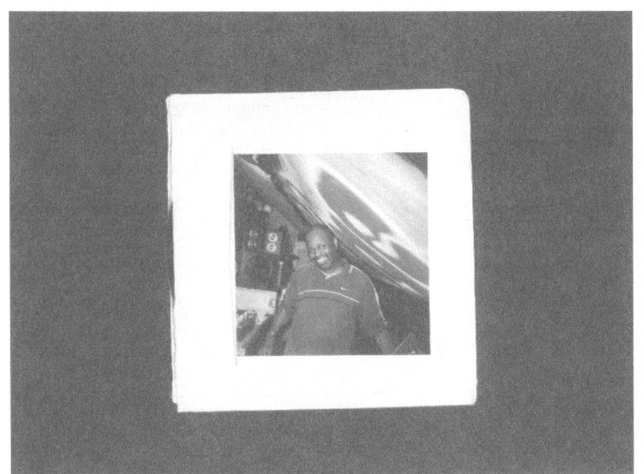

A single glass lantern slide from the collection of over 60,000 University of Chicago glass lantern slides at Rebuild Foundation's Stony Island Arts Bank. Courtesy of Rebuild Foundation.

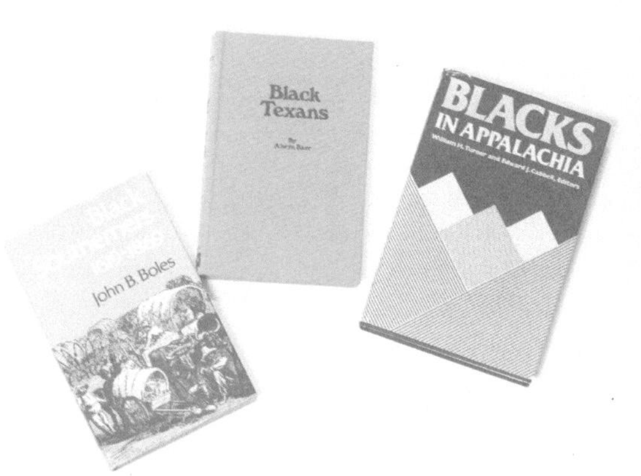

Books from the Johnson Publishing Company Library, one of Rebuild Foundation's four permanent archives at the Stony Island Arts Bank. Courtesy of Rebuild Foundation.

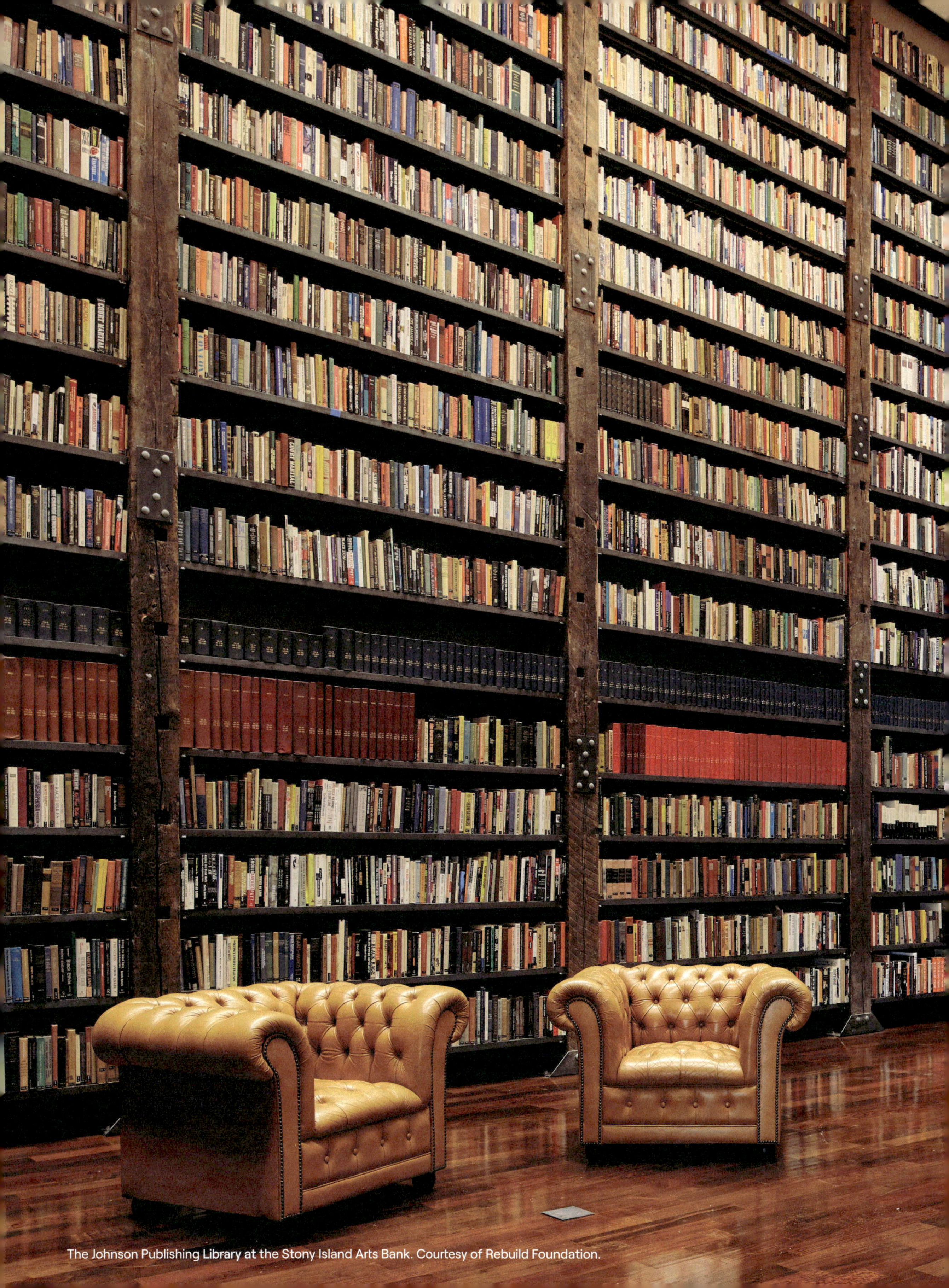

The Johnson Publishing Library at the Stony Island Arts Bank. Courtesy of Rebuild Foundation.

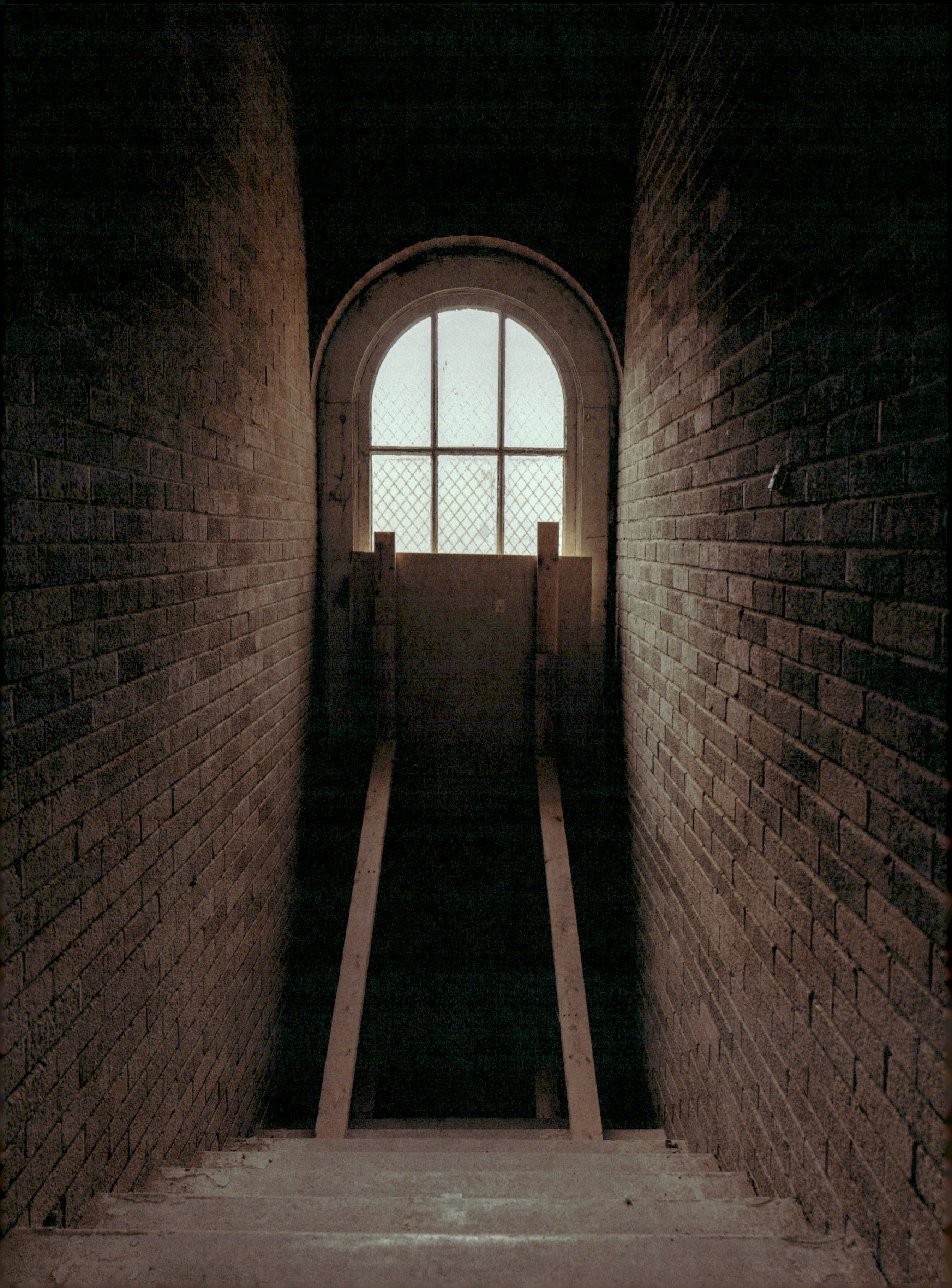

they are from in order to have a successful career or make money from their work. What is the importance of artists' relationship to the place they are in and/or from? Our Issue Two cover story with Lauren Halsey, for example, offered a great blueprint for an incredibly fertile and symbiotic artist-community relationship. What would need to change in order for more artists to feel able to "stay home"?

TG   I love Lauren, and I'd like to make this a little bit of a personal story. There's a generation between Lauren and I, artistically. And then there's a generation between me and, say, Rick Lowe, in terms of artists who stayed in a place and tried to do a thing that was about a place. What we share is a strand of ideology or philosophy that says it's okay to be where you're from and work out of that place as the principal fodder for one's artistic imagination.

I think that, because of individuals like Rick, Gordan Matta-Clark, Donald Judd, Martha Graham, Alain Locke, Mark Bradford, James Turrell, and Gertrude Stein, there have been people over time who understood the power of place. And by anchoring deep down in a place that they're from, or that they choose, they were able to build a world around them. I believe that sensibility is just *in* some people, and I think I have an artistic practice that is rooted in staying—the politics of staying, you might say. I don't think it's the burden of the artist to have to stay anywhere, but the artist has the ability to choose place as a strategy among other tools in their toolkit. And, by choosing place as a kind of artistic imperative, make things happen through it.

If there is anything I could offer young artists, I would say, be boldly where you want to be and really, really *be* there. I feel very fortunate that I was able to work through the trauma of home to be a stronger self.

NG   To close, I'm going off script. Theaster, during our photoshoot earlier this week, I asked you about your choice to be barefoot. Your response, which has stuck with me, was, "I'm country as fuck." We shared a laugh, but the conversation evolved to encapsulate what we each need, as a human, as a Black person, as an artist, to be boldly in our place. Prior to this call, I was telling Alice about that exchange and how often I observe that, when occupying predominantly white spaces, we feel a need to assimilate. Even for safety reasons, we feel we have to fit in. But the conversation that you and I were having was more around imagining, "What starts to happen when I control the space, and the place, and what do I need in order to be boldly there?" Is there anything you would add about how we do that—how we create those opportunities to be boldly ourselves?

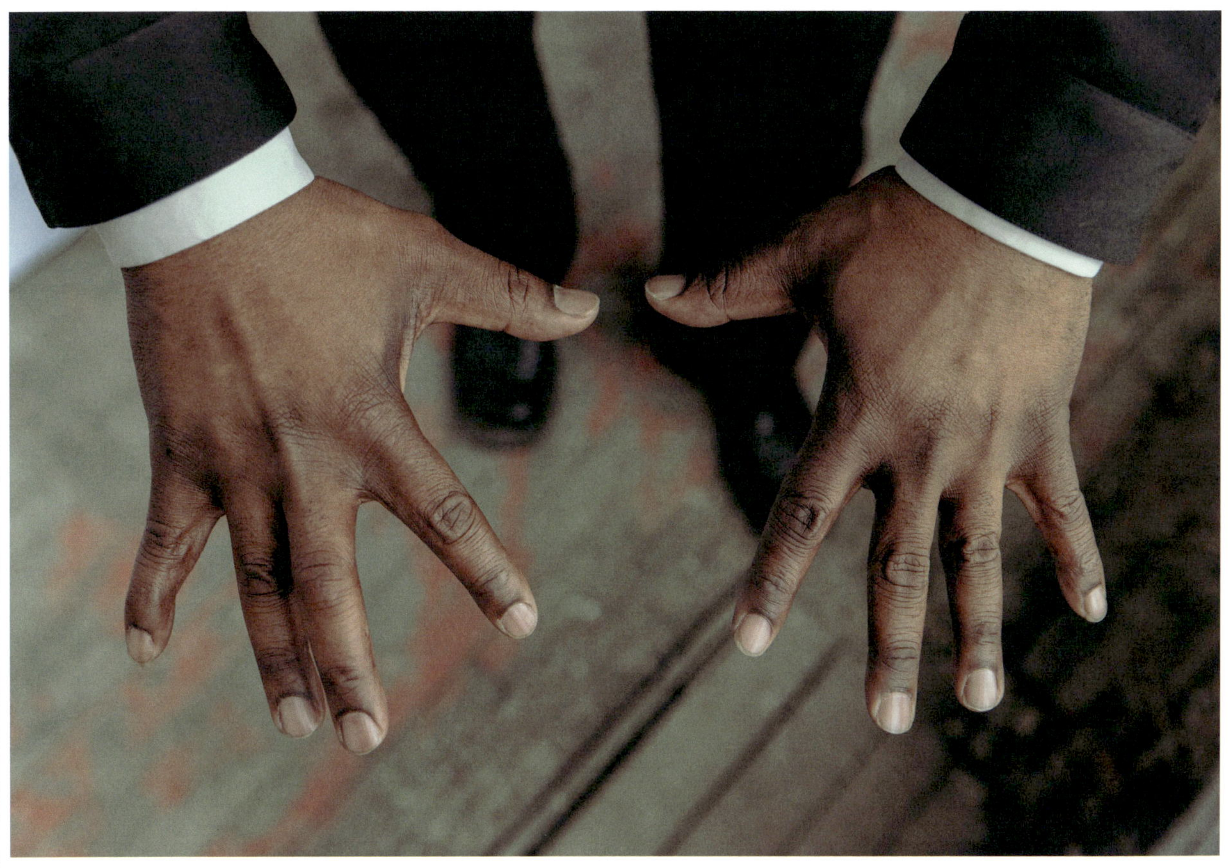

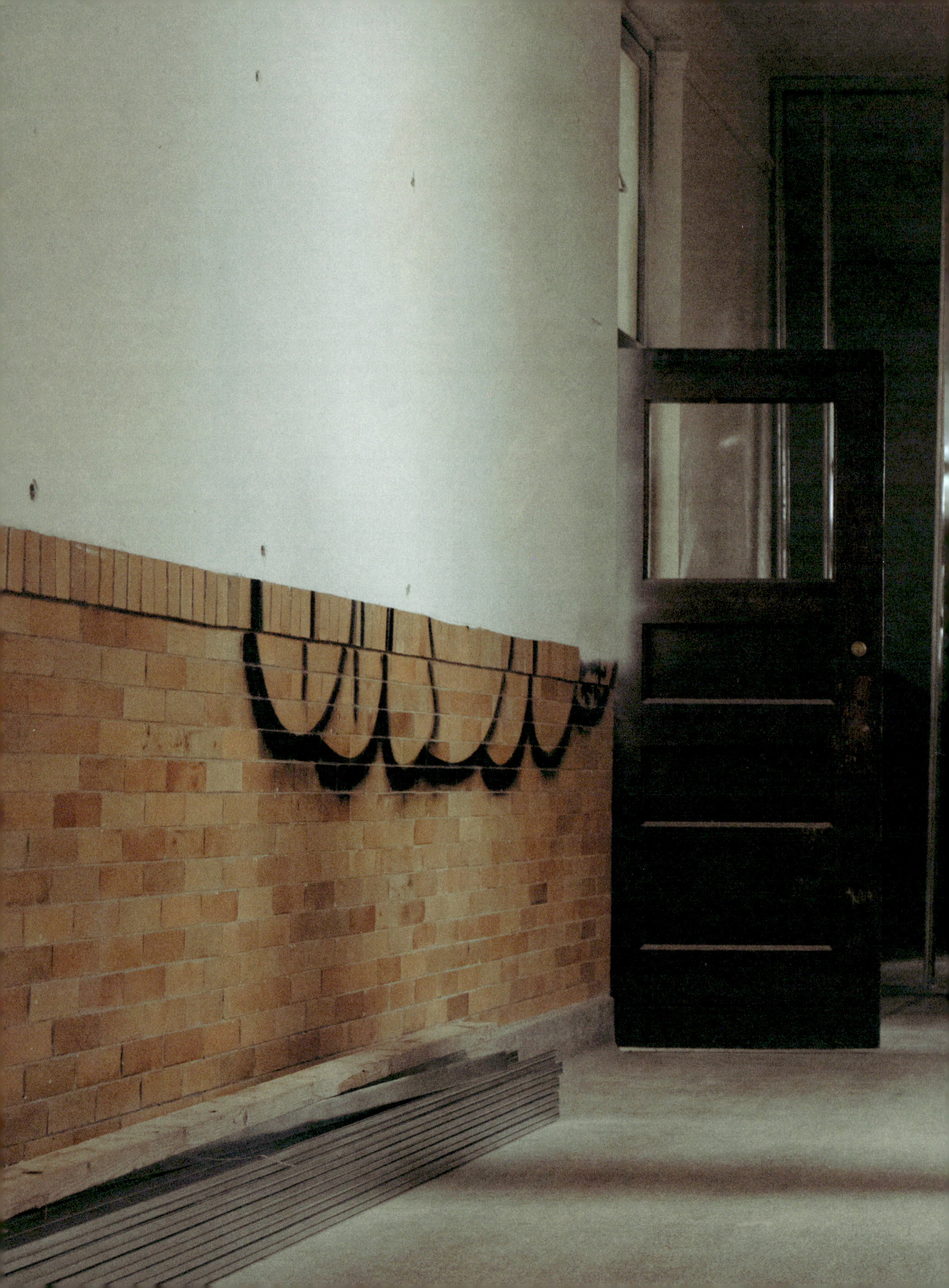

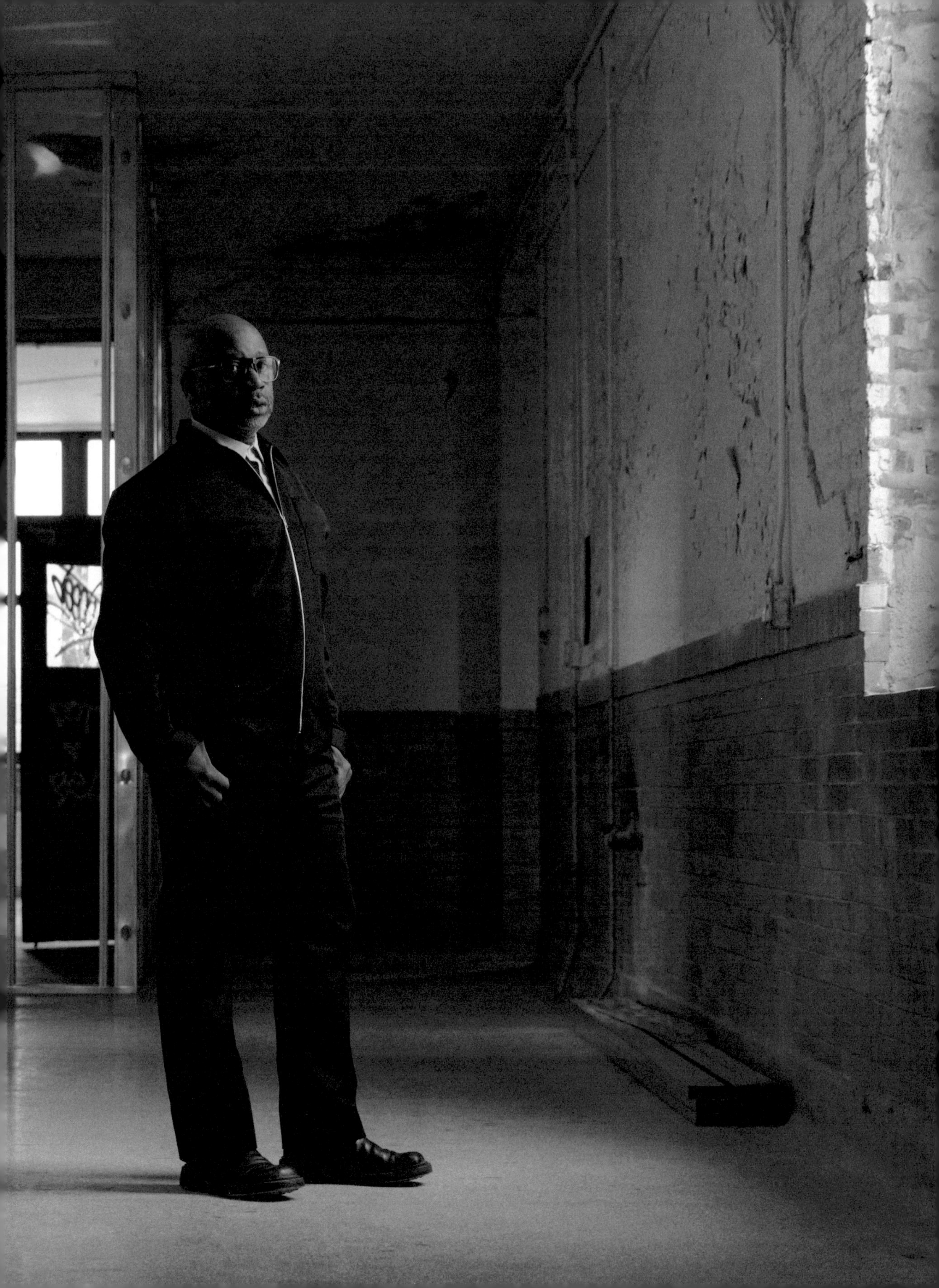

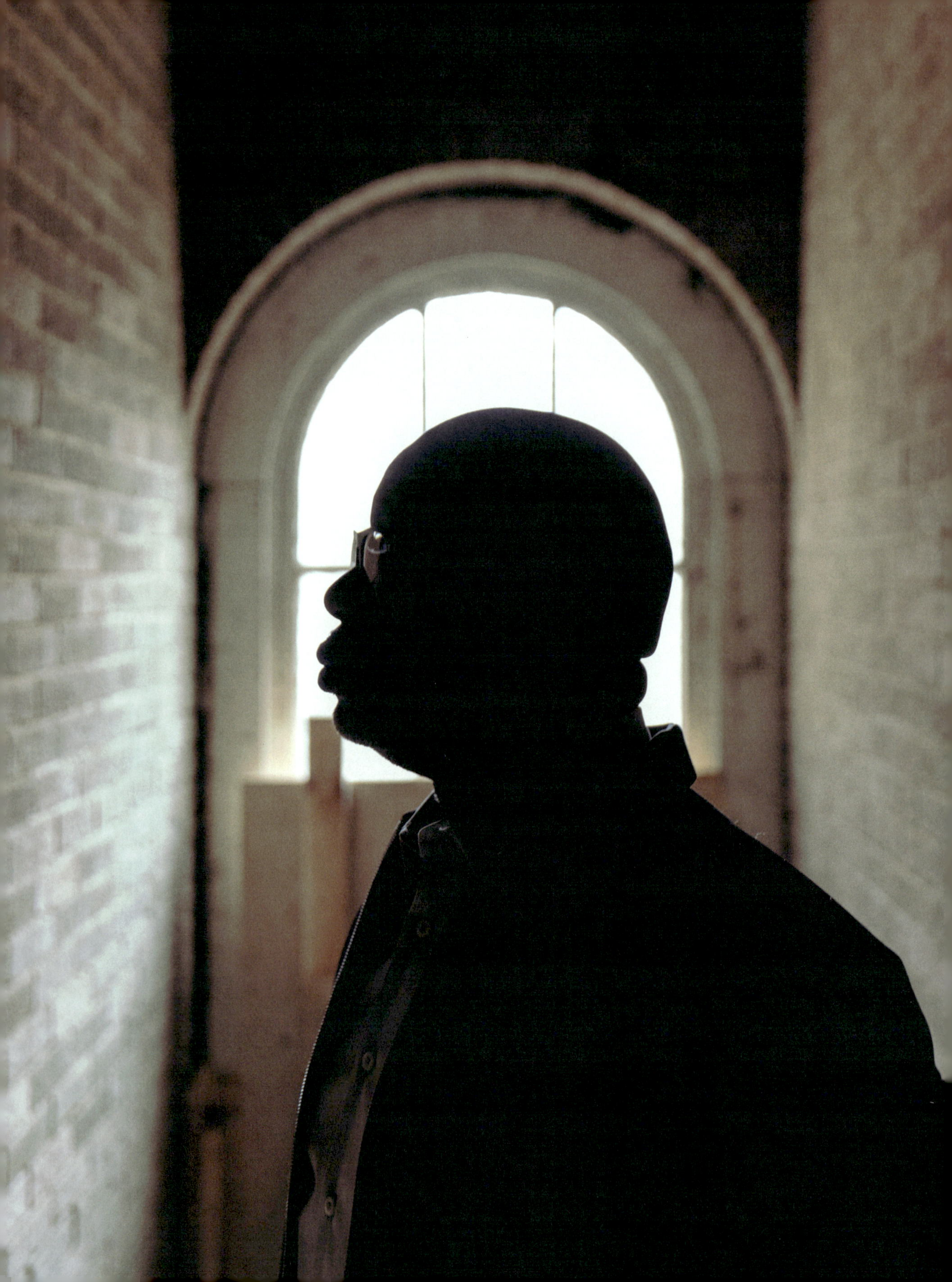

TG   Two things come to mind. The first is the work that actors and performers do to practice centering, so that they can deliver the best version of their craft. This is the ability to shut out the world and find the place within yourself that the good thing comes out of. Everyone needs strategies to counter the noise so that we can get in touch with our sense of self. Being barefoot allows me to access a different part of my brain and, on that day, I knew I especially needed that. I knew I wanted to deliver something very special from my heart, so I wanted to literally feel the ground of this space. In that moment and that place, I was flowing.

The other part has to do with courage—the courage to be oneself. I don't know if that's advice, but it's an admonishment. I think the more one practices being oneself, the more one traverses different states and discovers different aspects of being. Lately, when I'm in a room full of amazing people, I want to be the lo-fi dude, and that's after years of feeling like I had to be the hi-fi dude. Courage allows you to continue to ask yourself, who am I *today*? Who do I need to be for myself today? Who do I need to be to others today? More and more, who and how I want to be, wherever I am, is safe, prayerful, reflective, listening.●

Theaster Gates is a multidisciplinary artist and social innovator who creates work that focuses on space theory and land development, sculpture and performance. Drawing on his interest and training in urban planning and preservation, Gates redeems spaces that have been left behind. Known for his recirculation of art-world capital, he creates work that focuses on the possibility of the "life within things." In all aspects of his work, Gates contends with the notion of Black space as a formal exercise—one defined by collective desire, artistic agency, and the tactics of a pragmatist.

Where We Are Invited to Enter:

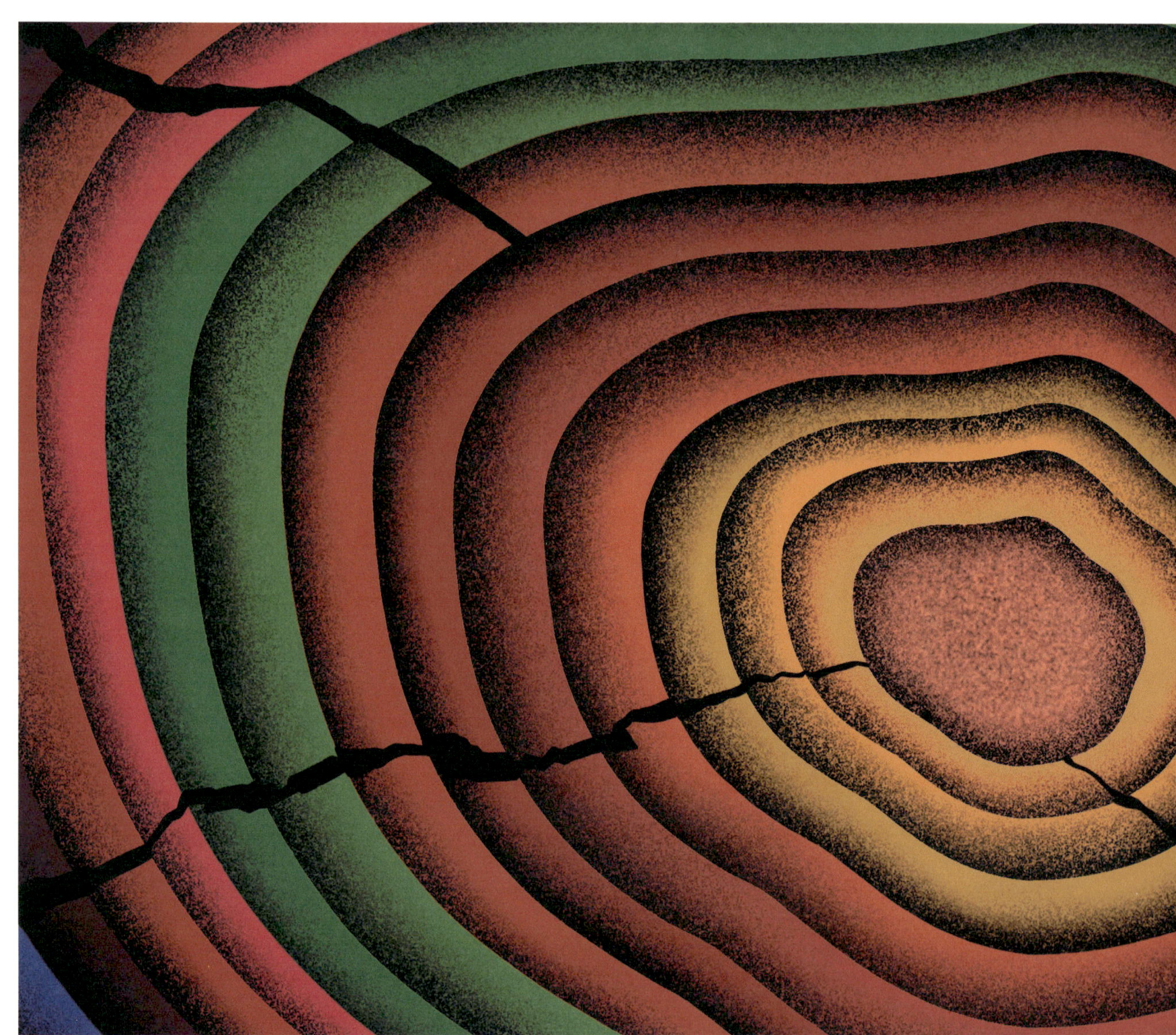

26

Sasha Costanza-Chock & Cara Page in conversation

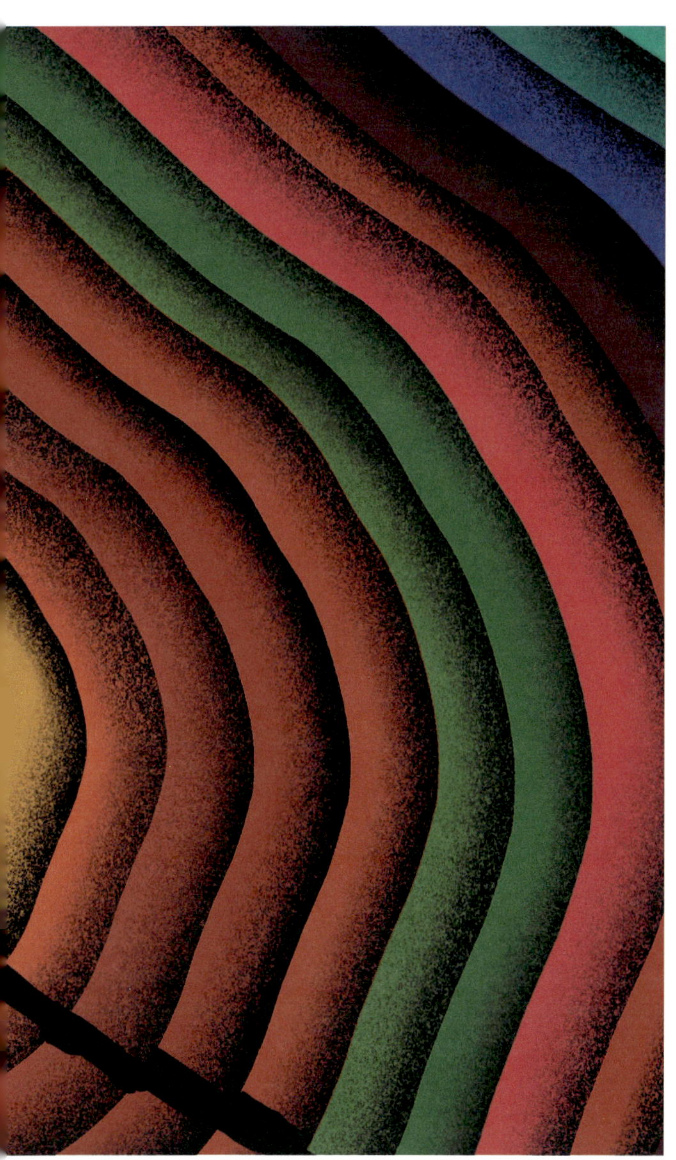

Moderated by
Alexis Aceves Garcia

Illustrations by
Jorge Vallecillos

ALEXIS ACEVES GARCIA   Before we get into our conversation, can you briefly introduce yourself and where you're currently calling home?

SASHA COSTANZA-CHOCK   My name is Sasha Costanza-Chock. I use they, she, elle, or ella pronouns. I'm a researcher and a designer, and my work is focused on supporting community-led processes to build shared power, dismantle the matrix of domination, and advance ecological survival. I'm a non-binary trans femme. I'm raced white in the logic of racial capitalism, and I'm known for my work on networked social movements, transformative media organizing, and design justice. I currently live in Cambridge, Massachusetts, on the stolen land of the Massachusett and Wampanoag peoples.

CARA PAGE   Greetings. Hi, everyone. It's good to be here. Thank you, Sasha. I'm Cara Page, and I am calling from the Lenape land of Brooklyn, New York, by way of my people—migrant sharecroppers from Florida and Georgia of Black and Seminole descent, and my European ancestors from the Northeast.

I am here as a Black queer woman and organizer, cultural memory worker, and healer by way of bringing cultural and spiritual practice as an integrative design strategy for movement spaces and community spaces. I seek to center collective care strategies that reimagine and expand what we mean by healing and care—not defined by the carceral state, by colonization, by slavery, by homophobia, by transphobia, by ableism nor by capitalism, but defined by our Indigeneity, by our sacredness, by our ancestral traditions of how we bring forth the ways we have survived attempted genocide, slavery, and capitalism.

AAG   This issue of *Deem* is centered around the idea of place and placemaking. What does place mean and/or represent to you?

CP   I love this question. When I think about place, it is always in relationship to where I am invited in, where I am given the permission to enter a space that I am not imposing on or controlling in any way. To me, place is about who I am accountable to and where I am invited in, based on my relationships: blood relationships of family, ancestry, and lineage, as well as chosen family and community. In the broader sense, I also think about place in relation to where my geographies are located, not just in terms of physical space, but also the space of time. Then there's another level of place, which is the ground I feel most connected to based on where my family has either been forcibly displaced to, or chosen based on access and privilege.

When I think about place in relationship to community, it is where we have chosen to build safety, care, and survival infrastructures that allow us to be ourselves and in relationship to each other. Place is understanding our interdependence. For instance, here I am in Brooklyn. This is a newer place for me but, by way of my family, many generations before me have lived here as part of the cultural, political lineage of Black people in this city.

I also come from New Jersey and Pennsylvania in terms of geographical place by way of my mother's lineage, all the way to the Mayflower (we think possibly), and all the complications of that inside of colonization and slavery. And then the end trails of forced migration from the South, where my people were fleeing lynchings and sharecropping and moving from North Carolina and Georgia up to New York and Newark. I am returning to that place, even though I was cut off by state and interpersonal violence. I've spent the last two decades retouching, reasserting, or reimagining what my rootedness and connection is to place in the South based on the ancestry of my people: Black and Seminole.

And, if I could add—Black, feminist, queer, trans space, which I've been a part of in Oakland, Atlanta, and here in New York City. It's interesting how place is sometimes prescribed as physical, but I'm talking about a spiritual, political, cultural belonging to a people and the power we're building together in those spaces.

SCC   I really value, appreciate, and am inspired by the way you located your ideas about place and rooted that in history, lineage, and ancestry. I feel like I have a lot of work to do to think more about my own ancestry and histories that brought me to where I am today and how that informs the ideas and practices that I have and communities that I'm involved in.

A part of my family were Jews in Poland and Russia who were displaced through pogroms, came to New York, and worked in the garment industry. I know that I have a great-great-great aunt who was an anarchist and involved in a plot to assassinate the tsar at the time, which was discovered. She was exiled and so came to work in the garment industry in New York. She was involved in organizing what later became the International Ladies Garment Worker Union, an early labor union.

On my father's side, I have an Italian family, Sicilian actually. Just before my grandfather passed away, about six years ago, I learned more stories from him about his grandfather, who was a migrant worker. He moved between different glass factories in the New York and the Pennsylvania areas. As the large glass ovens filled, they would be shut down to be scraped out by another set of workers and the glassblowers would move to another location. As automation arrived and transformed that work, he was involved in helping to organize a glassblowers union so that, instead of everyone being fired, some ended up maintaining the new generation of glass-blowing machines.

I have these histories of labor organizing and migration based on economic necessity, and histories of violence, including sexual violence, as a mechanism of ethnic control. Those histories of places shape who I am and how I show up in the world. But when I think about place and placemaking in the context of the work I'm doing with the Design Justice Network, I would say, first of all, that design justice is a framework for analysis around how design can distribute benefits and burdens between various groups of people. It's a framework that focuses very explicitly on how design reproduces or challenges the matrix of domination, which is Patricia Hill Collins's term for interlocking white supremacy, patriarchy, and capitalism. We can add

"Understanding the design apparatus is also about understanding how space and place are deeply embedded in colonizer ideas of who is even able to take space, to claim place, to be in relationship to our physical spaces without being policed, surveilled, owned, or exploited for the purpose of reproduction or labor to serve the elite."

ableism, settler colonialism, and other forms of structural inequality. Then, I think that includes that idea of analyzing how design distributes benefits and burdens according to the matrix of domination, and includes the context of the many ways design can impact place and placemaking. That could be very literally in terms of architecture, urban planning, or the built environment, but also in terms of the policies that shape places. Unfortunately, right now, too frequently that means destroying or dismantling healthy places in the interests of racial capitalism, empire, the ongoing process of settler colonialism, and so on.

The last thing I'll say about this is that design justice isn't just a set of ideas. It's a community of practice. I participate in the Design Justice Network, but design justice is also an idea that is circulating through many different overlapping networks of people. In terms of placemaking, the Design As Protest Collective is a group of anti-racist designers dedicated to design justice in the built environment. They've done a lot of thinking about and working around design justice demands for anti-racism in

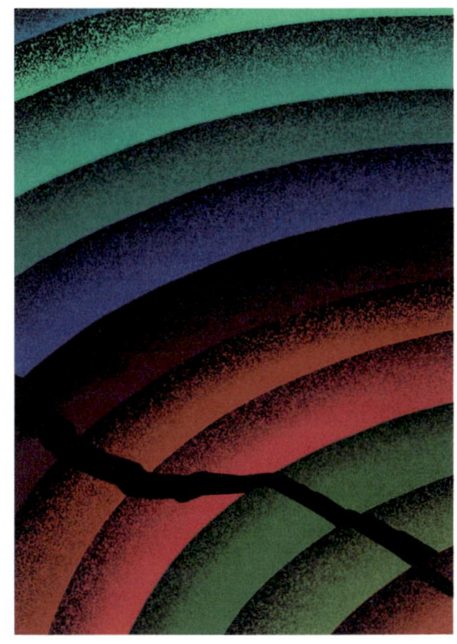

SASHA COSTANZA-CHOCK & CARA PAGE

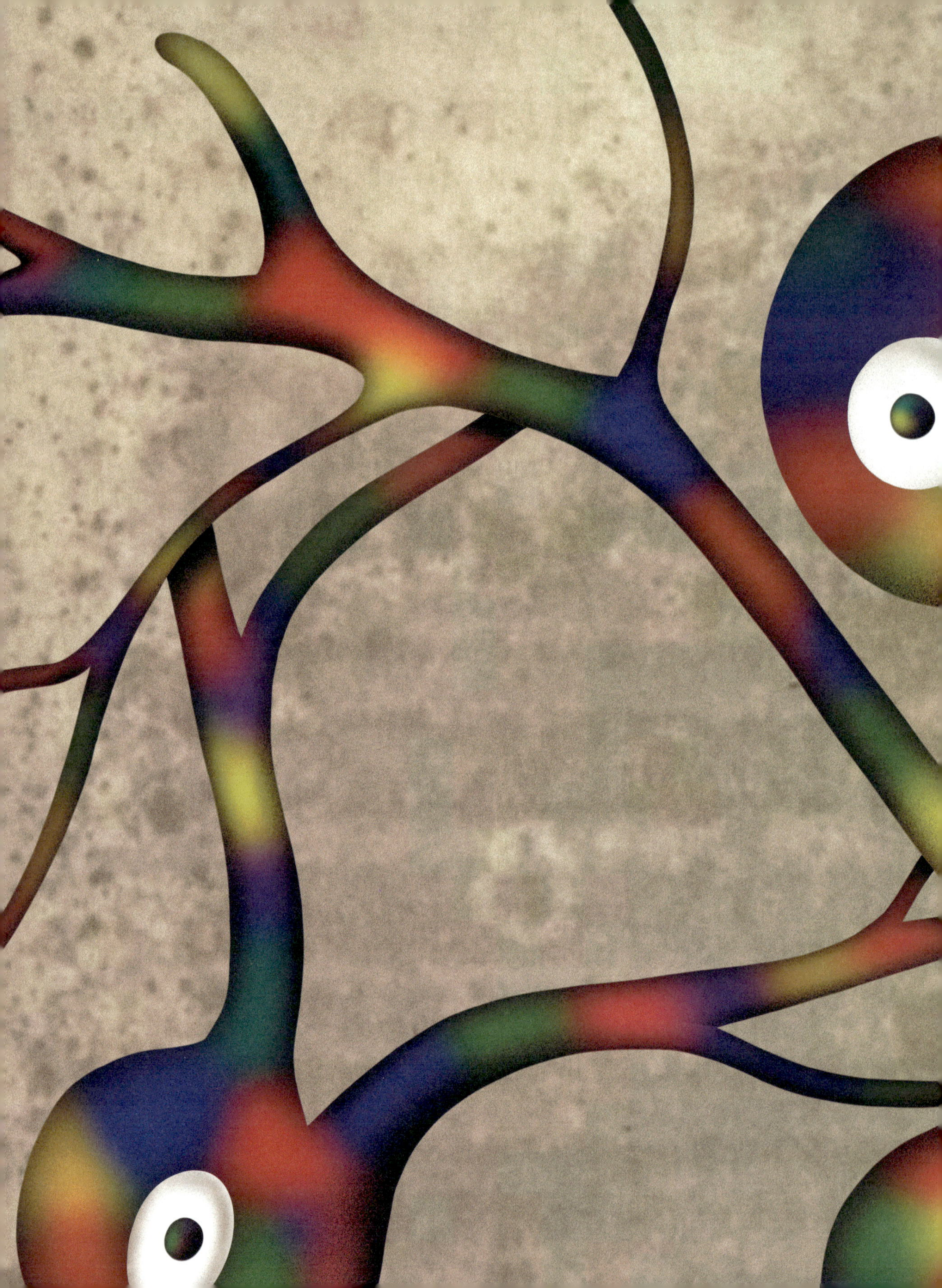

> "Why is it that I can't critique something without being 'anti,' when I'm actually for a future of science that remembers and draws on lineages and traditions of care from the same people, the same communities, that this system is trying to kill?"

the built environment, and they have those demands up on their website at dapcollective.com.

AAG   Thank you so much for your responses and Sasha, for illuminating the work of Design as Protest. Both of your practices make me hopeful that we can move from the individualism that capitalism propels, towards a future rooted in a more communal approach to care. How do the Changing Frequencies Project and the Design Justice Network embrace the speculative aspects of design as it relates to placemaking? How is placemaking also a form of worldbuilding?

CP   I don't necessarily consider myself a designer. I consider myself a cultural memory worker rooted in Black feminist radical traditions of care, safety, and culture. My work, Healing Histories, is housed inside of Changing Frequencies, which is a Black, queer, feminist-led project that designs and creates cultural memory work to disrupt violence, in particular from the carceral medical-industrial complex. I saw, as many others that I'm organizing and partnering with see, a huge gap in understanding around what it will take to build new places of care that are deeply centered in collective/individual autonomy and communal determination for our people, by our people, and that aren't rooted in an archaic way of thinking about health, based on a cis, able-bodied, heterosexual, Christian, and wealth-driven model of whose body is valuable and whose is expendable.

Understanding the design apparatus is also about understanding how space and place are deeply embedded in colonizer ideas of who is even able to take space, to claim place, to be in relationship to our physical spaces without being policed, surveilled, owned, or exploited for the purpose of reproduction or labor to serve the elite.

I'm deeply involved with political and cultural partnerships, like the Healing Histories Project, where we're building a digital timeline of the medical-industrial complex, from pre-colonization to now, in order to better understand its implications as an extension of exploitation, racial capitalism, and colonization. How we look at the timeline is rooted in a Black and Indigenous lens and examines the scientific racism and medical experimentation that affected queer, trans, and disabled people, sex workers, immigrants, Black, and Indigenous people. It documents the ways in which we have intentionally been surveilled, policed, and tested on by medical and scientific ideas and practices because of their need to design an "us" and a "them"—a hierarchy of bodies and of relationships to place that is deeply informed by who is genetically permitted and invited to live on this planet without being owned and controlled solely for the purpose of labor and building empire.

SCC   There are a lot of people in the Design Justice Network who would not say, "I'm a designer," which has made a part of our mission to work hard to intentionally expand the idea of who gets to be considered a designer. Design has a Latin root, *de signum*, which means to mark out. It's marking. It's planning. We all design by making plans for the actions we'd like to take, things we might want to build, construct, create, and form, places we want to build or develop, relationships we want to foster. We're designing things, spaces, connections. One of the things we do in the Design Justice Network is question and critique ideas that come from elite design institutions, like design schools or design publications, as well as the way the design industry structures activity around the interests of white supremacy, capitalism, heteropatriarchy, etc.

What would that look like if we reimagined who gets to be considered a designer? What type of activities and practices get valorized and

SASHA COSTANZA-CHOCK & CARA PAGE

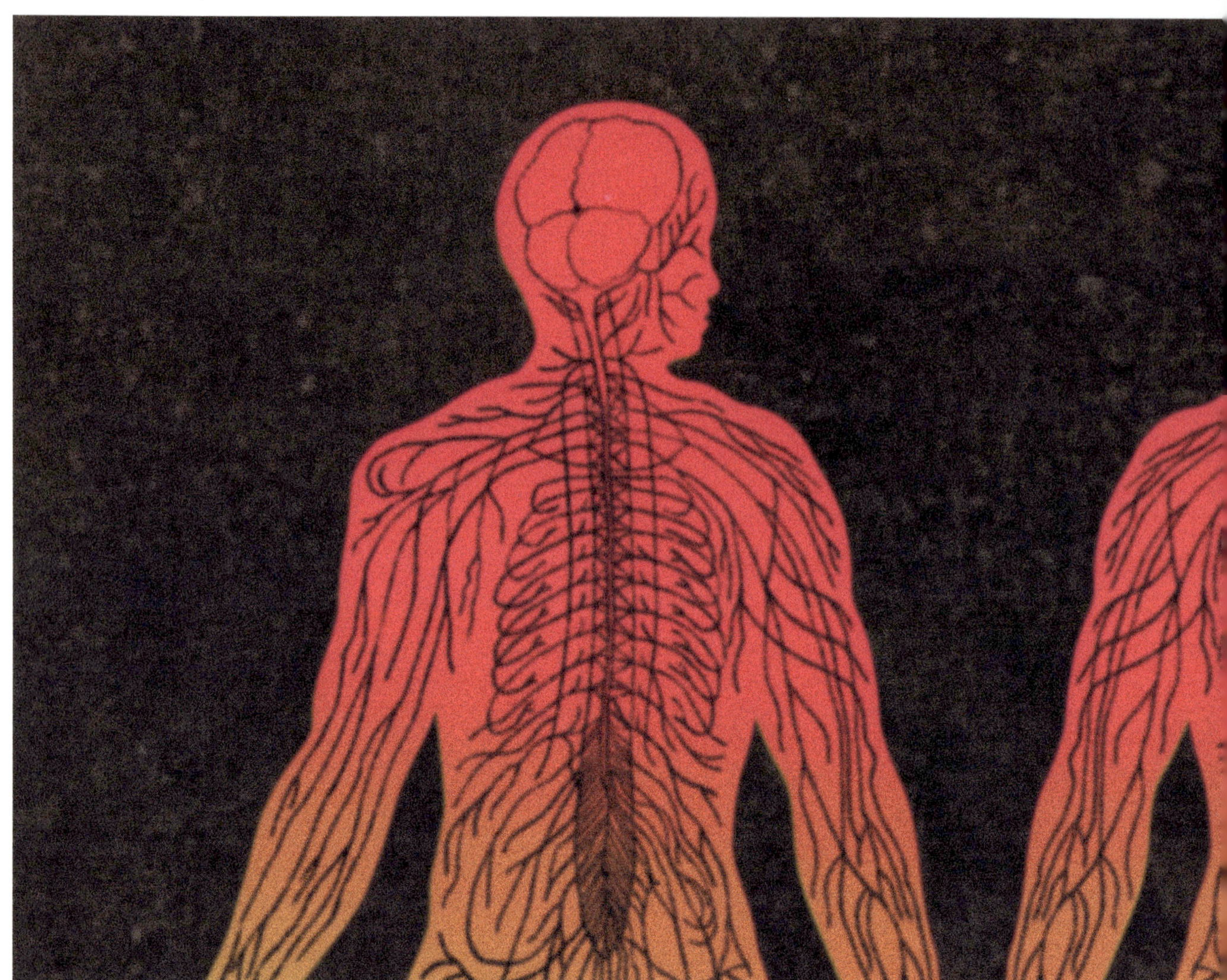

resourced? On the speculative design side of things, earlier today I was on a prep call for a workshop I'm going to be involved in tomorrow with Joana Varon from Coding Rights, which is a Brazil-based hacker feminist organization. We have a project together called The Oracle for Transfeminist Technologies; it's a card deck, partly inspired by tarot, a performance, and a participatory design workshop where you are dealt a hand of objects, values, and situations. People are invited to imagine the future design of transfeminist technologies and what that would mean and look like. What would these objects and systems do? What would they afford and enable and what other systems would need to be shifted to make it possible to create these things, these experiences?

CP I think there's something particular to the movement that is being built here that is sending us into the future, and I am entering into that conver-sation as an architect of social justice, as someone who considers myself a community historian and a curatorial archivist. I am entering through the lens of the medical-industrial complex, having met with farmers, healers, and health practitioners who are looking at the ways the medical empire has used DNA to both deconstruct and redesign new bodies, new DNA. Pulling from what white supremacy wants to reproduce as bodies, as foods, as seeds, I enter through the lens of understanding how we are deconstructing a design system around bodies, and concepts of the body, healing, and care, that have been devoid of conversations about belonging, place, dreaming, and future—Afrofuturism for me.

I was called anti-science because I was critiquing public health. Because we were producing a cultural, political critique of a system of care that does not know how to center immigrant, refugee, formerly incarcerated, detained, transgen-

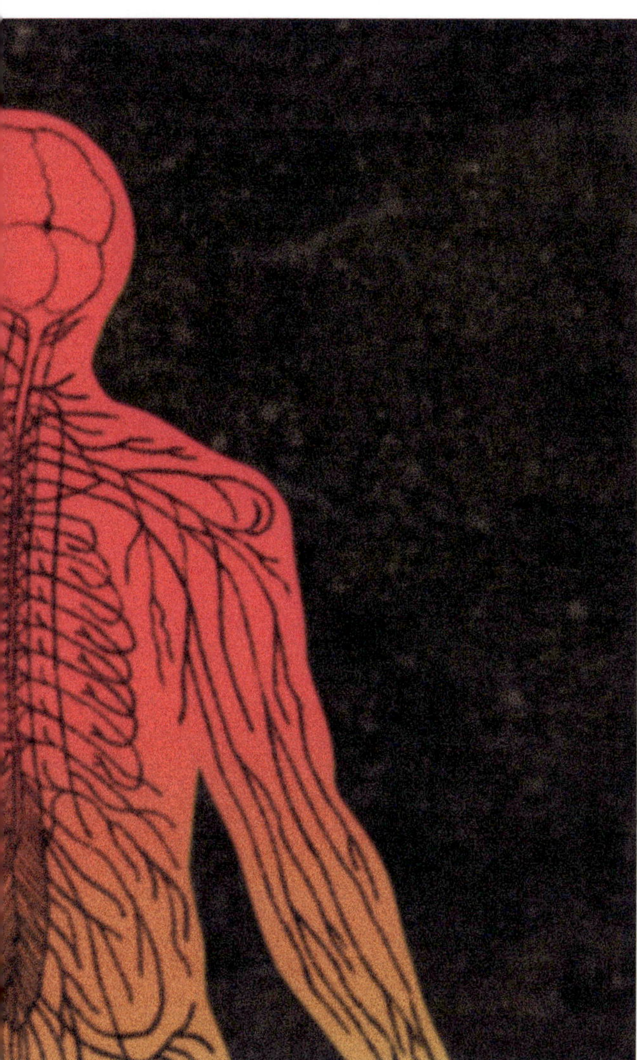

for decades, in the 19th and 20th centuries, tested and experimented on Black and white Southerners and Indigenous people in the state of Georgia. I'm using this virtual reality tool to ask how we heal and reclaim a place from which many of our people disappeared. I'm creating a map towards the future that doesn't reclaim the institution of psychiatric exploitation, but instead brings home the people who disappeared and were misremembered in that place.

AAG   What does care look like for you? What place do you associate with your own experiences of care?

SCC   For me personally, care lately has been making space and time for creativity, music, and beat-making. In the context of my political home, the Design Justice Network, I'd love to shout out and talk about the care circles that we've been doing, inspired and organized by our Steering Committee member Denise Shanté Brown. We currently have close to 500 people who are active members of the Design Justice Network, and they're either contributing money and/or time on a monthly basis to support the activities of the network. One of the things that's happened more recently is intentionally putting time, energy, and resources into Design Justice Network care circles.

We thought of it as a way for members to start cultivating conditions that would enable us to be in spaces where we could create the worlds that we want and need from a shared place of aliveness, nourishment, awareness, connectedness, and communal care. The care circles are places where our members come to slow down, to reflect on, and to witness more sustainable ways of doing design work. We want our members to be more open to the experience of receiving nourishment. Last year, we invited practitioners from healing justice frameworks to work with our members during a virtual series of 90-minute sessions. We're thinking about how to deepen and expand that work in our coming cycle of growth.

CP   For me, care comes in multiple ways based on the communities I'm working with. The Changing Frequencies Project has given me the opportunity to strategize with healing justice organizers, advocates, and practitioners, as well as health practitioners, to think about care strategies inside of COVID and the arc of where we were before the pandemic. That shit was already a mess. It just accelerated the level of demise and the disparities. And then, of course, the collective grief and trauma we all experienced in relationship to being told by the state what we could or couldn't do; the relationship between COVID care and big pharma; the loss of many community members to this pandemic and the policing that continues in our communities, whether we are in a pandemic or not.

der, gender-nonconforming, disabled, Black, and Brown people, youth, and elders? To understand this, one must first, or simultaneously, deconstruct how others are designing what the narrative is. Why is it that I can't critique something without being "anti," when I'm actually for a future of science that remembers and draws on lineages and traditions of care from the same people, the same communities, that this system is trying to kill? Just holding those complexities is very powerful.

I am also interested in using virtual reality as an experiential place that taps into our multisensory ways of learning and being. I want to take the militarization out of virtual reality and put back into it the practice and traditions of our communities. I believe in virtual reality—the possibilities of how you come in and out of space and place. In particular, I'm using it to bring people into one of the largest psychiatric hospitals in the world that,

     SASHA COSTANZA-CHOCK & CARA PAGE

For me, care is imagining what strategies we have to build collective safety, and how it is integral to our political liberation, including what we are co-generating beyond geographical borders. I'm in conversation with people from West Africa, South America, and parts of Asia. Finally asking and demanding, with healers and health practitioners across spheres and regions, what it means to build long-term care infrastructures that do not only respond to instances of violence—state, interpersonal, and colonial—or to a natural disaster, like a pandemic. How are we imagining what we're going to build for the future?

I'm also in relationship to mapping what has been working. I am co-writing an anthology with Erica Woodland, a Black trans organizer and healer and the founder of the National Queer & Trans Therapists of Color Network, on healing justice lineages. We are dreaming at the crossroads of liberation, collective care, and safety. That anthology will gather many voices across the US right now and look at the ways people are centering care in their political, spiritual, and cultural work as a liberatory practice for the present, past, and future. We draw on the traditions of the Black Power movements and from other communities who have used practices of care and safety as modes of liberation. We can build powerful possibilities for our future when we're mapping the power we already hold together.

SCC   When can we read this anthology? This is so exciting.

CP   Early 2023. It's coming. It features many writers who we are deeply honored are part of this anthology.

SCC   It's current events time. Elon Musk has secured financing to purchase Twitter. By the time this issue comes out, I don't know where that will have taken us. But this has reopened a long-standing conversation that I feel very invested in, as someone who works a lot with media and information technology for liberation, and who has a history of being in community with many others who do that.

We have long criticized what we see as the appropriation, by capitalism and the culture industries, of free software innovations, many of which originally came out of anarchist hacker communities. There's a section in my book, *Design Justice*, where I talk about an alternate origin history of Twitter itself. There was a demo design for Twitter, TXTMob—it was a small group messaging tool for direct action activists to evade police during the 2004 Republican National Convention in New York City—that some Indymedia (Independent Media Center) hackers were involved in making. TXTMob was used as a demo design and prototype back at the headquarters of ODEO, where Twitter was born as a project to redirect resources from a podcasting company that wasn't working out. These things that our movements create get picked up and turned into machinery for monetization, for surveillance, for violence that passes between online spaces and physical spaces, for reproducing all of the negative aspects of the matrix of domination and, by default, innovation, wherever it comes from.

Capitalism is a machine for thievery. For taking something and making it profitable for the same elite networks. Musk buying Twitter is a moment for education, thought, and experimentation. If we're leaving advice for readers of *Deem* on how to leverage collective care and take collective action, one thing I noticed in this conversation about the Twitter purchase is a back and forth like, "No, the only solution is the elimination of billionaires. No, the only solution is a publicly-supported social media platform. No, the only solution is tighter regulation on how these platforms operate. No, the only solution is everybody leaving and moving to more radical, free, open-source, federated alternatives." To me, as a non-binary person, my question is always, "Why is any one of these the 'only solution'? Why isn't it yes *and*?" Let's do all of the above!

Get yourself a critical lens that will enable you to say—let's tax the tech billionaires out of existence and use some of the money to create a public interest social media platform. Meanwhile, let's build radical alternatives that are decentralized and federated, and let's try lovingly and with care to work with our friends, family, and community to explore these other possibilities. We can build platform cooperatives and community-owned decentralized social media networks while we're also fighting for those other larger structural changes. We can own it and create it.

CP   Care is also about possibility. I'm loving what you're saying about responding to this Musk moment. This is not an isolated incident. We're going to see this happen more and more. This is the metaverse. We could deconstruct that or stress about it, but what is possible for us to create? I'm interested.

For care, it's the same principle. I'm always fascinated by all the energy required to deconstruct something. The answer is never binary. There are multiplicities and complexities in how we're going to create care because there's no one modicum model of it. We have so many traditions of care for our collective survival. Take our stories right here, of you and I, Sasha, of how our people survived. Where does care sit inside of our positioning based on our gender, our sexuality, our race, our identity—in other words, inside of the matrix of domination? What can we reimagine around care that doesn't limit us to just bodies, but expands our relationship to land, to work, to spirit, to economies that are deeply rooted in traditions of survival, and to transcendental economies that are not limited to profiting off of one for the domination of another?

To the *Deem* reader/listener, what are we co-creating? What are we co-generating that doesn't just ask the question, "How do we fix or cure?" but, "How do we imagine, dream, or reimagine?" How are we in the right relationship to the belonging of land, work, body, and spirit? How is that rooted in my care for *you*?

SCC   I love this. I feel like we need to have another conversation.

CP   We just started.

SCC   Now I'm like, how might we imagine a metaverse that is constructed around meeting everyone's access needs?

CP   Yes, exactly.

SCC   That is constructed around caring for one another and being in the right relationship to the stories there.

CP   To the stories of land, of beings, of seeds. Yes. Love that.

SCC   Let's do that next time.

CP   Next time I'll be there to build it with you.●

Cara Page is a Black Queer Feminist cultural/memory worker, curator, and organizer. She is founder of Changing Frequencies, a Black Queer Feminist-led abolitionist organizing project that designs cultural memory work to disrupt the harms and experimentation of the medical-industrial complex towards organizing transformative and healing futures. She is also cofounder and core leadership team member of the Kindred Southern Healing Justice Collective and the Healing Histories Project.

Sasha Costanza-Chock (they/she/elle/ella) is a researcher and designer who works to support community-led processes that build shared power, dismantle the matrix of domination, and advance ecological survival. They are a nonbinary trans femme. Sasha is known for their work on networked social movements, transformative media organizing, and design justice and is a member of the Steering Committee of the Design Justice Network and a Faculty Associate with the Berkman-Klein Center for Internet & Society at Harvard University. They are the author of two books and numerous journal articles, book chapters, and other research publications, including their latest,* Design Justice: Community-Led Practices to Build the Worlds We Need, *which was published by the MIT Press in 2020.*

      SASHA COSTANZA-CHOCK & CARA PAGE

REVER ENCE OVER REFER ENCE

Ramsay Taum speaks with
Isabel Flower about the
meaning of place-based values

Illustrations by
Cory Kamehanaokalā
Holt Taum

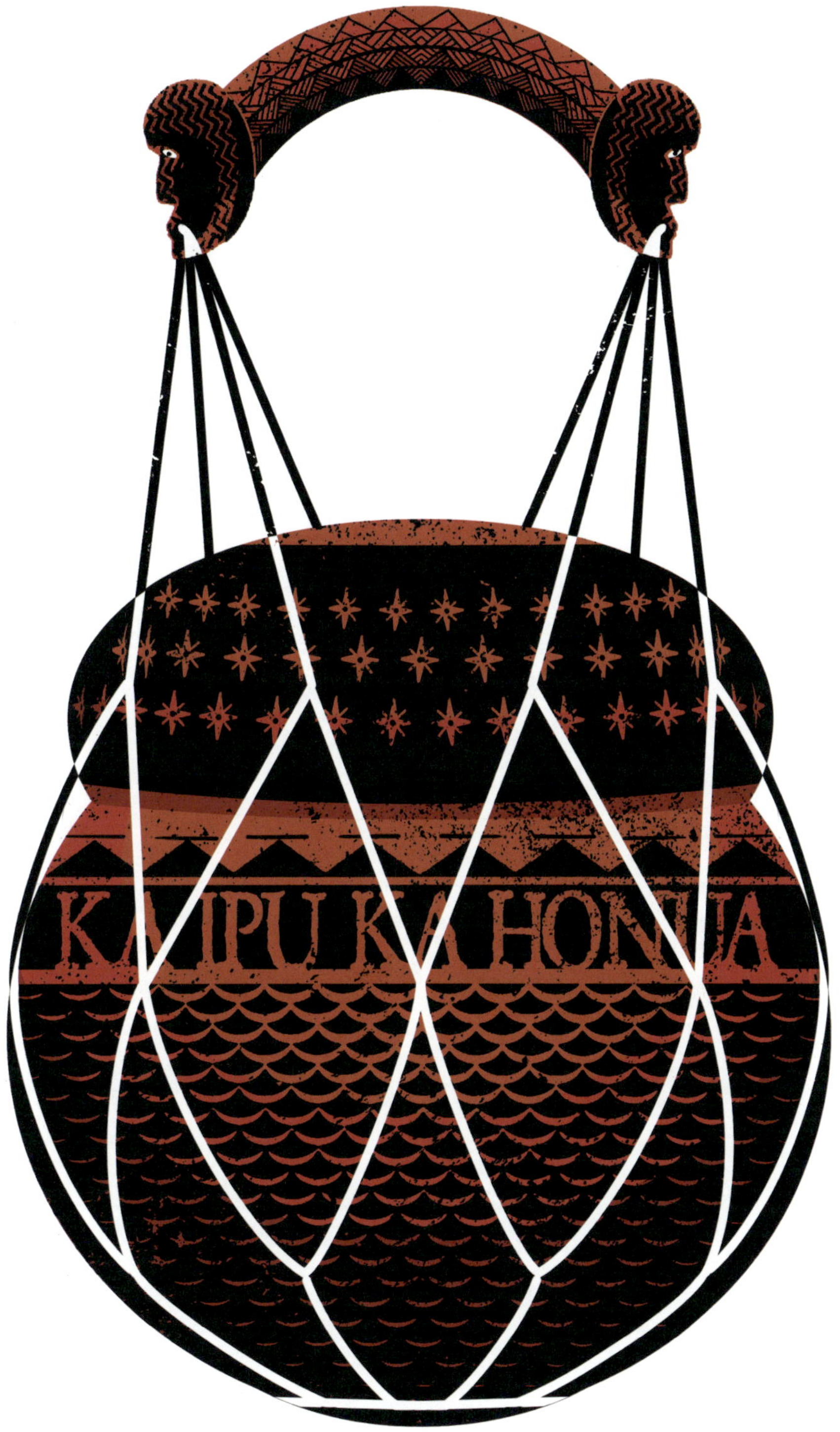

Ka ipu ka honua, 2022

This first image is inspired from an old Hawaiian chant for the god Lono, comparing the earth to a hanging gourd, and the gourd's cover to the starry sky. This gourd then hangs from a rainbow as the '*Auamo* (burden pole). This is my humble attempt to translate our ancestors' visual poetry, which reflects Uncle Ramsay's mana'o on the Hawaiian understanding of our place in the cosmos. "The gourd is this great world; its cover the heavens of Kuakini. Thrust it into the netting! Attach to it the rainbow for a handle!"

—all captions authored by the artist, Cory Kamehanaokalā Holt Taum

RAMSAY TAUM

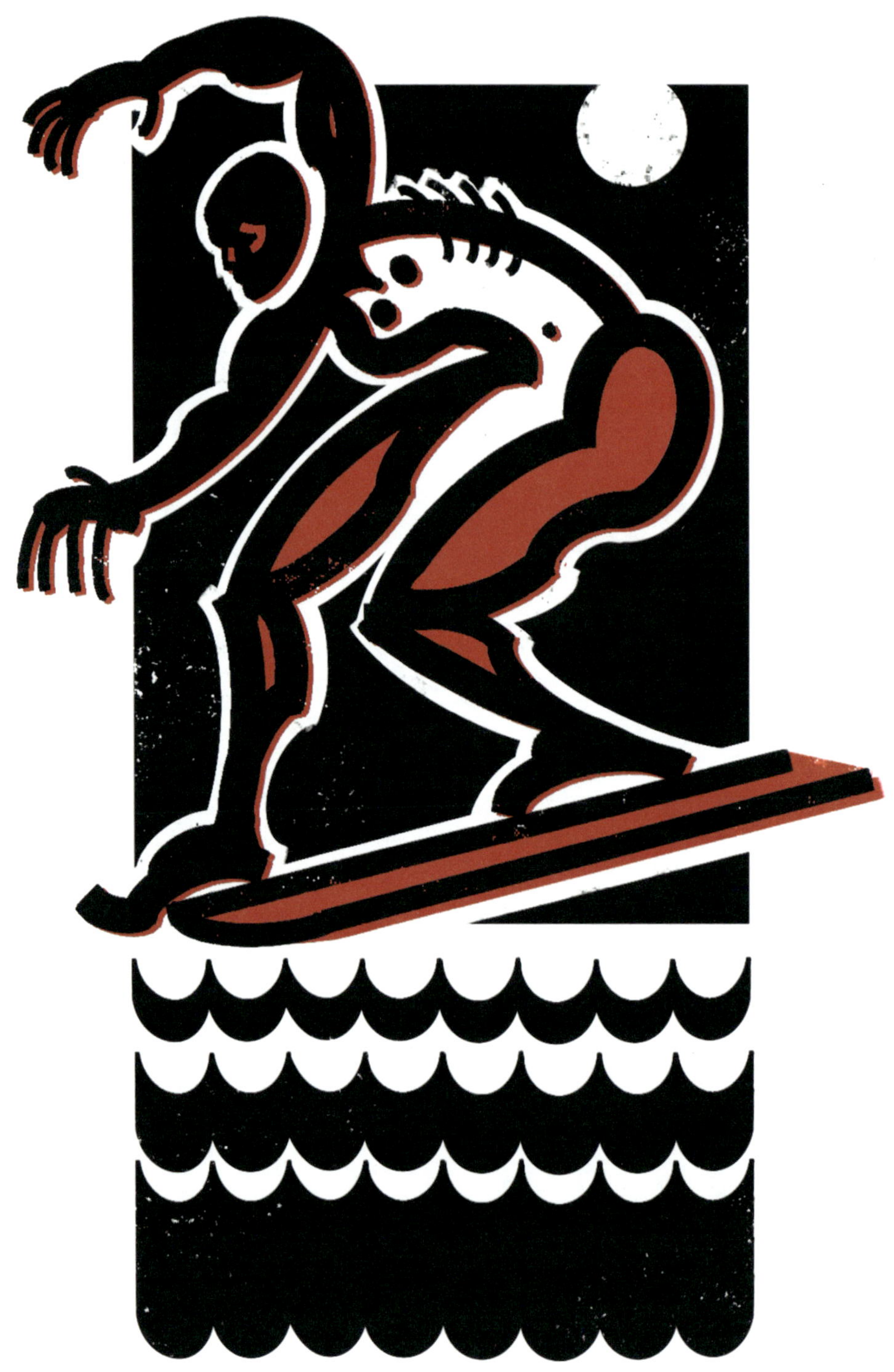

Kapolioka'ehukai, 2022

This image is dedicated to the many stories about renowned Hawaiian *wahine* surfers throughout time, from the days of old to modern legends. I hoped to illustrate this sport of the chiefs, and daily ritual of our ancestors, that has since become popular around the world.

ISABEL FLOWER This issue of *Deem* is centered around the concept of place. I want to start by asking what place means to you personally and, if it's relevant to your answer, what differentiates place from space?

RAMSAY TAUM Thank you, Isabel, that's a wonderful question and reflects a priority that favors relationships rather than transactions. A "place" is where one has a relationship with "space" and the people and things in it. There are places where you experience something specific to you—such as an external connection to your internal space. I like to call it an inside job. What and where is that place that allows you to engage whatever you want or need at that moment? Your residence, for instance, is a place you may look to for sanctuary. In that place there are spaces where you experience and engage in activities that enhance the sense of safety, calm, quiet.

I think place and space go hand in hand, but space is more like a container, a holding environment, while place provides context and content. Depending on what experience I'm looking for, there are different spaces that I seek out and, within those spaces, there are places I'm attracted to.

IF I'd like to talk a bit about Hawai'i. As an archipelago, I think there is a special kind of relationship to place because there is a natural isolation. Rather than a politically or culturally constructed sense of a border, there's a real physical barrier between this place and other land. How do you think Hawai'i's geographic physicality affects the kind of place it is, and the relationship of the people who live there to it?

RT This is another great question, and I'm not sure we have enough time to answer it completely. Hawai'i is a series of mountain tops we perceive and experience as islands. It is quite literally placed in the middle of the ocean, and what we see on the surface is just a small part. The islands themselves reach deep into the sea. Consequently, we live on mountain tops, which is not so different from the human condition. We tend only to see what's above the ocean's surface, yet, like Hawai'i, there is so much of us that lies beneath the water.

Since we live "in" the ocean, we have a special relationship with it. What we do to it, we end up doing to ourselves. There's no getting away from it. We are in it. You become very mindful of that relationship. In the middle of the sea, while we may be

"Hawai'i is considered the most remote inhabited place on the planet. You don't get here by accident."

That's one way of looking at it. With that said, I also think the ultimate space is the internal one. The space between my head and my heart. That space that allows me to think, feel, and connect the two. If you're not in a place that allows you to become centered, that allows that connection, then that's not a very good place for you. That internal alignment is what allows me to be present and to fully engage with the people I'm with or the activity I'm trying to experience. There are places that have and create that space.

IF That was beautifully articulated. It's been interesting to hear different people's take on this because there's been a lot of interpretation. This morning, I spoke to an artist who feels that place is wherever she has a memory. I feel like there's a relationship between your two perspectives.

RT Thank you. I think if I were to simplify it further, I would probably end up at the same place. It is all about memory. Certain places and spaces trigger us, and fundamentally, that's what everything is—memories we are recalling or creating.

IF I guess place is made when our sense of meaning is activated.

RT Absolutely.

under the influence of the external environment, we are equally in sync with the internal space as well. Hawai'i is considered the most remote inhabited place on the planet. You don't get here by accident. It takes intent. You also don't leave here by accident, either. That, too, is intentional. If you plan to come and stay here, there are challenges you must acknowledge and navigate.

Another way to explain what Hawai'i means to us is to look carefully at its name. It is our home, it is our mainland, it is our main place. The name itself reveals its identity and our relationship to it. For instance, we can break it into three words: *ha-wai-i*. How you say the name activates it.

The first word—*ha*—refers to life-giving breath, air. It is the first thing you receive when you come to the planet, and the last thing you give back. Something you always share and can never own. Giving and receiving is foundational to the principle of *aloha*, which *is* Hawai'i. It's a reciprocity agreement, it's a relationship with others as well as with this place. It's breathing in and breathing out. *Ha* is also the space, the atmosphere between you and I. It's the air that connects us. Isn't it funny how, anytime we damage that space, we use expressions like, "let's clear the air between us," because we recognize the importance of that space.

The second word—*wai*—refers to fresh water. Life in this archipelago, or anywhere on this planet, doesn't succeed without water. We are also surrounded by saltwater called *kai*. While *wai* is fresh, *kai* is salt. This reflects the dualities of life— soft and hard, in and out, up and down, external and internal. A balanced ecosystem requires living in alignment with your surroundings, because if you don't, you can't live here; the island won't allow you to because you won't have the necessary resources to do so.

The last word is *i (ee)*. The *i* references the creative forces that some would call God: the divine thought process, inspiration, the spirit that comes from within us, the big "I."

Ha-wai-i, the place of air, water, and spirit— that's where we are. That is our connection to our place.

IF That's probably a profoundly different way of thinking from the average person whose mainland is the United States. We tend to think of ourselves as being separate from nature and needing to return to it—this is an idea poignantly expressed by Mia Birdsong in our last issue—instead of acknowledging that we were never not part of it, even when we might feel otherwise.

RT That's exactly what I mean when I say we are *in* the ocean. Yet we say we need to save the earth. The earth is fine. The earth isn't going anywhere, but we might be. What we really mean is that we need to take better care of the earth if we want to survive.

IF When I was preparing for this interview, I discovered your work described as "sustainability, cultural and place-based values." What are some of the place-based values that you center around?

RT The reason it's phrased as cultural *and* place-based values is because I believe it should be "*and*" rather than "*or.*" I'm suggesting those are the values we give priority to in the places we are, and culture is the reflection of that relationship.

Take the expression, "You are what you eat," for example. I can assure you that my relationship with my food is important, as you'll find is true for most Indigenous people. Some of us even refer to primary food sources as a relative of sorts. My Native American cousins might say, "my brother the bear" or "my brother the deer." For us, it's taro. *Hāloa* is our elder brother and we know that when we "care for our brother, he will care for us for life." Caring for the land, caring for the air, caring for the water, caring for your food, caring for who you feed—this is what keeps us together as community. This is what makes us "we." If I'm getting my food delivered, then I might only be thinking about sus-

taining the delivery system, rather than the source of the food itself. What you perceive as directly connected to you changes your behavior. You begin to act differently.

Hawai'i is no different than anywhere else, but our priorities are. The shift comes when place is based in reverence, not reference. When we order food from across the ocean because we built condominiums on the land that used to feed us, we have changed our priorities. It's easy to see what our priorities are—just look at how we treat the land and sea. Place-based values come alive when we give priority to the relationship between our resources and one another. Someone who is living in the city versus someone who is living in the desert has a different priority regarding water, right? They both value water, of course. But the person who travels miles to get it and who is aware of its scarcity I think values it a little more than the person who can go to the tap and turn it on. That's what place-based values are: What do you eat? Where does that come from? Where are you born? Where do you sleep? Where do you die? Where are you buried?

IF Part of what inspired us to choose this theme was noticing that most of our conversations about design occur through virtual interactions and I think there is often a disconnection or disassociation from physical place. We may not even know where the people we're speaking to are at the time of our conversation. That is the nature of modern life and the ability to move around so easily in a globalized world.

RT In Hawaiian, we have a way of referring to ourselves before we give our name. If you asked one of my elders—my *kūpuna*—who they were, they wouldn't say their name. What they'd say is, "I am Hawai'i. I am the son of my father and of my mother, who are the sons and daughters of..." Our genealogies connect us to place. I belong to my place, which is also a family, a culture, and an identity. Like you said, today's world is, in many ways, placeless. Or our sense of place has been relocated to the virtual space of computers, which allow us to be in many places at once. But life always comes back to a few questions, like, who are you? And often that relates to, where are you, and why are you there? What do you value? What do you prioritize? Many of our conflicts in life are not so much about values as they are about priorities.

IF You've anticipated my next question, which is around how our late capitalist and globalized world divorces us from place so dramatically that the kind of work you do is both lacking and essential. Historically, this divorce goes back much further than just capitalism and globalization—it is also a product of imperialism and colonialism. What are some strategies you employ in your work to address this?

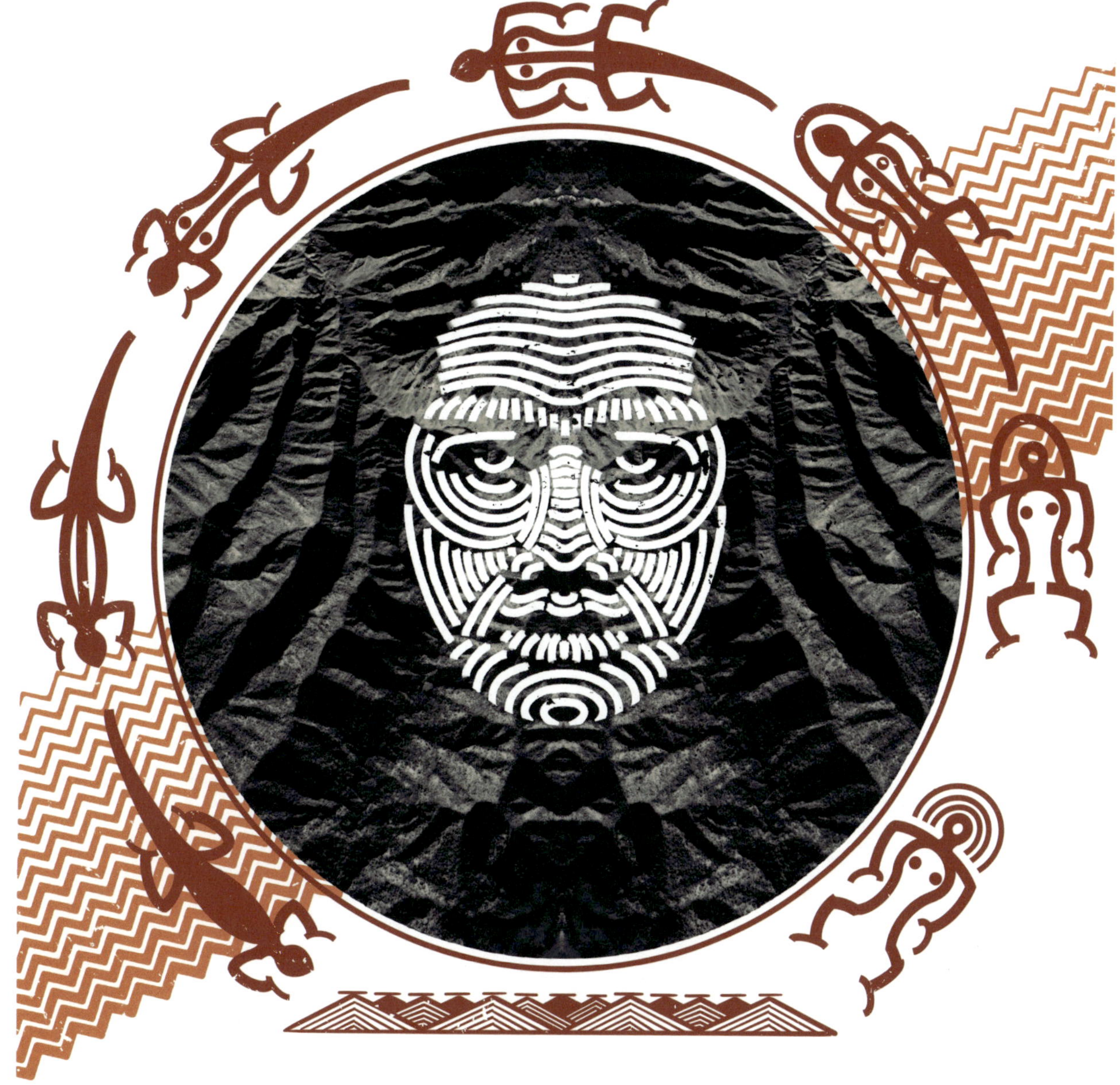

Kameha'ikana, 2022

Kameha'ikana is one of the names for the wondrous (literal translation of the word *kāmeha'i*) goddess,
Haumea. On the Ko'olau side of O'ahu, one of her body forms is as a *Mo'o Wahine* (Lizard Woman),
as well as in the plant form of the *Ulu* (breadfruit) tree.

RT   Something important about Hawai'i is that we're still in a natural space that is, for the most part, dictated by natural time. Yet the average person's experiences of work are dictated by artificial spaces and artificial time. I try to help us recognize how we try to find authenticity in an inauthentic space. Why do I bring a potted plant into my apartment when I could easily step outside? Because my priority today is to be in front of my computer, inside, so I'm trying to create an external relationship with outside. Now I've just inconvenienced the plant. Now I've put the environment in my service, rather than the other way around.

What I try to address are questions such as: How do I serve my community and my space so that the relationship is a reciprocal one? This pertains directly to the "isms" you're talking about. Capitalism and commercialism tend to edify the

RAMSAY TAUM

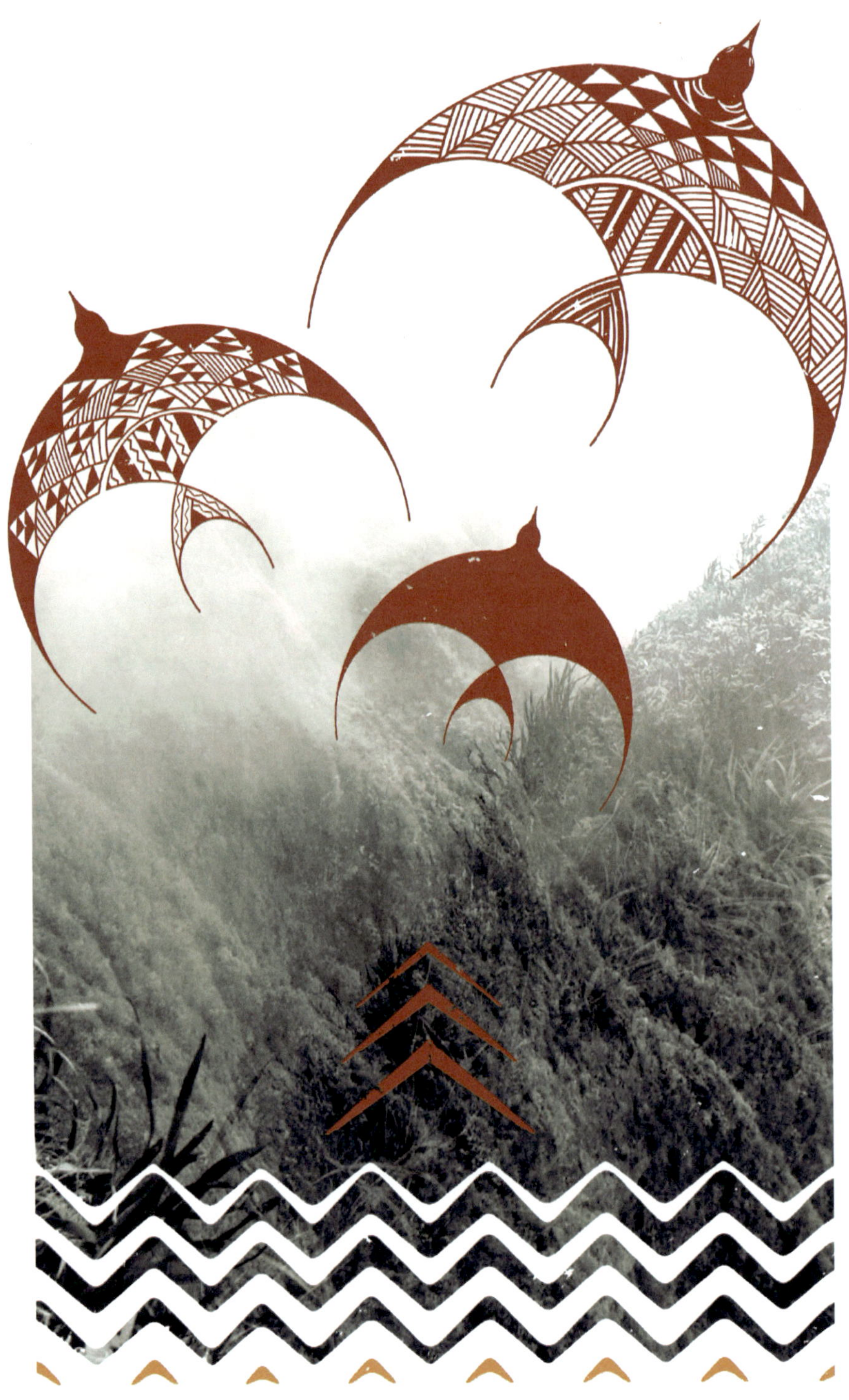

Kani Kīwaʻa ka manu i Waolani, 2022

This is loosely translated as, "the cry of Kīwaʻa, the mythical bird of the heavenly mountains."
This and the previous illustration are inspired by the profound beauty of the Koʻolau mountain range. Uncle Ramsay, and our
Taum ʻOhana, grew up beneath the shade of the tallest peak of the Koʻolau mountains in Maunawili Valley.

extractive nature of the other "ism" you mentioned, imperialism. The doctrine of discovery, the ideology that everything is there to serve you, including people. The ideology that bigger is better, that building a 100-story building gives you power. Does that power become an identity? Does it give us a sense of belonging? It's full circle, right? Most of us are looking for belonging, but we've become enamored by *belongings*. In the process of extraction, do we ever return what we take in full measure? Sustainability is balance. It's taking and returning, giving and receiving. It's not independence. It's interdependence. I know we can't go back, but I think we can go forward, perhaps by bringing forward practices from the past that were more in alignment with a sustainable way of life. It's really shifting our mindsets from "carrying" capacity to "caring" capacity.

IF I love what you said about needing to look back to go forward. In design, there is often an emphasis on needing innovative solutions for our times. I think more and more we are realizing that some of the answers lie in history, in reacquainting ourselves with the past.

require you to figure out how to carry, because it's already done. Caring capacity versus carrying capacity is the same as accountability versus accounting; capitalism is an accounting procedure, not an accountability procedure.

IF When we were working on the concepting for the issue, I was thinking that place is at the intersection of time and space. I think that's kind of what we're talking about, because it's impossible to think about the meaning of place without considering time in the way that you're describing, without letting go of some sense of its linearity or finiteness.

RT I'd suggest that place is also time. It's made from the time you spend somewhere and what you do with it. Of these little things I say—some of my students call them "Ramsay-isms"—I think the most important one, the one I'd like to leave you with, is the idea of shifting from reference to reverence. Let's not just refer to things, but instead adopt a more spiritual and sacred relationship with them. That's a big part of being in Hawai'i because our relationship to place is sacred. It's also the difference between being self-centered and being centered in self. What gives me the ability to be centered is

"Life always comes back to a few questions, like, who are you? And often that relates to, where are you, and why are you there?"

RT A lot of my work is about that, but it's not about going back anywhere specific. It's about paying homage to what got us here. Let's not forget that. Let's not put our ancestors out of the house. They say, "the past is in the past," but the past is actually the present. It's right now. We're living it. We're living in the resultant conditions of what occurred before, whether it was yesterday or 50 years. Right now is an expression of what we did yesterday and the day before. But we must still ask ourselves, how do I want to live tomorrow?

IF Thinking about it that way changes one's perception of what a consequence is. The modern YOLO rhetoric of "living in/for the moment" sort of misinterprets what it means to be present. Of course, the philosophy of *presence* has been an integral concept to many intellectual and religious traditions, especially Eastern ones. But I think our contemporary sense of being present—which is sometimes to live without accountability, to make decisions without considering consequence—is not the true or intended meaning.

RT Yes, and that's the difference between caring capacity and carrying capacity. Sustainability has become about carrying capacity. But if you care enough, you're going to choose behaviors that don't

knowing myself: learning how not to be a victim of externalities, but a creator of and respondent to what's going on in me. Finding that internal compass within and creating places where I can go, when I need to retreat, reform, transform. At their best, the places we make hold the space for that.●

Ramsay Taum is mentored and trained by respected kūpuna (elders) and a practitioner and instructor of several native Hawaiian practices: ho'oponopono (stress release and mediation), lomi haha (body alignment), and kaihewalu lua (Hawaiian combat/ battle art). Taum is a locally, nationally, and internationally recognized cultural resource, sought-after speaker, lecturer, trainer, and facilitator, especially when working with Hawai'i's industries, where he integrates native Hawaiian cultural values and principles into contemporary business. In 2009, he was recognized by the University of Hawai'i as a Star of Oceania, an honor presented every three years to extraordinary individuals of Oceania for their work and service-related contributions to raising greater awareness around Oceania and its people to the nation, region, and world.

LIZANIA CRUZ: ARTIST TAKEOVER

The work of Dominican-born artist Lizania Cruz uses audience participation to investigate notions of being and belonging within the public sphere. In 2018, she created the participatory installation, *Here & There*, inspired by the following quote from cultural theorist Stuart Hall's posthumous 2017 memoir, *Familiar Stranger: A Life Between Two Islands*: "…identity is not a set of fixed attributes, the unchanging essence of the inner self, but constantly shifting the process of positioning. We tend to think of identity as taking us back to our roots, the part of us which remains essentially the same across time. In fact, identity is always a never-completed process of becoming—a process of shifting identifications, rather than a singular, complete, finished state of being." Cruz invited participants to fill in the statements, *HERE I (AM/CAN BE)___* and *THERE I (AM/CAN BE)___* through a website, and these statements were then silkscreened onto fabric and hung in the 2018 exhibition, "Familiar Boundaries, Infinite Possibilities," at the August Wilson African American Cultural Center in Pittsburgh. For this issue, Cruz has shared a selection of the responses she received.

HERE I AM FREE AND TRUE
THERE I AM AN OUTSIDERS IN RUINS

HERE I AM WHERE I COME FROM, WHAT I INHERIT
FROM MY PARENTS
THERE I CAN BE UNLIMITED, EVERYTHING,
CONTRADICTIONS, FULLY

HERE I AM A FRENCH AFRICAN WOMEN
THERE I CAN BE A UNIVERSAL, GLOBAL CITIZEN

HERE I AM A MANAGER
THERE I AM A SISTER AND A DAUGHTER

HERE I AM YOUR BARISTA
THERE I CAN BE INVISIBLE

HERE I AM LIMITED
THERE I CAN BE AN ANIMATOR

HERE I AM RESERVED
THERE I AM WILD AND FREE

HERE I AM AN ILLEGAL ALIEN
THERE I AM A HUMAN BEING

HERE I AM BLESSED IN THE CITY AND
BLESSED GLOBALLY

THERE I AM POWERFUL AND RELEVANT
TO THIS GENERATION

HERE I AM THEY THEM THEIRS
THERE I AM EL

HERE I CAN BE HALF-MOON; IN-THE-MAKING;
INCOMING, INCOMPLETE
THERE I AM HALF-PERSON; UNBELIEVING;
STILL-LIFE MONSTROSITY

HERE I AM LINGERING
THERE I AM DELAYING

HERE I AM NO LONGER AFRAID OF BEING HARASSED
THERE I AM YOUNG, VULNERABLE, PREYED UPON

HERE I AM RELATIVELY FREE
THERE I AM RELATIVELY SUPPRESSED

HERE I AM STRUGGLING TO SPEAK IN
MY SECOND LANGUAGE
THERE I AM ABLE TO SPEAK MY TRUTH
IN MY MOTHER TONGUE

HERE I AM FREE, BUT LIMITED
THERE I CAN BE DIMINISHED, BUT ENDLESS

HERE I CAN BE A REFUGEE
THERE I CAN BE RESIDENT

HERE I AM FLOWING AND FLUID, I LET
THE CURRENTS GUIDE ME
THERE I AM STIFF AND STALE, THE WIND
DOESN'T MOVE ME

HERE I CAN BE STILL AND DOUBTFUL
THERE I AM ANYTHING BUT

HERE I CAN BE FOCUSED
THERE I AM LOST IN THE NOISE

HERE I CAN BE LOUD AND NOT AFRAID TO BE MYSELF
THERE I CAN BE QUIET AND TIMID

HERE I AM TIMID
THERE I AM BOLD

HERE I AM CONSTRAINED AND IMPOVERISHED
THERE I CAN BE AT HOME, CREATIVE AND FREE

HERE I AM A PERSON ON A TRAIN
THERE I CAN BE ANOTHER PERSON IN A VERY BIG CITY

HERE I AM SOMEONE ELSE
THERE I CAN BE THE BEST VERSION OF
ME THAT I REMEMBER

HERE I AM JUST LATINA
THERE I CAN BE COLOMBIAN, BOGOTANIAN,
CARIBBEAN, SOUTH AMERICAN

HERE I CAN BE A STRONG WOMAN
THERE I CAN BE MADE TO FEEL INFERIOR

HERE I CAN BE ME
THERE I CAN BE ME

HERE I CAN BE WHATEVER I WANT TO BE
THERE I CAN BE SOME OF WHAT I CAN BE

HERE I AM AN IMMIGRANT
THERE I AM FREE

HERE I AM ERIN, THE QUIET, SMALL ASIAN GIRL
THERE I CAN BE AGNES, A FEARLESS,
EMPOWERED LEADER AND SPY

HERE I AM RESERVED, PROFESSIONAL,
ONLY SPEAKING ENGLISH
THERE I CAN BE MYSELF — EXPRESSIVE AND JOYFUL
IN MY NATIVE TONGUE

HERE I AM MOUTO! JE VAU DE L'OR! A MOTO! I AM
A GOLD MINE!
THERE I CAN BE DIED BY NOW DJA NOUBI?

HERE I AM A STUDENT
THERE I AM A CITIZEN

HERE I AM NOT WHITE ENOUGH
THERE I AM NOT LATINO ENOUGH

HERE I AM JEWISH AMERICAN
THERE I CAN BE ANYTHING

HERE I AM INDOCUMENTADO PERO BIEN BENEFICIAL
AL SISTEMA
THERE I CAN BE UNREMARKABLE, WITH NO NEED TO
FIGHT FOR MY EXISTIR

HERE I AM AFRICAN-AMERICAN
THERE I AM A MOOR, YORUBA, YE YE OSHUN,
ISIS, DAYO, IMAN

HERE I AM INDEPENDENT, DIRECT, SEXY, IN MOTION
THERE I AM NAIVE, UN-LADY-LIKE, HEADSTRONG, STUCK

HERE I AM GAY
THERE I CAN BE QUEER

HERE I CAN BE FREER FROM DAILY THREATS OF VIOLENCE
THERE I AM CLOSER TO MY ROOTS

HERE I AM STUCK IN A LOOP
THERE I AM FULL OF THE SUN

HERE I CAN BE QUESTIONED OUTWARD AND INWARDLY
THERE I AM UNQUESTIONABLY ACCEPTED

HERE I AM KIDNAPPED
THERE I CAN BE HOME

HERE I AM A JOB TAKER
THERE I AM A PROVIDER

HERE I AM BLACK
THERE I AM AFRICAN

HERE I AM HOME, BUT NOT ALWAYS WELCOME
THERE I AM A WRAP

HERE I AM STILL ON A JOURNEY
THERE I AM ON A PURSUIT OF HAPPINESS

HERE I AM BILINGUAL
THERE I AM IMMIGRANT

HERE I AM WHAT THEY IMAGINE I AM
THERE I AM FREE IN MY TRUTH

HERE I AM A BLACK WOMAN
THERE I AM HUMAN

HERE I AM THEREFORE I THINK
THERE I CAN BE CREATIVE

HERE I CAN BE INDEPENDENT ECONOMICALLY BUT
LONELY
THERE I CAN BE RESTRICTED BUT FEEL THE CULTURAL
WARMTH

HERE I AM THE WIFE OF AN IMMIGRANT
THERE I CAN BE THE IMMIGRANT

49

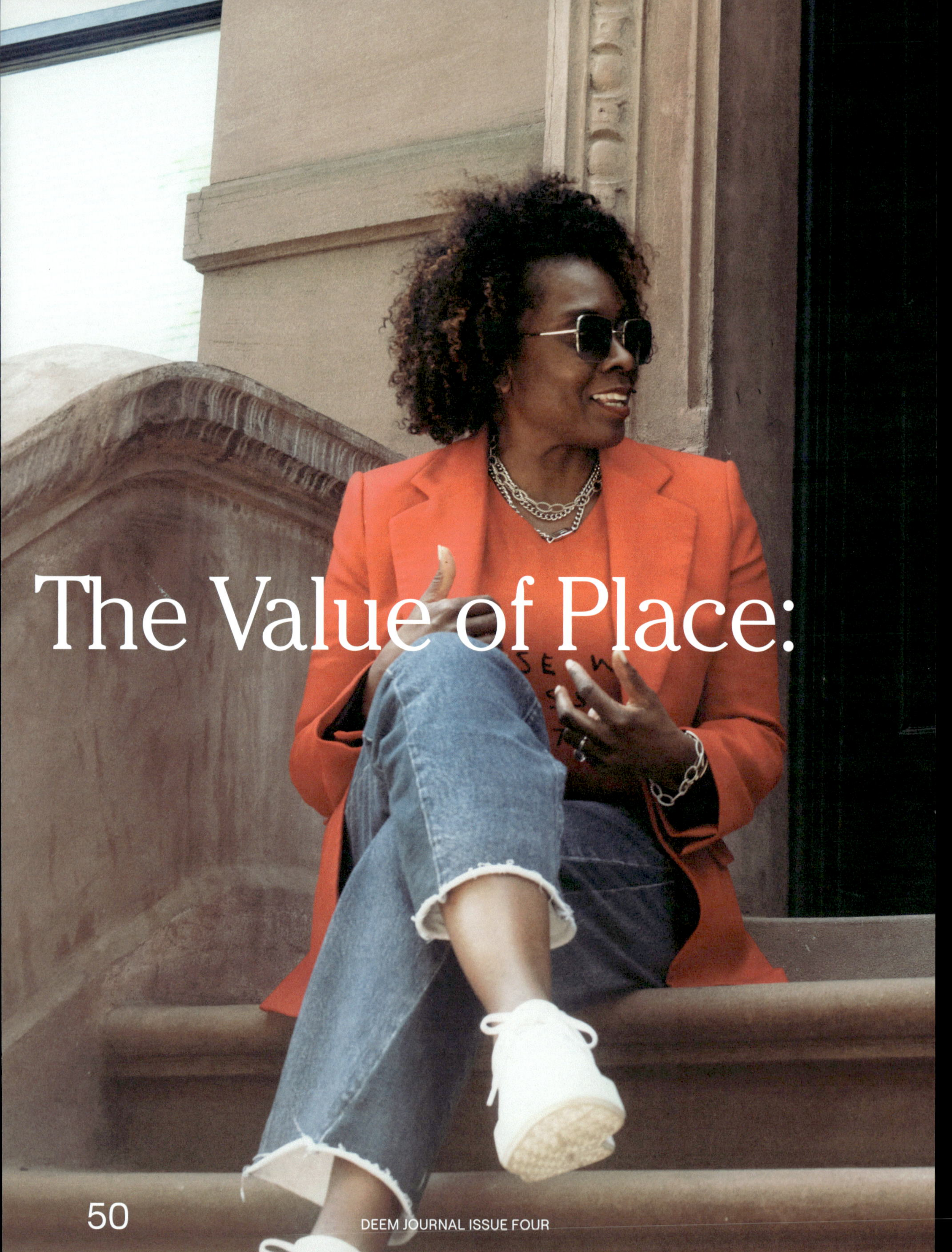
The Value of Place:

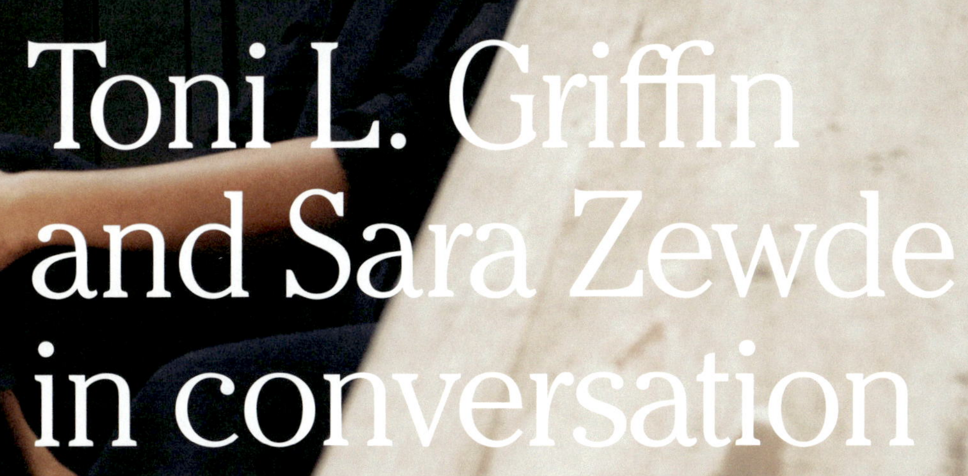

Toni L. Griffin and Sara Zewde in conversation

Photography by
Guarionex Rodriguez, Jr.

From left, Toni L. Griffin and Sara
Zewde in Harlem, New York City.

TONI L. GRIFFIN   What's been cool about living in Harlem—I've been here now 12 years—is that it's dotted with so many creatives working in the built environment space, including many of my former students. In general, I think Black architects, planners, and designers are becoming more visible. I did a NYCxDESIGN poster this past year where I wove designers' names through the streets of Manhattan, including yours. I have to get you a copy.

SARA ZEWDE   Yes! I need one.

TLG   There really is a little creative Renaissance happening here.

SZ   I'm curious how you ended up in Harlem. I ended up in Harlem sort of randomly. I read this book by Sharifa Rhodes-Pitts called *Harlem Is Nowhere* (2011). Have you read it?

TLG   I haven't, but I've heard of it.

SZ   I grew up in Louisiana and there's this coffee shop in New Orleans that I love and used to work at all the time. There was another woman who was also always there, working on a laptop. One day I was like, "What are you doing?" and she said, "I'm writing a book about Harlem."

TLG   Oh, wow.

SZ   The book is about whether Harlem is a real place, or whether it's an idea. I was so fascinated with this question that I was inspired to open my design practice here. As Black designers of the built environment, this very question that the book proposes is often at the crux of our thinking. We have this sense of what places can be, despite what they are, and the huge chasm in between.

TLG   I think for places that are very culturally rooted, either by their inhabitants or by their identity, which sometimes are one and the same, it's both. They're physical locations and ideas, even ideals. I think designers working on physical space are wrestling with all three of those things simultaneously. We're asked to talk about context and history, we're asked to consider, understand, and address current conditions, and we also have to figure out how to push all those things forward into a proposition that changes a space into a place, or that extends the meaning of that place, or both.

What drove me here was not so much professional as personal. I was coming from working for Cory Booker as planning director during his first term as mayor of Newark. That was after living in DC, New York and, before that, my hometown of Chicago. I'm from a gritty, racially segregated place. It's black and it's white—there's no in between.

The first time I lived in New York, which was after the Loeb Fellowship at Harvard GSD, I loved being in a city where I could see people who looked like me, but also spoke different languages and represented so many different cultures. In the Midwest, you don't get the same sense of the richness of Black Americans or the many variations on the Black experience in America.

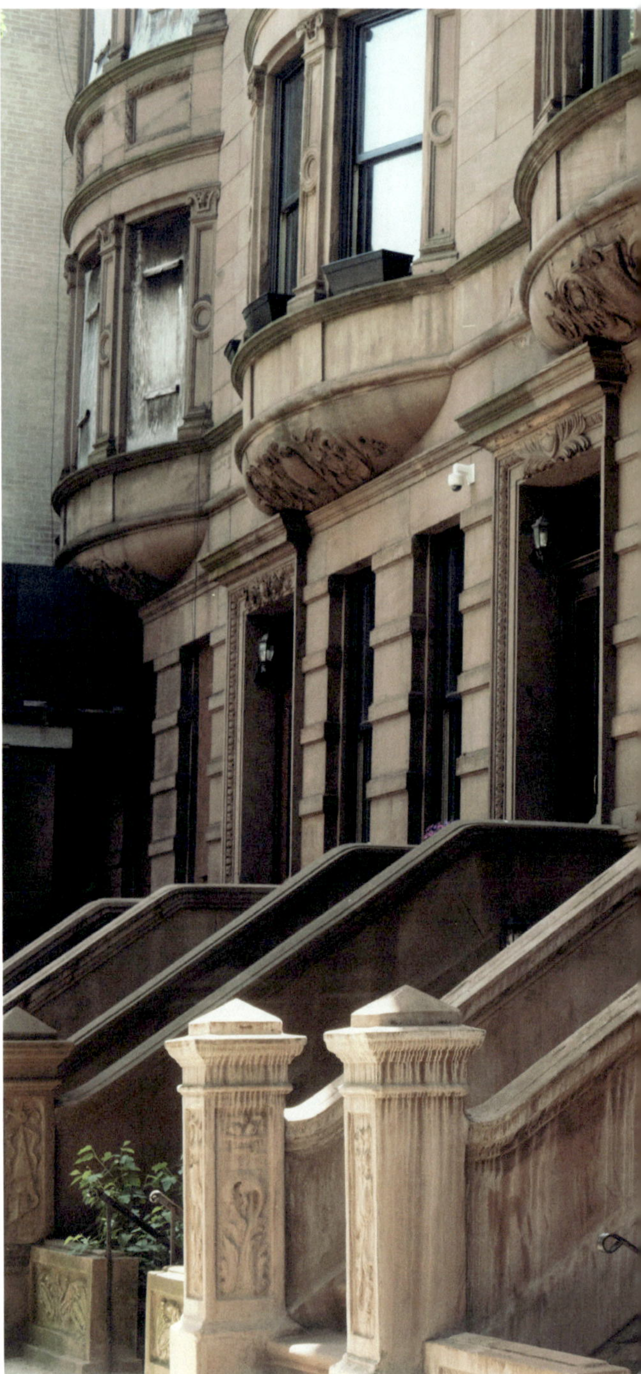

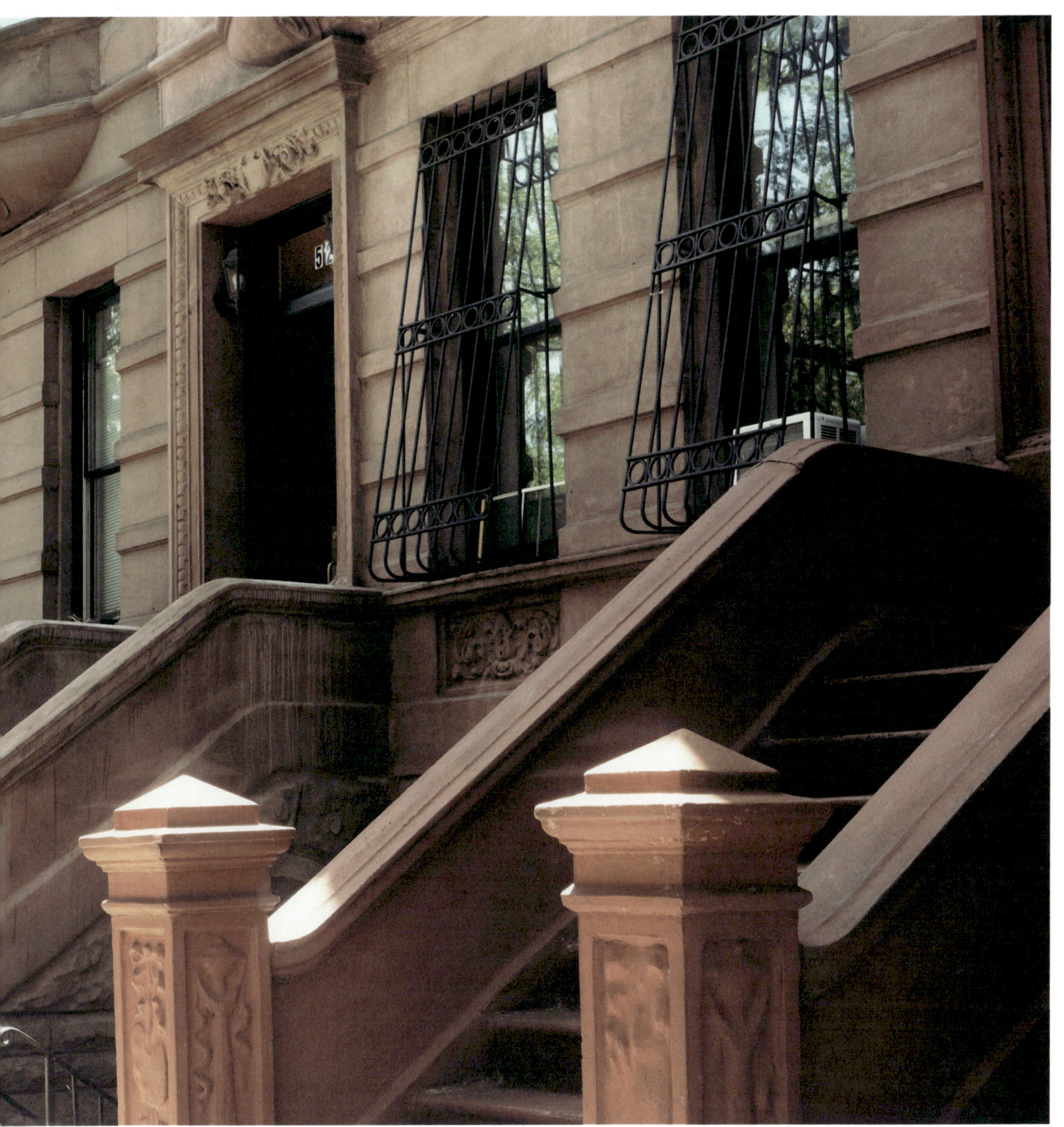

TONI L. GRIFFIN AND SARA ZEWDE

Coming back here a second time, after living in Newark—which is a very Black and Brown city, but also a very economically depressed city—I was just like, you know what? I don't want to live in the hood and I don't want to live in an all-white neighborhood. I don't want to live somewhere where I can't walk out of my house and go buy a gallon of milk. I want amenities *and* I want to live among people who look like me and share similar experiences to me. I want accessibility, identity, community, and coexistence. I want balance. I'm going back to Harlem.

SZ You moved here for personal reasons, but I'm curious as to what Harlem has given you professionally. What inputs has it provided to your practice?

TLG Super interesting question. It's complex because, shortly after I moved, I wrote an article for *The Huffington Post* questioning, "Am I a gentrifier?" I was two years into living here. This block in particular—120th Street and Lennox—was, at the time, predominantly Black, but still mixed race. I was grappling with the decisions I made about leaving Newark and recognizing that I, in fact,

"Economic displacement, when rents go up, means that a broader span of people are subject to being priced out... Cultural displacement, however, is the loss of an identity, of tradition, of community."

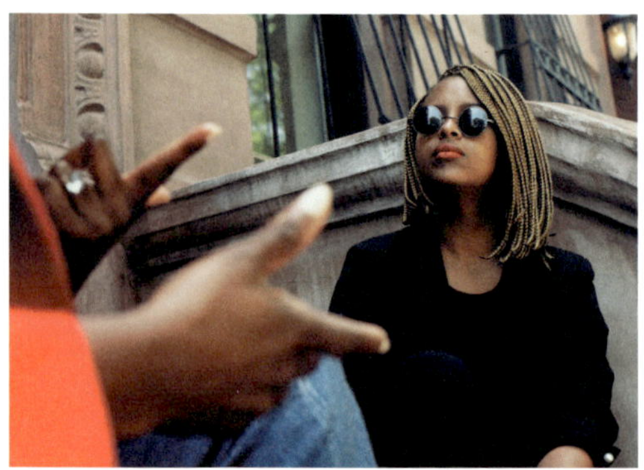

was a gentrifier, what that meant to me, and how we unpack what gentrification truly is. It's a term that people tend to use in a very binary way, and in a way that's most often negative. Gentrification is white folks moving into Black neighborhoods, displacing poor people, and especially displacing poor Black people. I was teaching a course on gentrification at the time, so I was thinking, "Okay, I'm living this, but what do I actually want to say about it?"

As I've watched this neighborhood transform for over a decade, I've thought more about the complexity of what neighborhood change means alongside aspects of displacement or dislocation. Economic displacement, when rents go up, means that a broader span of people are subject to being priced out. You and I were just talking about rents going up on commercial space nearby, so perhaps you have been gentrified out of an office. Cultural displacement, however, is the loss of an identity, of tradition, of community.

The threat of that loss comes when a different population moves in, who are not of the identity of people already in place; people who don't understand that identity, and perhaps also actively don't want to understand it. Then there's also civic displacement, a change in whose voices

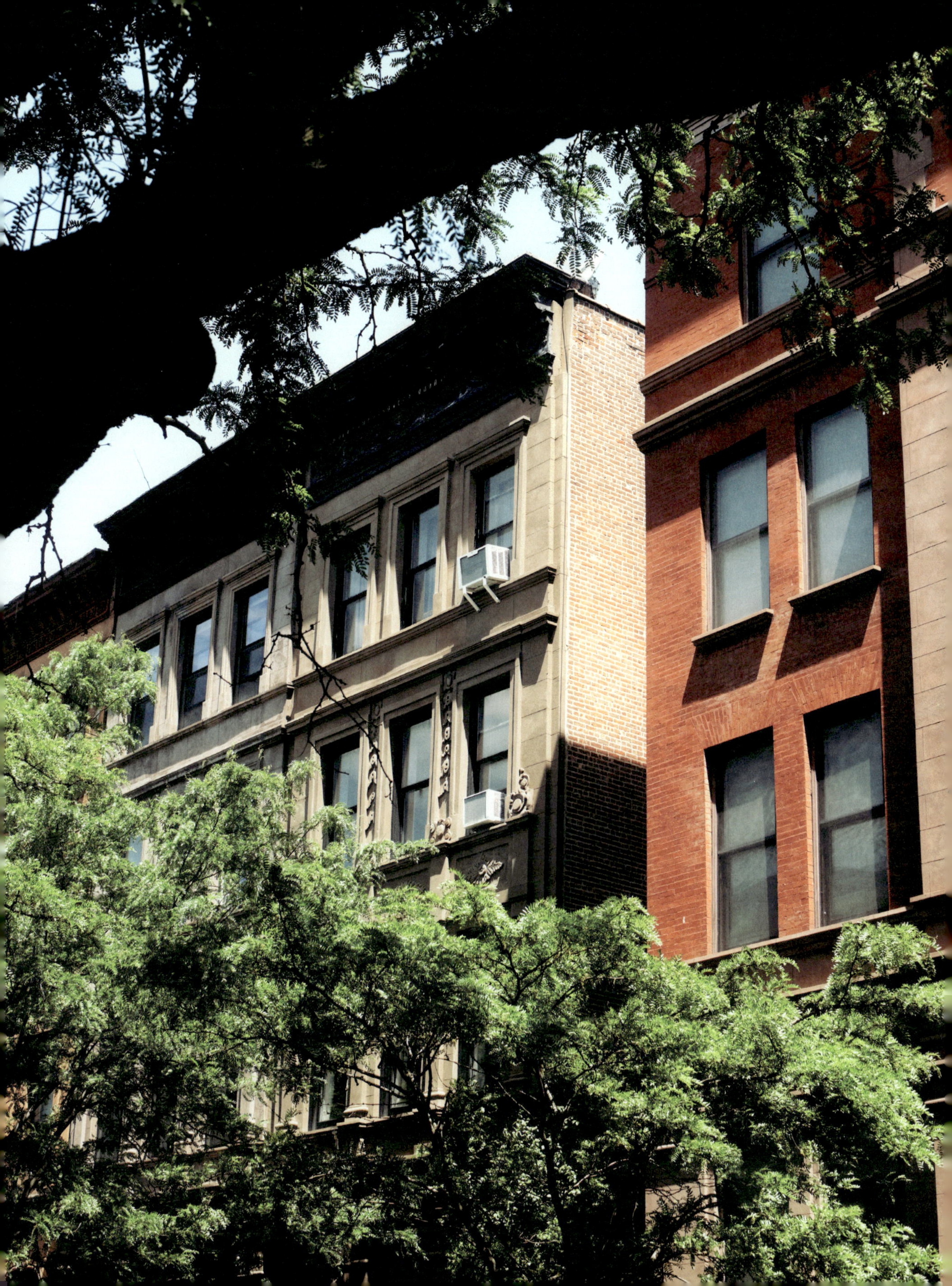

are shaping decisions within that community, both at the elected level and within the day-to-day negotiations that neighbors have with one another. Certain bodies bring with them power and resources to affect decision-making and change; Black residents in gentrifying neighborhoods must fight for the value of their Blackness, and their needs, against the inherent value of whiteness and white people's ability to mobilize their structural advantages to prompt services and changes in the neighborhoods they're moving into.

There are so many Black creatives who are an active part of this neighborhood change, living with and around us—gentrifiers and legacy residents. I feel so inspired, not just by the history of this place, but by the future possibilities of what this cohort of designers might inspire for one another.

SZ   That's the very value of place that is coming under threat given how digital our social lives have become during the pandemic. I think we've become more uncoupled from our value of place. What you're describing, on the other hand, suggests that there is an inherent and non-quantifiable value to being in a place, in union with one another, on an everyday basis.

To your point about gentrification, I try not to use the word because it's—

TLG   So loaded?

SZ   Well, yes, and it combines all the different dynamics of change that you described into one idea. In my office's projects across the country, in places that are experiencing rapid change, those dynamics are not always the same. Sometimes rents are going up but racial demographics aren't changing. Sometimes an area is simply densifying or, sometimes, people associate a particular aesthetic with gentrification. Sometimes it's the displacement of people that have many generations of connection to a place by newcomers with no legacy there. Combining all those different forms of change into one word prevents us from being able to identify the specifics of the type of change, and what its causes and implications might be.

TLG   Absolutely.

SZ   Toni, I would argue—and I'm curious what you think about this—that you're not a gentrifier, and here's why. I think gentrification, or very rapid change within a neighborhood, is possible because certain neighborhoods are artificially undervalued. Harlem has great building stock. It's in Manhattan, it's close to Central Park. Why is it artificially lower in value, relative to the rest of Manhattan? Because of the color of the skin of the people who live here. And, historically, it was always a mixed-income neighborhood. In fact, what makes a neighborhood stable is being mixed income. I think that having mixed income Black neighborhoods, like Harlem, is key.

TLG   It is essential.

SZ   So, in my opinion, your presence here is quite the opposite of what people would associate with gentrification.

TLG   That's interesting, and yet if you took race off the table and looked at my profile through the lens of how gentrification has historically been defined—which is around income—you and I are both part of a population that has a higher income than the historic baseline, and our income profiles are driving up the value of property and goods. In a way, I think we are feeling this erosion of place because we've started treating place, and home, as a commodity tethered to a market. We buy real estate as an investment for generating wealth rather than for the establishment of rootedness or a multi-generational sense of home. This commodification of place is what leaves us vulnerable to the erosion of place that you're talking about.

Now, when you put race back on that table, what's interesting is that Black folks with means have been buying assets in Harlem for decades. What's troubling is that this did not bring with it the escalation of value such that those who owned here saw their wealth increase decades ago. But it's notable that only when other bodies, different bodies, started to acquire assets here did the market then respond with a validation of Harlem as a commodity. That's the rub.

I've found that a lot of my students are very much interested in understanding involuntary displacement versus voluntary displacement, and how cultural displacement occurs within the involuntary category. The fight against the erosion of identity and ideals makes clear why a deeper understanding of what place means is so important. How do you come into a place and understand the fullness of what you're dealing with?

I think the public realm is where all these contests ultimately play out. As a landscape architect, how do you grapple, take on, or reject the term *placemaking*? Because I haven't found the term useful in my practice.

SZ   I'll put it this way. I think the aesthetics that are now associated with placemaking are more about making legible the value of a place to outsiders. Some of the most important Black cultural landscapes are parking lots. You know what I mean?

TLG   Yes.

SZ   Or a sidewalk. The placemaking lens is about saying, "This parking lot has value."

TLG   It's something.

SZ   As a landscape architect, we have interesting conversations about bolstering place in a way that's beyond placemaking. It's about rooting people's rituals of everyday life in space, and I think that ties into the kind of neighborhood change that we're talking about—anchoring it, mitigating it, evolving it.

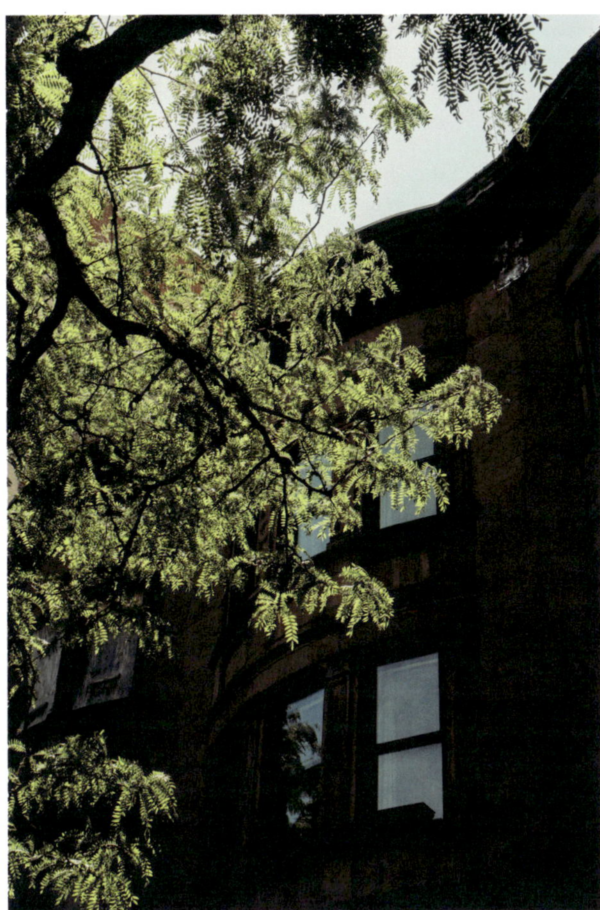 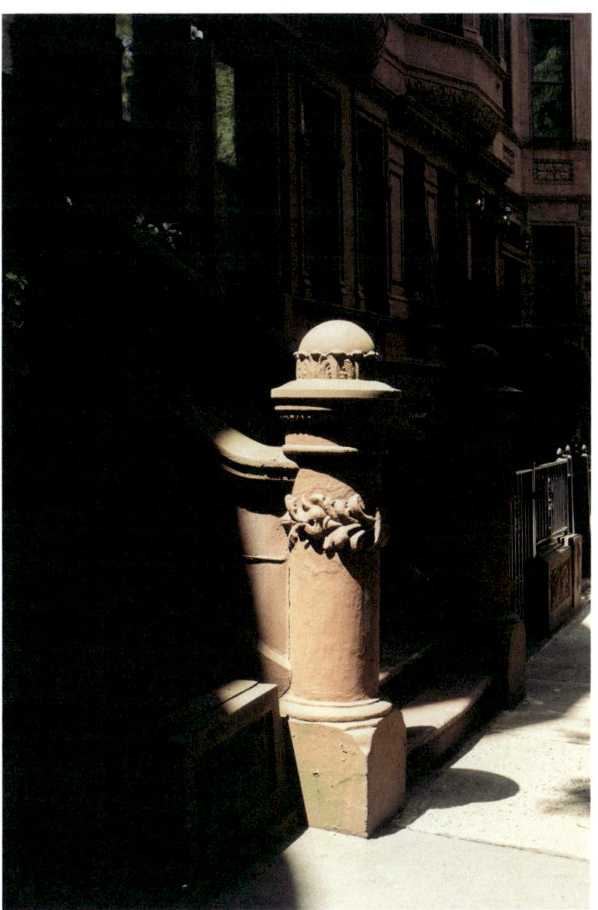

Speaking of asset generation, this block is one of the most highly valued in Harlem. Why? Because of the park. Not coincidentally, my block, which faces Central Park, is also one of the most expensive blocks in the neighborhood. There's a value that landscapes in the public realm create, a value that can be wielded. You and I, Toni, have always wanted to work together, yet we haven't. But we have this opportunity, because when design and policy come together, we can craft the kind of mechanisms that would allow for a neighborhood to be invested in by the residents it has historically been tied to. That takes both design and policy working together really, really intimately, and I feel the potential for that has yet to be explored.

TLG We will find something to work on together. I have no doubt about it. I find it interesting that when I read RFPs for the public space projects that are defined as components of the civic infrastructure of a neighborhood, they inevitably have to take on more than just the boundary of the public space. There are also the conditions of the neighborhood, such as the understanding of populations around that public space and who is its intended user, that

TONI L. GRIFFIN AND SARA ZEWDE

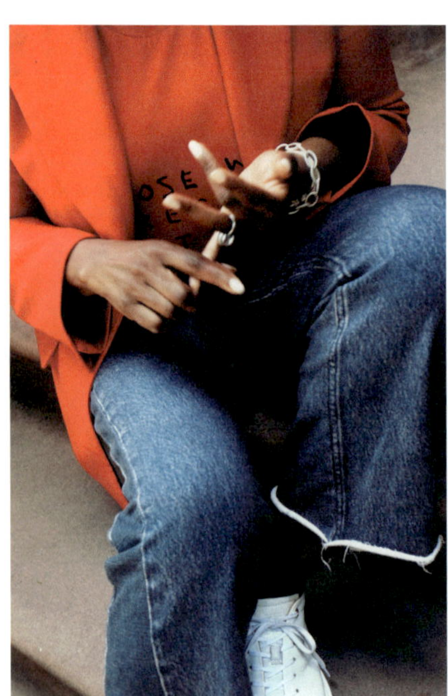

require a broader interrogation of the context in which the park sits.

Finding a way to help the people we work with, and for, understand that their neighborhood environs shape their landscape is where I hope we can create an opportunity to collaborate. The success of these types of projects requires additional investments and strategies that help lessen vulnerabilities, such as involuntary displacement, and ensure that those who we're designing for can actually be a part of that place once it's finished. When I worked in the public sector, I could shape policy, direct the way governments hire people like us, and help create the type of multidisciplinary teams that I knew were needed to design projects for our communities.

SZ   I've been doing research on the formation and early history of the discipline of landscape architecture. Our profession was founded by people who were engaged in politics. They were engaged in city building. We are, currently, 11 blocks from America's first public park, and it's 840 acres large. That's a city building project. Over the last two years, we saw Central Park become a mental health facility and a field hospital. Our parks and our public spaces are not just nice amenities—they're essential to city function and infrastructure. I had to go back to the history of the profession to be energized by that legacy, and it has emboldened my belief in the role landscape architecture can play in city building and neighborhood shaping.

TLG   It's something I've really been inspired by, too. We both wrote an essay in this issue of *Harvard Design Magazine*. Mine was rooted in the narratives of neighborhoods surrounding historic parks, which brings me to this topic of place and stories, which I find you always bring into your projects. Narrative is so important. History is your entry point to narrative, data is mine. You and I could look at the same data, but you may tell a very different narrative with the data than I would. I'm trying to teach my students how to learn to shape their own narratives, and for those of us who are working in Black neighborhoods, I'm encouraging the unearthing of hidden narratives—not the pervasive narrative of what a place looks like and projection of what you think is happening in it. For example, a new narrative we incorporate into our work in Black neighborhoods is that vacant land is actually an asset, not just the representation of disinvestment, devaluation, and extraction. Land is inherently valuable because it holds the potential for future valuation, and Black people should be a part of that.

Do you find that your use of narrative and storytelling is ever oversimplified as an engagement tactic versus as a legitimate aspect of the design process?

SZ   In a word, yes.

TLG   It becomes tactical rather than a substantive component of the design ideation.

SZ   Unfortunately, it's because there are not so many examples in which the narrative-centered aspects of the process have really borne out into a design that's resonant to those things. Again, I'm hoping to raise the expectations for design and our ability to do that. That's why I teach—because understanding people in place must be translated not only into design and detail, but also into construction.

The place you live in tells you something about yourself, your story, and whether that story is valued by your society. I don't take it lightly when we build a curb. Why is it six inches high? Is there a story there? Can we rewrite it and design this street to be reflective of another story? The idea of narrative is relevant to every phase of what we do, and at every scale.

By the way, Toni, I thought it was so interesting that you described your entry point into design as being from data, and mine from history. I don't know if you know this, but I have a background in statistics.

> "The place you live in tells you something about yourself, your story, and whether that story is valued by your society. I don't take it lightly when we build a curb. Why is it six inches high? Is there a story there? Can we rewrite it and design this street to be reflective of another story?"

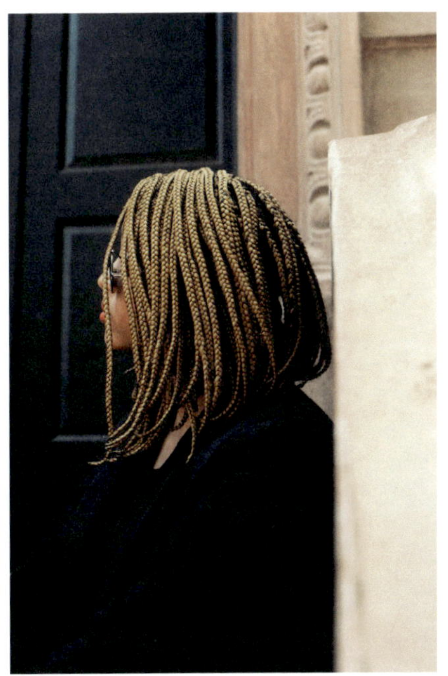

TLG   I did not. Another reason we need to work together.

SZ   In my view, statistics are a creative practice. Statistics are not so much a science but an art—the art of identifying a pattern and crafting a story about it.

TLG   That's such a powerful tool when you are working with community sectors. Sometimes I bristle at using the word "community," because people tend to think I'm only talking about resident folk, but I'm actually talking about all the different sectors that *make* a community, such as government, business, nonprofits, faith-based institutions, philanthropy, *and* residents—each of these are part of shaping place, the responsibility to use data accurately and thoughtfully, and the stories we tell about both people and place. Historical narratives, cultural narratives, data narratives—they're all intermingled. Most of the cities I work in have contested legacies and deep histories of racial segregation, extraction, and discrimination. Even today, the undercurrent of that tension makes its way into community decision-making processes. The different stakeholders in these conversations experience place quite differently. The use of data and narrative can help to balance power dynamics, because if everyone is armed with the

TONI L. GRIFFIN AND SARA ZEWDE

same information and has the ability to share their stories, it helps legitimize varied life experiences and perspectives and ground people in common facts, which I find can be very powerful.

SZ   When we talk about Black places specifically, there's a tradition of storytelling that far predates Black people's presence in the Americas. Stories have long been a primary vessel for understanding who we are in the world. Walter Hood and I were having a conversation about the difference between a narrative and a story.

TLG   What'd you come up with?

SZ   He likes to use the word "story" because of the understanding that a story is fabricated. There's a usefulness to a liberated relationship with what we tell ourselves about who we are and where we live. Whatever you call it, I think it's about having an idea, a framework, a concept that people feel is flexible enough to put into and take out of. It's not about a didactic way of telling, like something written on a plaque, but more about forming a relationship to the built environment that is about dissonance.

TLG   Yes. Narratives can be the projections that we associate with place. Those projections can perpetuate actions based on false information, while stories can help to enrich, dismantle, or create alternatives to harmful narratives.

I have one last question for you. What are you hopeful or excited about in terms of your creative process and the places you're working in?

SZ   I want to raise our expectations about what design can offer people. I believe that landscape design has the ability to elevate people's sense of belonging in the world. I want to fully express that in the built environment, raise expectations, and hopefully prompt us all to engage more in the places we live.

TLG   Similarly, I feel that these last 10 years—in my practice, urbanAC [Urban American City], and at the Just City Lab at Harvard—have been a space for reflecting on the impact of what I've done across my career and how I want to find opportunities to push further, because I'm not satisfied that I've adequately expressed these aspirations in the built world yet.

I'm eager to figure out, as you explained, how that can manifest beyond a plaque or a marker or an object in public space, or even just the fact that I engage Black and Brown people in the process. To me, that is an insufficient representation of the belonging of Black and Brown bodies in the public realm. I think there's a deep culture of Americanism rooted in white supremacy that makes this difficult to unpack, and maybe it's naive of me to think that the built environment alone can satisfy what it truly means to belong in a place. But I continue to be super excited about projects that afford me the chance to poke at that possibility.

SZ   Let's do that.●

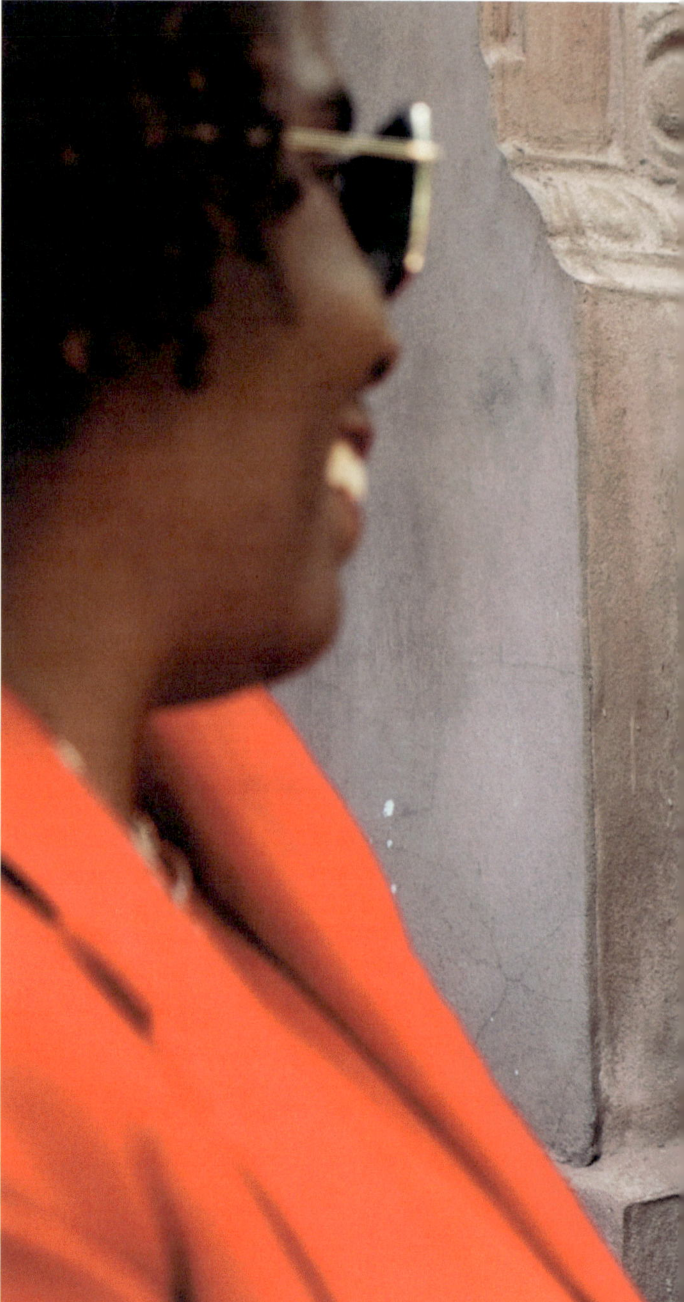

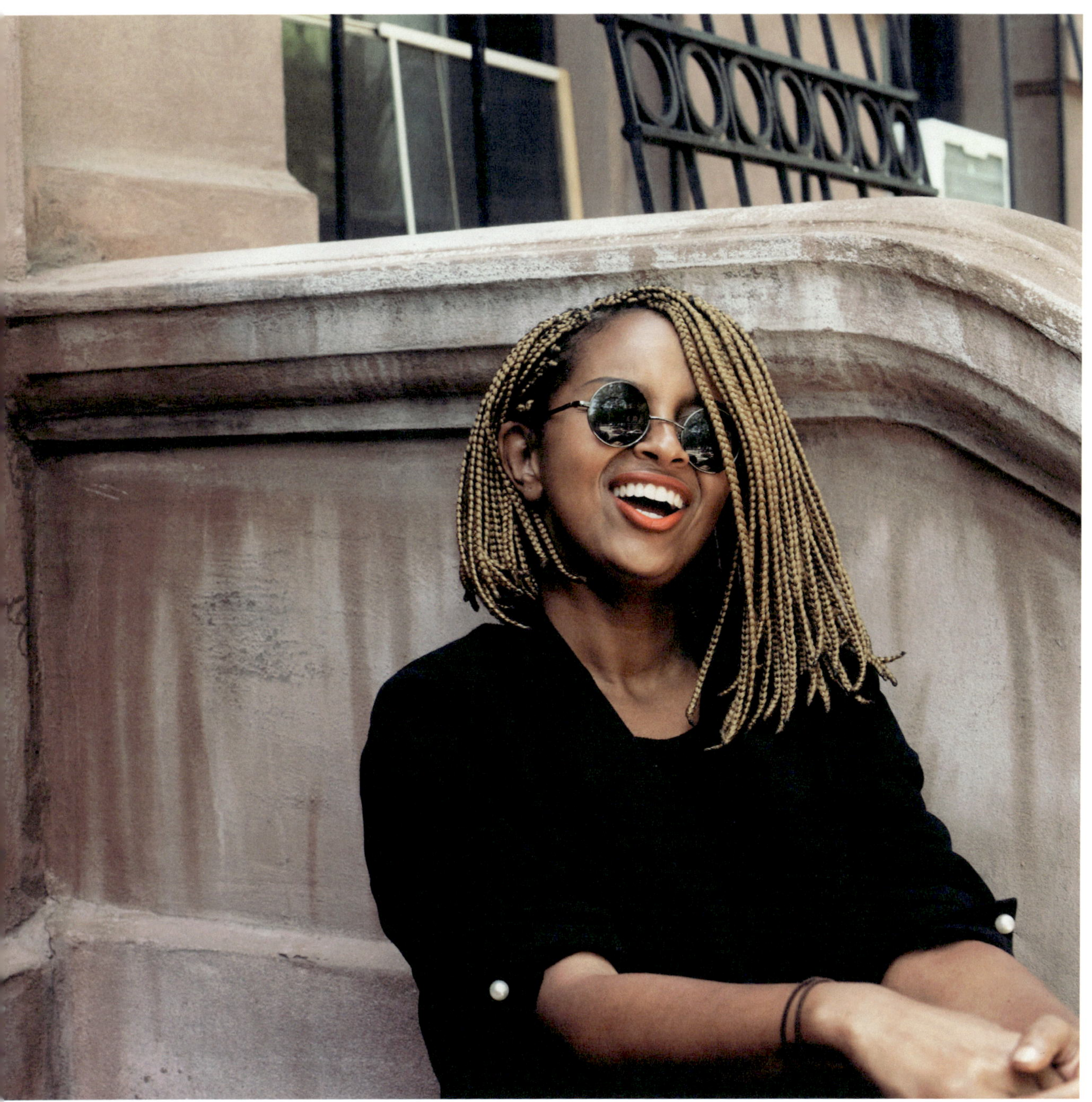

Sara Zewde is Founding Principal of Studio Zewde, a landscape architecture firm based in the Harlem neighborhood of New York City. Parallel to practice, she also serves as Assistant Professor in Practice of Landscape Architecture at the Harvard University Graduate School of Design.

Toni L. Griffin is founder of urbanAC LLC, a planning and design management practice based in New York that works with public, private, and nonprofit partnerships to reimage, reshape, and rebuild just cities and communities. The practice designs and leads complex and transformative social and spatial urban revitalization projects rooted in addressing historic and current disparities involving race, class, and generation. She is also a Professor in Practice of Urban Planning at the Harvard University Graduate School of Design and founder and director of the Just City Lab, an applied research platform that investigates the ways design can have a positive impact on addressing the conditions of injustice in cities.

DREAMPLACE: Doreen Chan on the subconscious as meeting space

As told to
Isabel Flower

One of my solo shows was about my daddy passing and the grief that, for a long time, I was unable to deal with. That show was called "How to Close a Window." Another was about my break-up with my ex-boyfriend, after we had spent a lot of time together in his parents' very small apartment, which is a typical situation for Hong Kong. That show was called "Hard Cream." The first show was about grief, and the second was perhaps more about memory, but both reflected how I was struggling to handle a change. I guess you could call that trauma.

I feel like I make art to help myself deal with trauma. These two exhibitions were very personal. When Lalie Choffel, the curator from Charbon Art Space in Hong Kong, asked me what I wanted my show to be about, I chose my daddy because I knew his death was something I needed to deal with but hadn't. Every time he was mentioned I would cry, because the image I had in my mind was of him lying inside his coffin. I was always scared of how I would handle my grief once it was triggered by a conversation or a thought. I created a task for myself—to help myself not have only this one picture in my head. I spent time sorting through my memories of him instead of interviewing my mom or his family and friends. The material for the show was the experiences we shared, which were stored in my memories. For "Hard Cream," which happened at HB Station, I used a similar method. I created the work with my memory, by going back to bring something up. I went back to the memory and felt it all over again. Then, the emotion that was produced by whatever I brought up was transformed into the idea or concept in my work. Sometimes it could feel a bit dangerous to do it. Sometimes it made me a bit depressed. But it is also a process that can help me digest. It helped me be able to talk about my daddy to you now.

For me, a place is a space that contains memory. I think that, in general, dreaming happens in a space that is always there. But when the dreamer remembers a dream and thinks about it, it becomes a place. Beginning in March of 2020, I started remembering my dreams every night. This was partially the trigger point for the idea for my current project, HalfDream, which is a lot about the collective experience of social events. HalfDream, which I will tell you more about in a few moments, felt like a way to explain my psychological condition at the time. I moved to Chicago in August of 2019, during the peak of the social movement in Hong Kong. I was worrying a lot about everyone back home and I felt very powerless being in the US. Then COVID arrived, and I was trying to figure out what my place was, especially as a foreigner who didn't really know the culture. I was thinking about the dreams I was having; they were very intense, and I wondered if others were dreaming the same way that I was, or about the same things.

I used to think of myself and introduce myself as a visual artist, but HalfDream is different from my previous work because it's an online platform that is developed for a general audience and, lately, I am more like a project manager. HalfDream collects dreams from people all over the world and connects them to other people who are dreaming about similar things. I guess it is a form of social media, but it connects people based on shared experiences rather than what we might perceive as a shared identity. We have tried to make this a safe and intimate space, as we are dealing with something very personal, and it's been very special to develop the user experience with my team. Without my team, and the support of the Burger Collection and TOY Meets Art, this project would not have been possible.

HalfDream users can share their dreams in writing or through voice recordings, by uploading images or videos from their daily life that relate to the dream, or with a function we created that allows you to draw a scene from a dream. This helps to reveal and address if and how the experiences in our waking life affect and inform our dreams. All these processes help our users to revisit and remember—we even have an audiovisual exercise that helps you to do this, as many people forget their dreams quickly after they wake up. We also offer a reminder option to prompt people to record their dreams early in the day.

Another function of the interface lists common dream elements that people can choose from—these details inform the design of what we call "dream generated objects." These are abstracted visual expressions of different parts of the dream, which also serve to create intimacy between people without relying on facts that might reveal information about who they are. Every dream also has its own QR code which can be printed out and shared in public places. Even though the platform is online, I still want there to be a strong connection to real life, beyond the screen. I want to link dreams back to neighborhoods, communities, and physical places. The hope is to match people with similar dreams into pairs or small groups. They are then invited on a virtual journey where for 5-7 days they will each complete one offline exercise per day, which we then forward to their dreammates. We hope this generates a connection both between the dreamers and to their waking lives. At the end of this period, they will have the option to exchange contact information.

Many of the details around how HalfDream functions are specifically designed to hide the identities of the dreamers, at least in terms of how society tends to construct these categories. Dreams have an interesting relationship to ideas about the self, and to online experiences in general. While most online experiences involve and/or are influenced by others, dreams are solitary and can feel out of our control, except in the case of lucid dreaming, which has recently been cultivated as a tool for treating PTSD. Another way to think about this is around how our online experiences—such as how we use search engines—are mediated by AI. These machines track patterns from our behavior that are, in ways, subconscious. All of the data about what we do in virtual space—such as what kinds of things we click on—very much influences our psychology. It is reflected back to us like a mirror that repeats and reinforces certain thoughts and memories. This is a lot like dreaming to me. As an artist, I care very much about people's well-being. In choosing dreams as a medium, I am hoping to facilitate people to construct and make meaning within their own dreamplaces, in ways that will actually affect their lives.●

Doreen Chan's artistic practices focus on investigations of personal perception, materiality, and daily details that are often overlooked. Primarily a lens-based and site-specific artist, in her current participatory art project, HalfDream, she blends her deep desire to connect people and the progressive development of her artistic practices with a focus on reexamining the tensions between interpersonal relationships, personal memories, and immediate environments. Chan was listed as a finalist in the Three Shadows Photography Award in 2015, the Art Sanya Huayu Youth Award in 2019, the VH Award in its fourth year, and has received the Pritzker Fellowship.

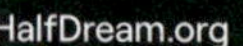
HalfDream.org

Image from Doreen Chan, HalfDream, single channel video, 5'37", 2021 Commissioned by VH AWARD of Hyundai Motor Group.

HALFDREAM
Wake up before your dream ended?
Find someone with the rest of the story.
Participatory art project,
"Archive of Dreams"

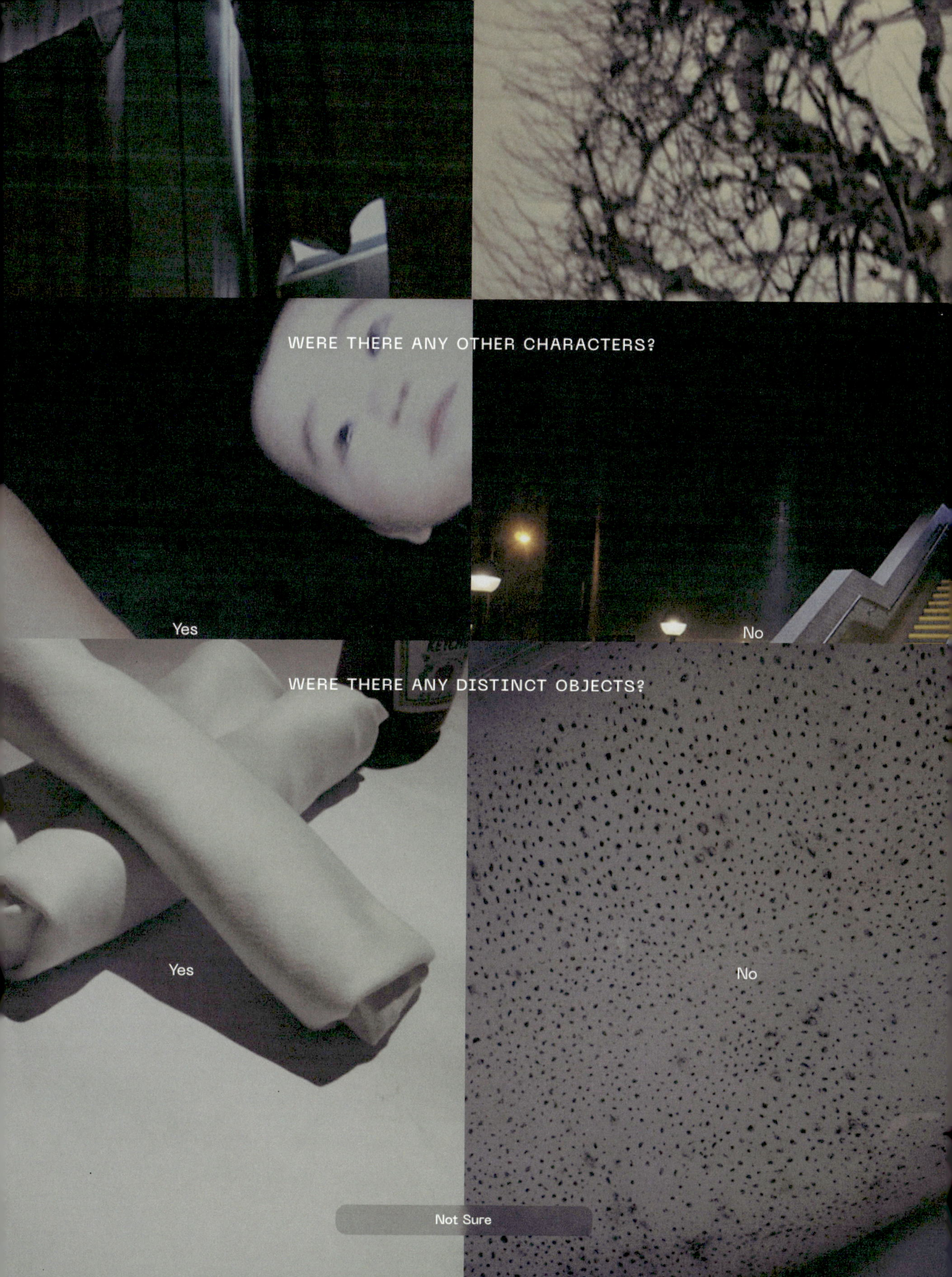
WERE THERE ANY OTHER CHARACTERS?
Yes
No
WERE THERE ANY DISTINCT OBJECTS?
Yes
No
Not Sure

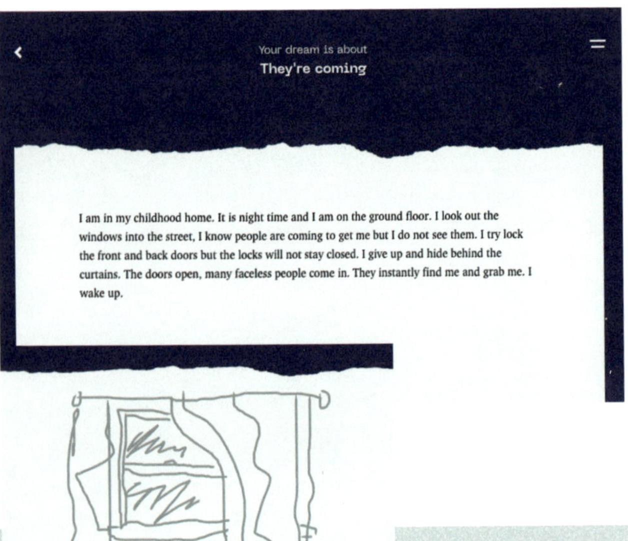

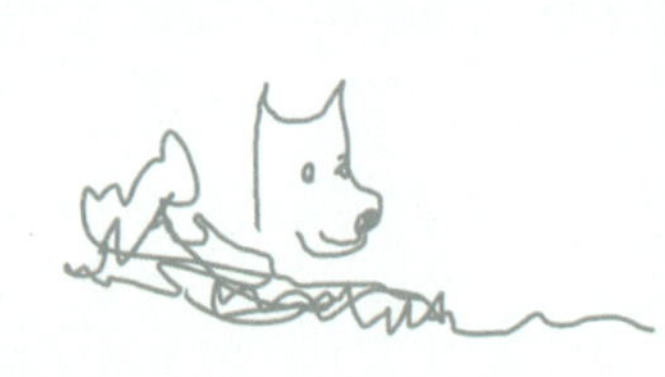

Dream testimonies and
dream-sharing capabilities
from HalfDream.

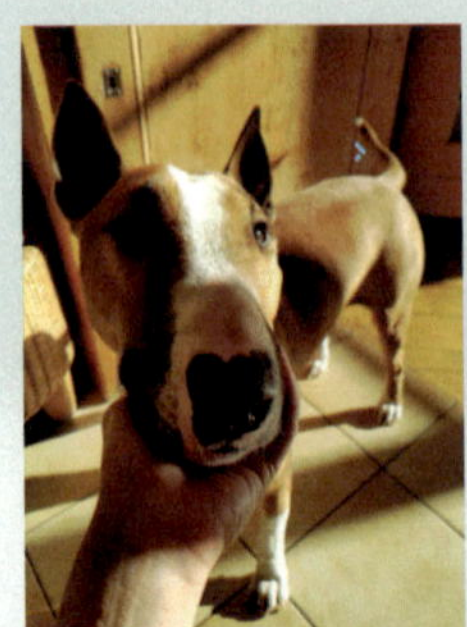

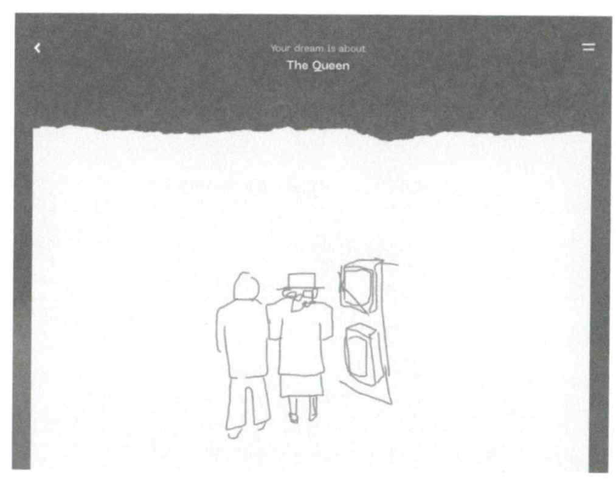

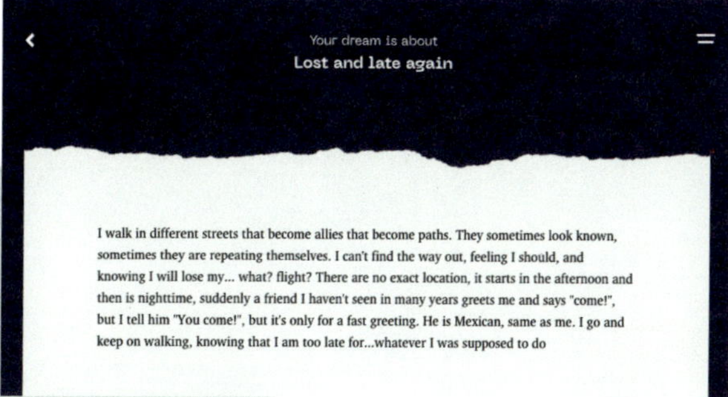

I walk in different streets that become allies that become paths. They sometimes look known, sometimes they are repeating themselves. I can't find the way out, feeling I should, and knowing I will lose my... what? flight? There are no exact location, it starts in the afternoon and then is nighttime, suddenly a friend I haven't seen in many years greets me and says "come!", but I tell him "You come!", but it's only for a fast greeting. He is Mexican, same as me. I go and keep on walking, knowing that I am too late for...whatever I was supposed to do

I was seated between my two sisters on a cold wooden pew in the middle of a Catholic Mass. Like the other worshippers, our family was facing the front of the church, attentive. During a pause in the prayers, I turned and yelled as loud as I could in the ear of my Left Sister. It was a single, derogatory swear word. It was an accusation. Then I swiveled my neck 180 degrees and screamed the same B-word into the ear of my Right Sister. I went back and forth screaming at them alternately without ever moving my shoulders, just my chin. It was very rhythmic. There was no reaction, in fact, it was as though time had paused for me, and everyone in the church was frozen. The echoes of my cussing floated above our heads up into the dark ceiling of the nave. I felt vindicated.

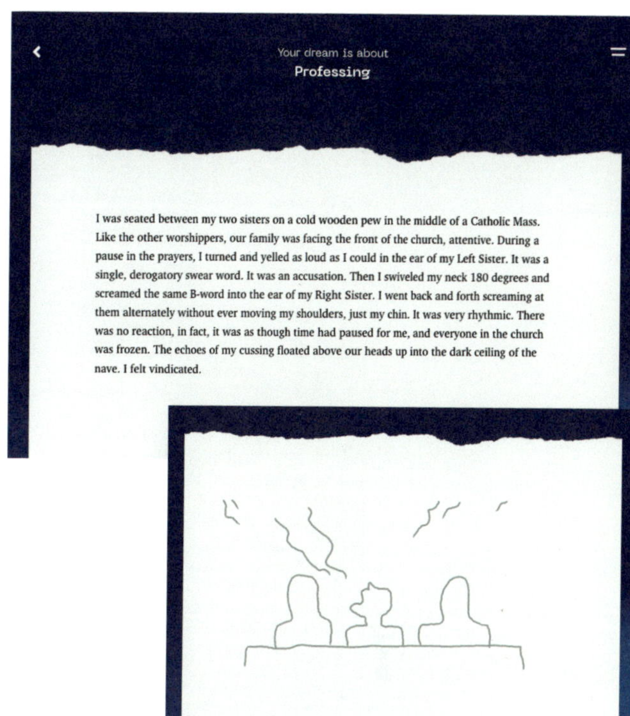

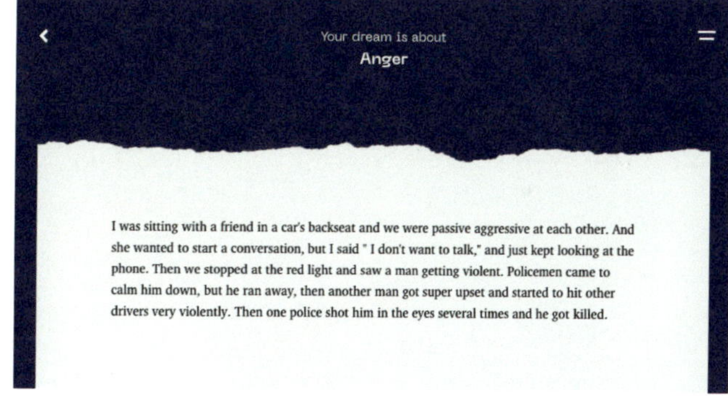

I was sitting with a friend in a car's backseat and we were passive aggressive at each other. And she wanted to start a conversation, but I said " I don't want to talk," and just kept looking at the phone. Then we stopped at the red light and saw a man getting violent. Policemen came to calm him down, but he ran away, then another man got super upset and started to hit other drivers very violently. Then one police shot him in the eyes several times and he got killed.

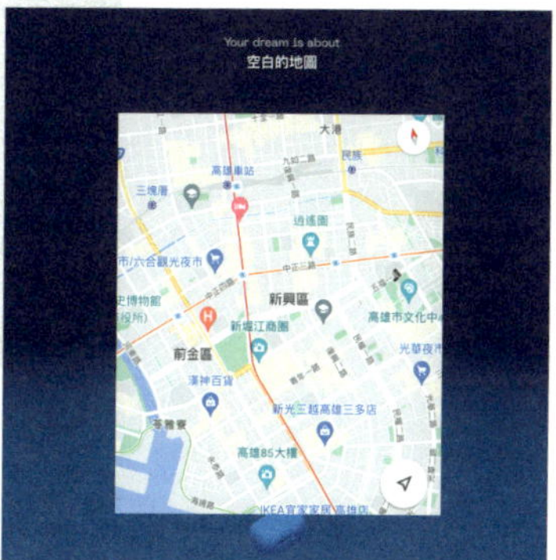

I was working in my living room, typing a text on my computer. This is not the place I usually work because I have my office upstairs. There were two enormous wild boars in the living room too, roaming around. It felt strange. I did not let them enter but I knew my husband did. My husband was actually working in my office and I could hear him above me. I wanted to go to the toilets but it meant walking through the living room and I was afraid of the boars. I called my husband: "I want to go to the toilets! What shall I do? They are blocking the way!" He just said, very serene: no worries. I felt he let me down. Then I saw them climbing the stairs. "They are coming!" I shouted. Next, I opened a door and entered the apartment of a very old friend, who I haven't seen for years. He was writing too, but sitting on the floor, surrounded by two fluffly rabbits. His wife welcomed me. She was so thin I could not help saying it. I could feel her bones when I touched her shoulders. She resembled a ghost and she did not reply. I have never liked her, but felt sorry for her. I thought she had wasted her life. "What is going on?" I asked my friend. He did not care answering and was caressing his rabbits. "They are too big, they are going to explode." I said but I knew this was meaningless. I felt embarrassed and stood, immobile. I thought that this situation was really stupid and that this was going nowhere.

DOREEN CHAN

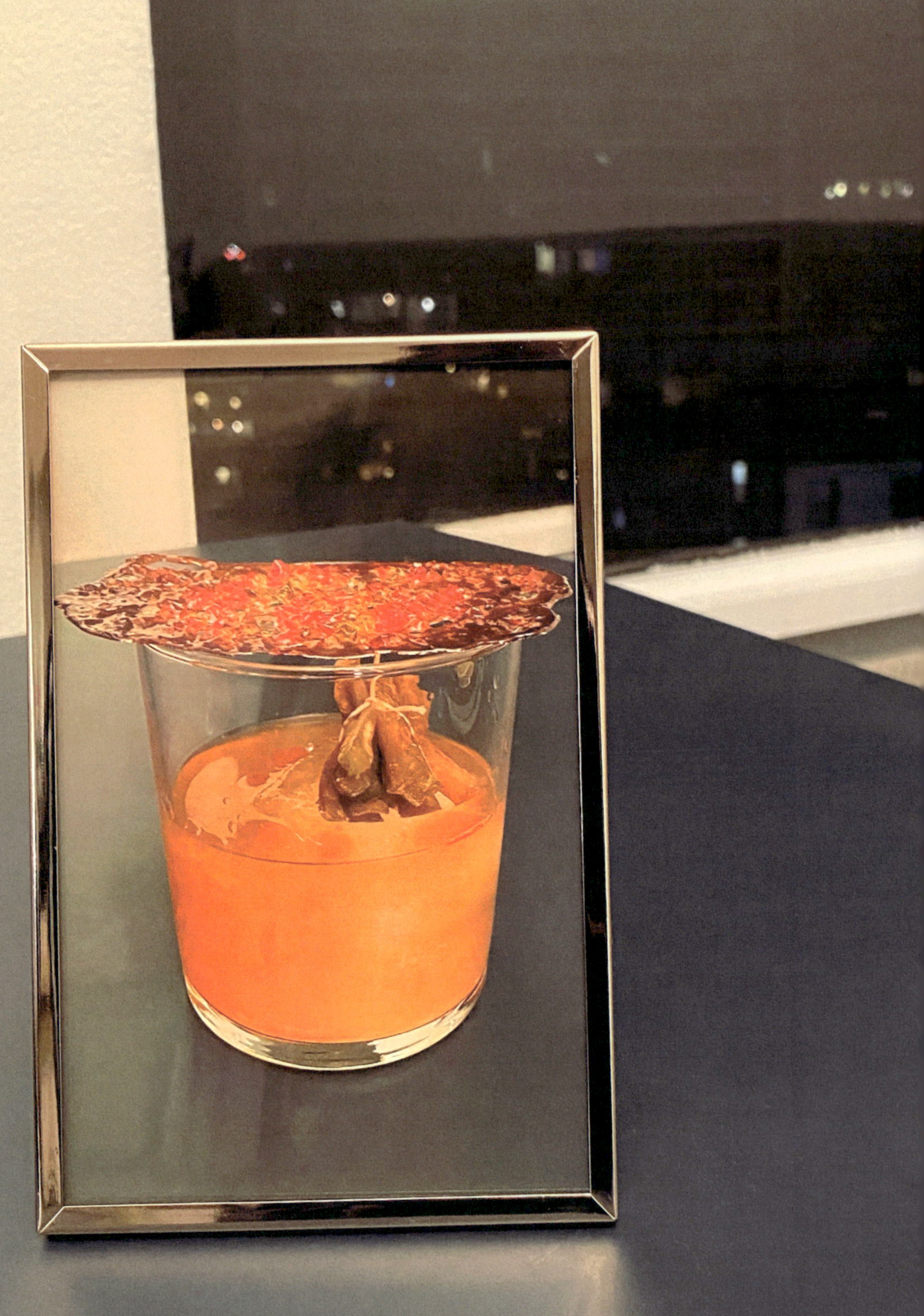

A cocktail based on a dream shared for HalfDream.

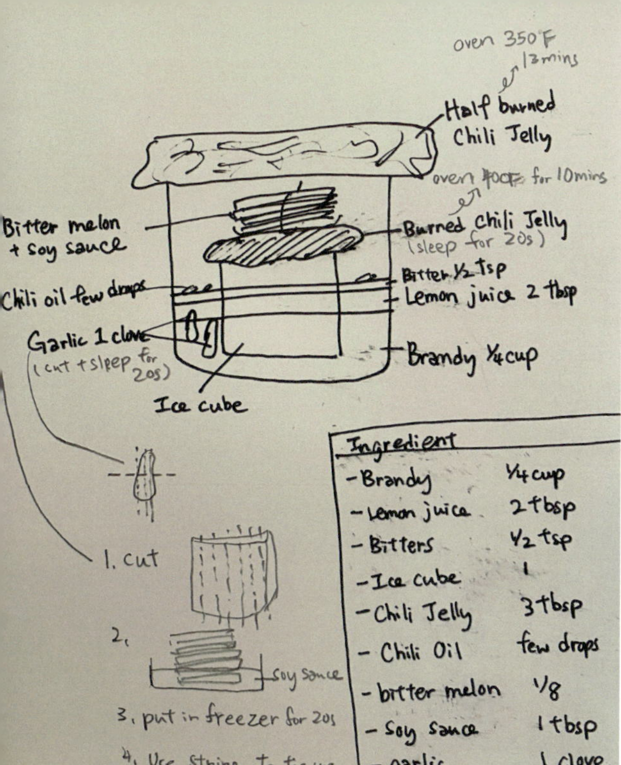

Recipe for a dream-based cocktail.

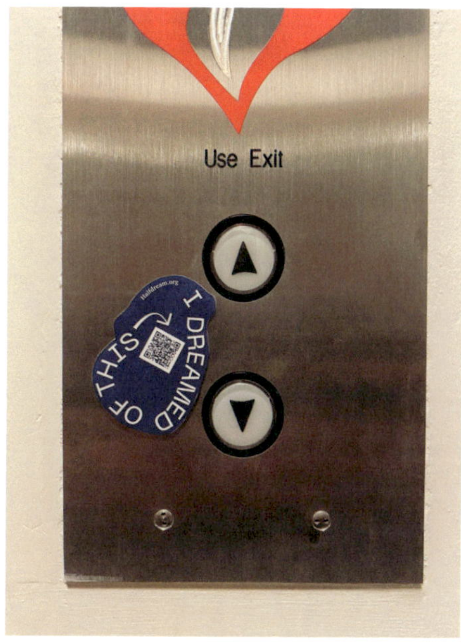

QR code sticker for a dream.

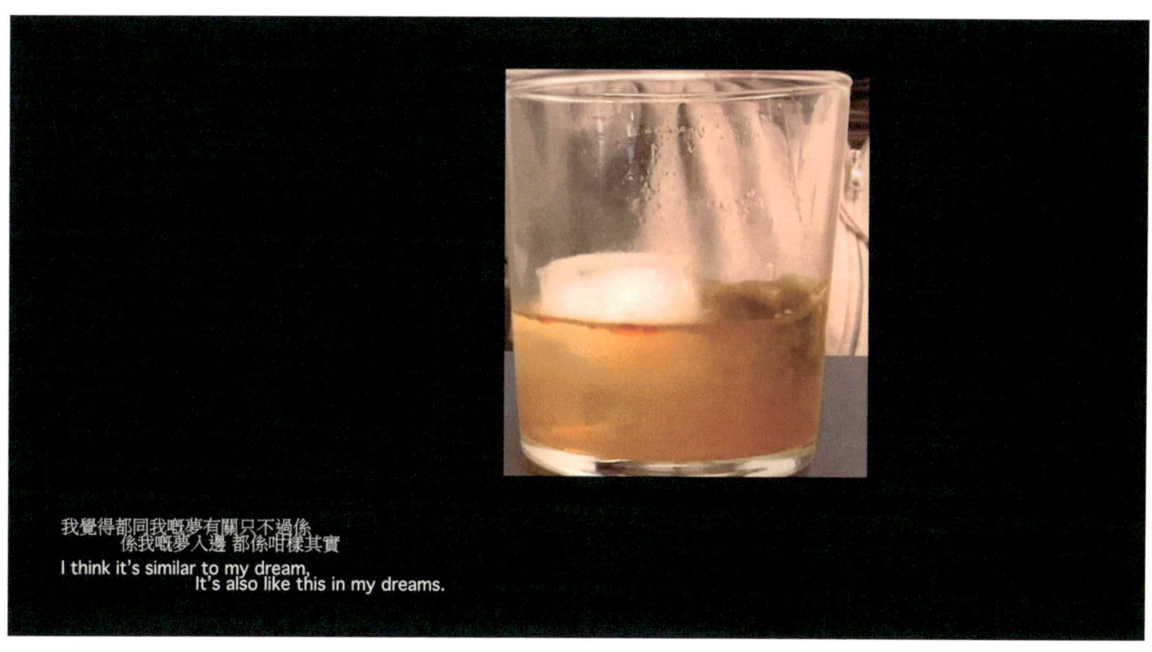

A conversation with the dreamer, while drinking a dream-based cocktail.

DOREEN CHAN

Teaching the Way We Needed to Be Taught: Valencia Gunder in conversation with Marquise Stillwell

70

MARQUISE STILLWELL   Tell us a bit about the work that you've long been involved in to combat poverty and homelessness. Give us a little bit of how you got there and what that looks like today.

VALENCIA GUNDER   I work amongst the most vulnerable population here in the United States—those who are unhoused. People are supposed to have housing, food, and water: the three basics. Yet, here in the US, there are many people who do not have those things. Back in 2010, I was one of those people for a short while, and it was devastating. I think about it all the time and the inaccessibility of solutions and programming, even stuff that is designed for that specific community. This was 11 or 12 years ago now and I was in Tallahassee, which is a medium-urban city about eight hours north of Miami. It ain't rural, but it ain't quite urban. It's right there in the middle. At the time, I promised myself that when I got on my feet, I was going to help. I was going to do something. In 2014, I organized a day around feeding folks in my community who were hungry. I put it on social media and all these volunteers showed up. We ended up serving bagged lunches all day. I thought it was going to be a one-time event, but here we are, eight years later, and I'm still out here feeding, serving, supporting.

MS   Hearing you speak, it's clear you have a spirit of service and what I call deep EQ. An empathetic mindset is very different from a charitable one. How do you find a way to serve that preserves the fundamental dignity of the people you're working with?

VG   I always tell people that I don't do charity. I do passion work and I create models of self-determination. I believe that everybody wants to take care of themselves. I have never met an unsheltered person who likes being unsheltered. I have never met a hungry person who likes being hungry, ever. Now, if they have access to the tools and resources to get these things for themselves, I'm quite sure

they'll do it. They might need some support and some guidance, but they'll do it.

When we go out to serve, it's always through the mindset of self-determination. I like to show up and treat people exactly how I would want to be treated if I was in that situation. How would I want somebody to talk to me? How would I want somebody to hand me a plate of food? How would I want somebody to treat me if I wasn't feeling my best or my strongest? I feel it is also my duty as a human being to support other human beings on this earth because I'm not self-made, I'm community-made. My community pours into me. My community

71

chose me to be a leader in this movement space and my community supports the upkeep of The Smile Trust, which is the nonprofit I created to provide services to people who are unhoused.

MS   You really turned a moment into a movement. How do you instill this approach in others?

VG   I teach by showing up. I've been serving on the same corner in the same community for the past eight years. When you show up the same way over and over again, you build consistency, and consistency between people creates family. It's not just for the people we serve, but also for the volunteers. I've been so proud that we've had many of the same volunteers for the last eight years, too.

This is a humanizing experience. None of it is transactional. None of it is hierarchical. I'm serving food and picking up trash just like everybody else. I embrace my volunteers, just like I embrace the unsheltered population. It's just showing up in that type of love. That has become what I look for all the time, including in my personal life.

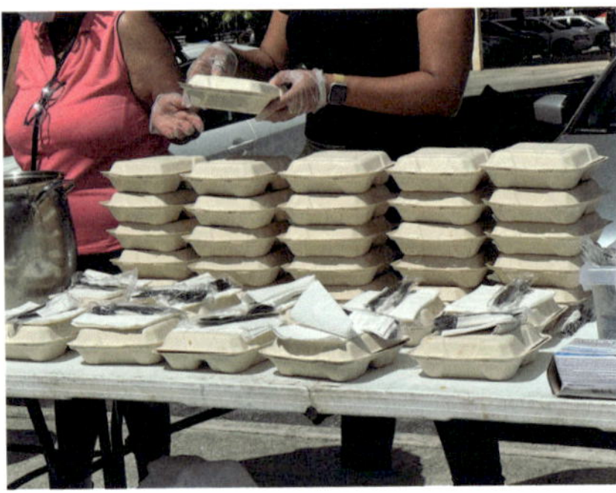

Courtesy of The Smile Trust Inc.

MS   That's what I meant when I said the moment became a movement. But also, how is dignity specifically sustained? The issue in so many kinds of organizing is sustainability.

VG   One thing that seems to surprise people is that I don't want to be doing service work for the rest of my life. I can't wait for the day when people just have what they need and they don't need to wait on Valencia, their government, or nobody else. I don't feel like anything I build belongs to me, nor does it need me to function. Everything that I create or learn to do, I teach other people as well. I didn't go to Smile Day this past Sunday because I wasn't feeling well, but everything happened right on the money. It went smooth because everyone involved knows how to serve. I think that's so important—teaching people tools and solutions and then stepping out of the way and letting them make it their own.

MS   I come from the "each one, teach one" generation but, in many ways, we've become selfish. Part of *Deem*'s vision is to return to that mindstate, which is why we invite

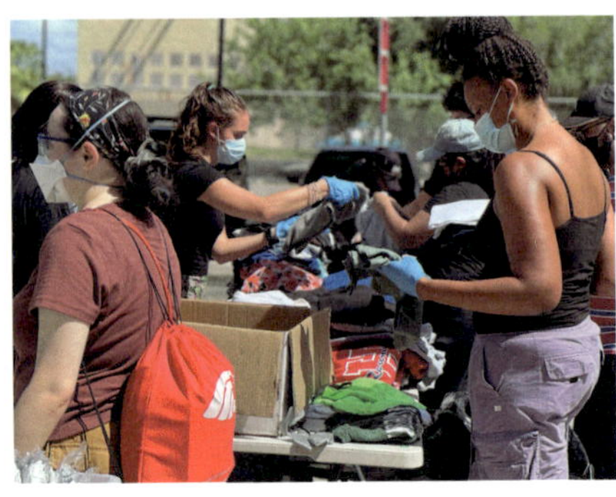

Courtesy of The Smile Trust Inc.

individuals like yourself to share their perspectives and experiences. This issue of the journal is themed around place, and I'd like to shift now to talk about climate gentrification, which is a major concern regarding our current and future places. These changes don't happen overnight. When and how did you first start to observe climate gentrification in effect?

VG   I'm from Miami. My family's been here for many generations, and some are even Indigenous to this land. My family and I have seen many iterations of this place. As a child I lived in Liberty City, which is a historically Black neighborhood on the inland side—what I call the *real* Miami.

I always tell the story about how my grandfather, during the crack era, said, "They're going to come steal our communities because it don't flood here." I was like, "Chill out, granddaddy, ain't nobody want to live here!" I didn't see the beauty in that place when I was growing up. We were under-resourced and I didn't feel I had access to the larger landscape. I went off to college, came back, and one day at a community meeting I heard all these people saying the same thing my grandfather had said. Mind you, this is 10 or 15 years later. I now have my formal education and training in agricultural business, so I'm hearing the conversation differently and realizing, wow—this is real.

By the time I got home, a lot had changed. Miami was already a different place. Wynwood,

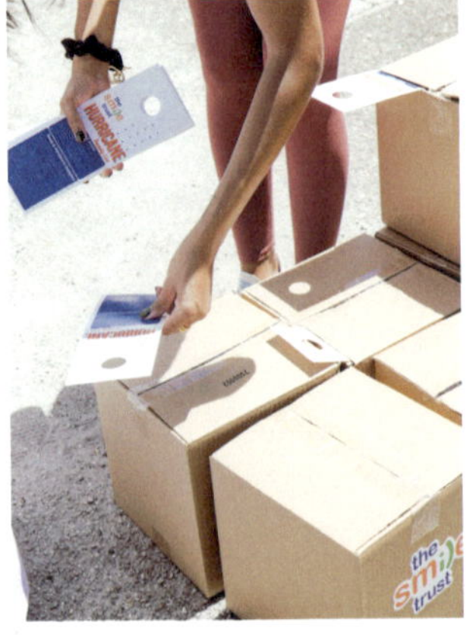

Photograph by Melody Timothee.

which used to be a Dominican community, had become an art district. These days, a house in Little Haiti is running you a half a million dollars. These drastic shifts happened extremely quickly. It was very confusing. Even the infrastructure of some of the roads changed. I would drive around and wonder, "Where are all the fruit trees?" Miami is, first and foremost, a *tropical* place. It's a paradise. We have tangerine and mango trees you could pick the fruit right off and eat. When I came back, I was like, "Why am I buying oranges and mangos in a grocery store?" I had never seen or purchased a mango in a grocery store in Miami. Capitalism had finally come to play. In addition to that, the climate itself had noticeably changed. It was always warm, but I don't remember the extreme heat. That changed the vegetation as well. I was experiencing the combined effect of many forces at play all at once.

MS Climate gentrification has a few different acceleration points. You have the acceleration of the climate itself, and you have the acceleration of the people moving in and out. Then there's the added pressure that storms are hap-

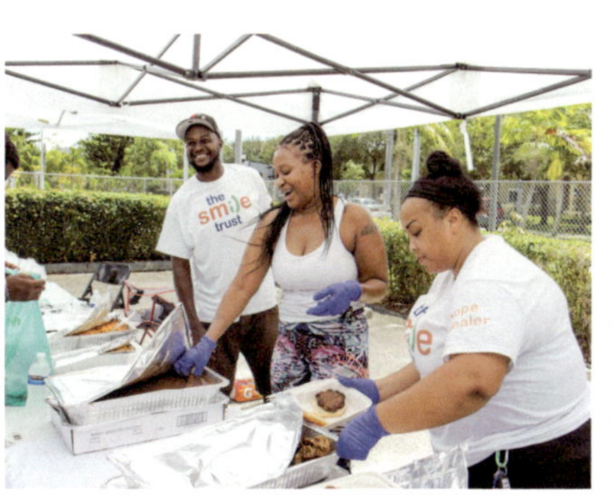

Photograph by Melody Timothee.

government to even begin to admit that we were in the middle of a climate crisis. This was in 2012, 2013. Mind-boggling. Then it was trying to teach our government that what people were feeling without having scientific data was a real thing. Because, at one point in time, feelings were not included. Even now, feelings are not really relevant to the decision-making spaces within our government. When we weren't being heard, we had to get proof—we had to make it—because I don't play that.

"It's absolutely mind-boggling to navigate the state government and climate deniers when we are ground zero in the world for sea level rise."

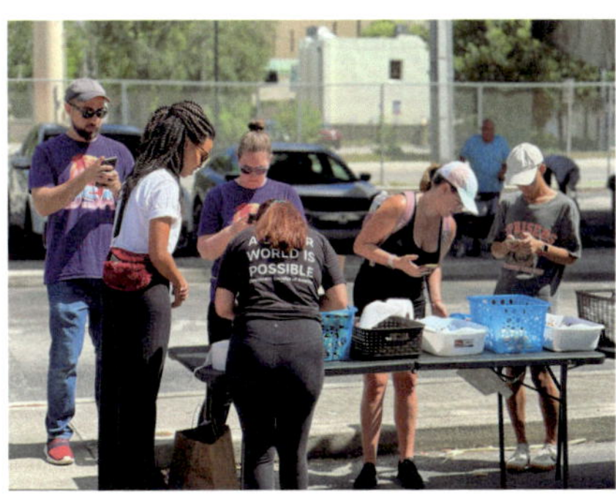

Courtesy of The Smile Trust Inc.

pening more frequently. How are you seeing some of those pressure points affecting policy responses? Do you feel like we're needing to fight a lot faster now than before?

VG It's hard. We in *Florida*. It's absolutely mind-boggling to navigate the state government and climate deniers when we are ground zero in the world for sea level rise. I'm not going to lie to you—when I first got into climate justice work, it was a lot of a few things. It was a lot of pushing our local

MS I've noticed that there are many design elements in the way you think and speak. How have you harnessed design tools to build evidence through aggregated storytelling?

VG The summer of 2016 was the first time I felt like I finally stepped into my power around storytelling, and it wasn't even about climate change. It was about Charles Kinsey, a Black man who was shot and almost murdered by the Miami police. We took to the streets. We shut down highways. Within a week, with the support of Color of Change, we got 50,000 signatures out of Miami-Dade County to challenge what the city insisted was the constituency's popular opinion around policing. That was the first time I realized the extent to which our people do believe in change, yet it's not often that they're asked their opinion. But we can collect their stories and get their opinions and use *that* as the data. We can do our own polling.

I've been using this approach ever since. I did it when it was time to talk about climate gentrification. When we're moving through

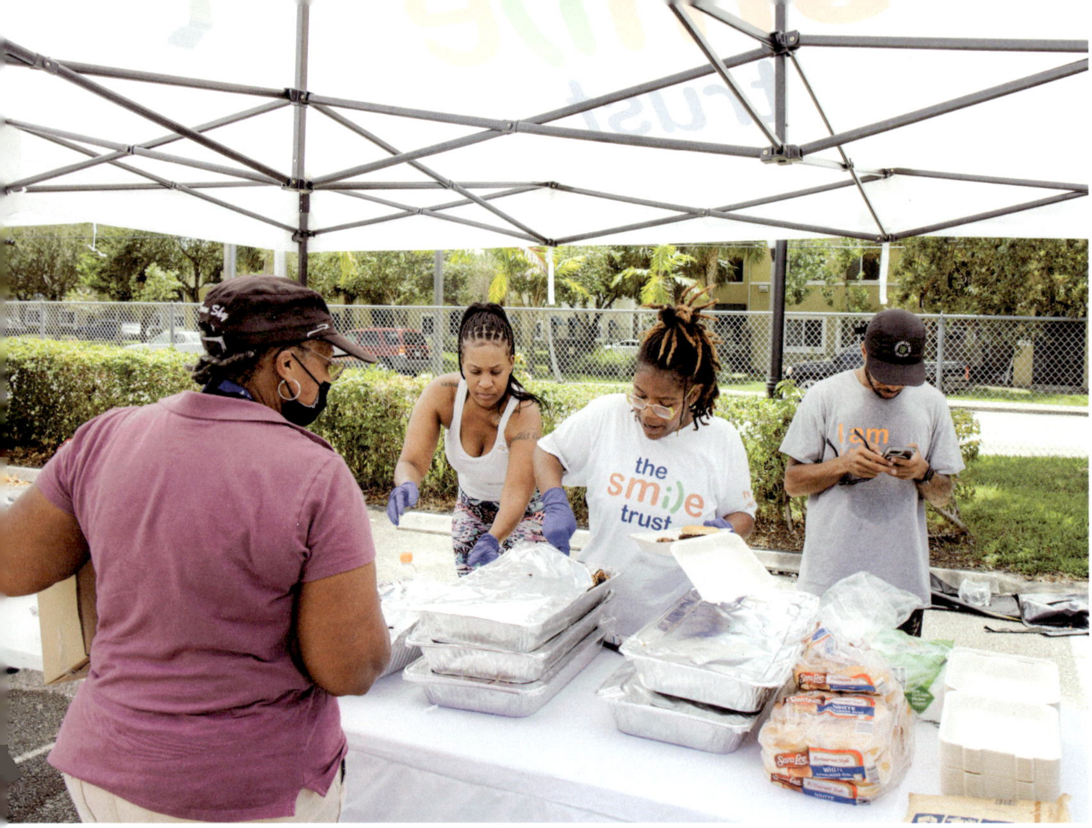

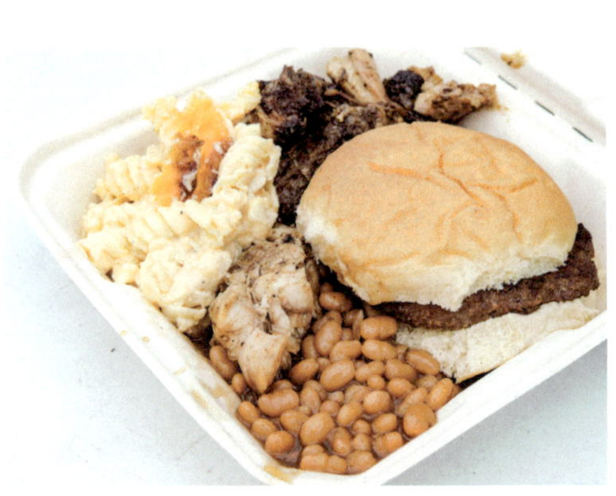

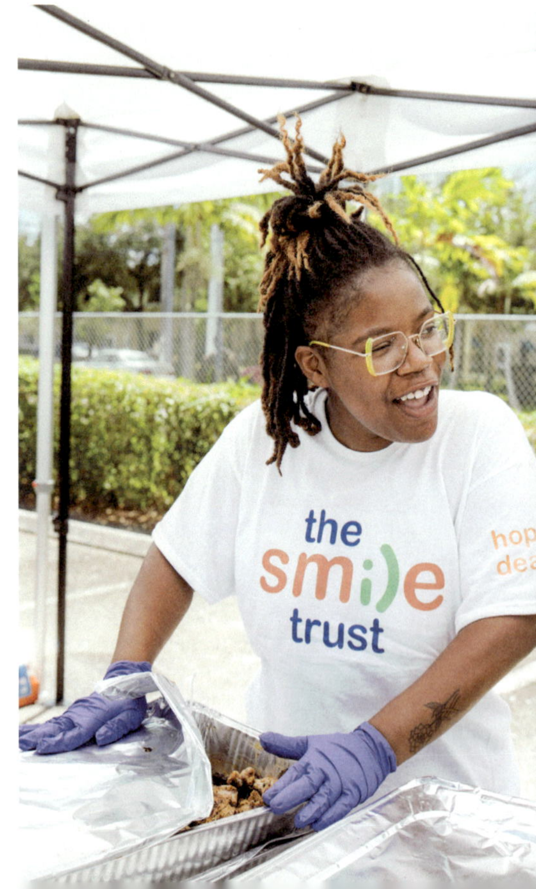

This spread: Volunteers at work at The Smile Trust's September pop-up event in Fort Lauderdale, FL. Photographs by Melody Timothee.

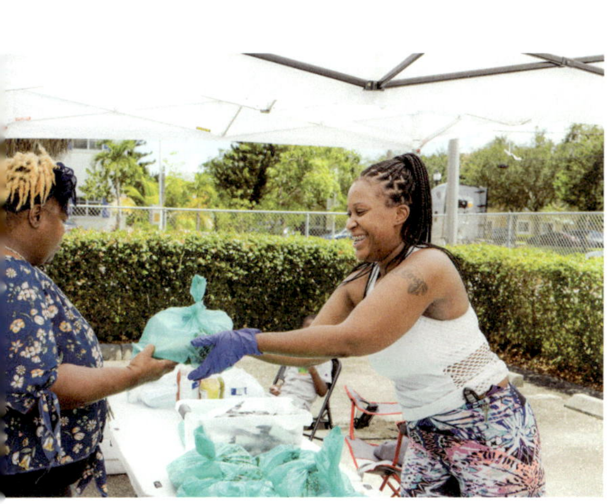

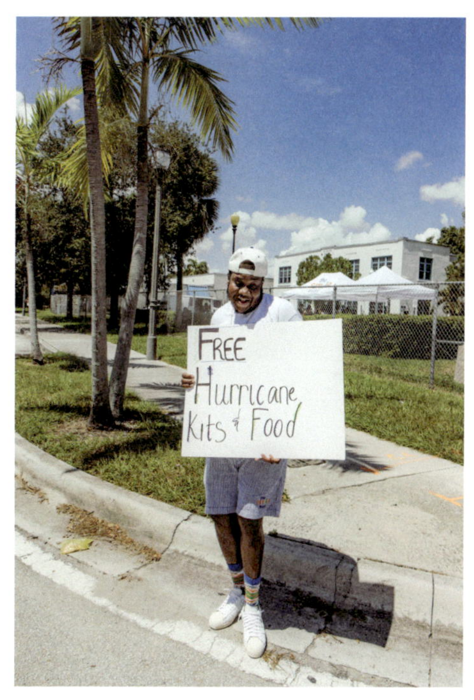

VALENCIA GUNDER

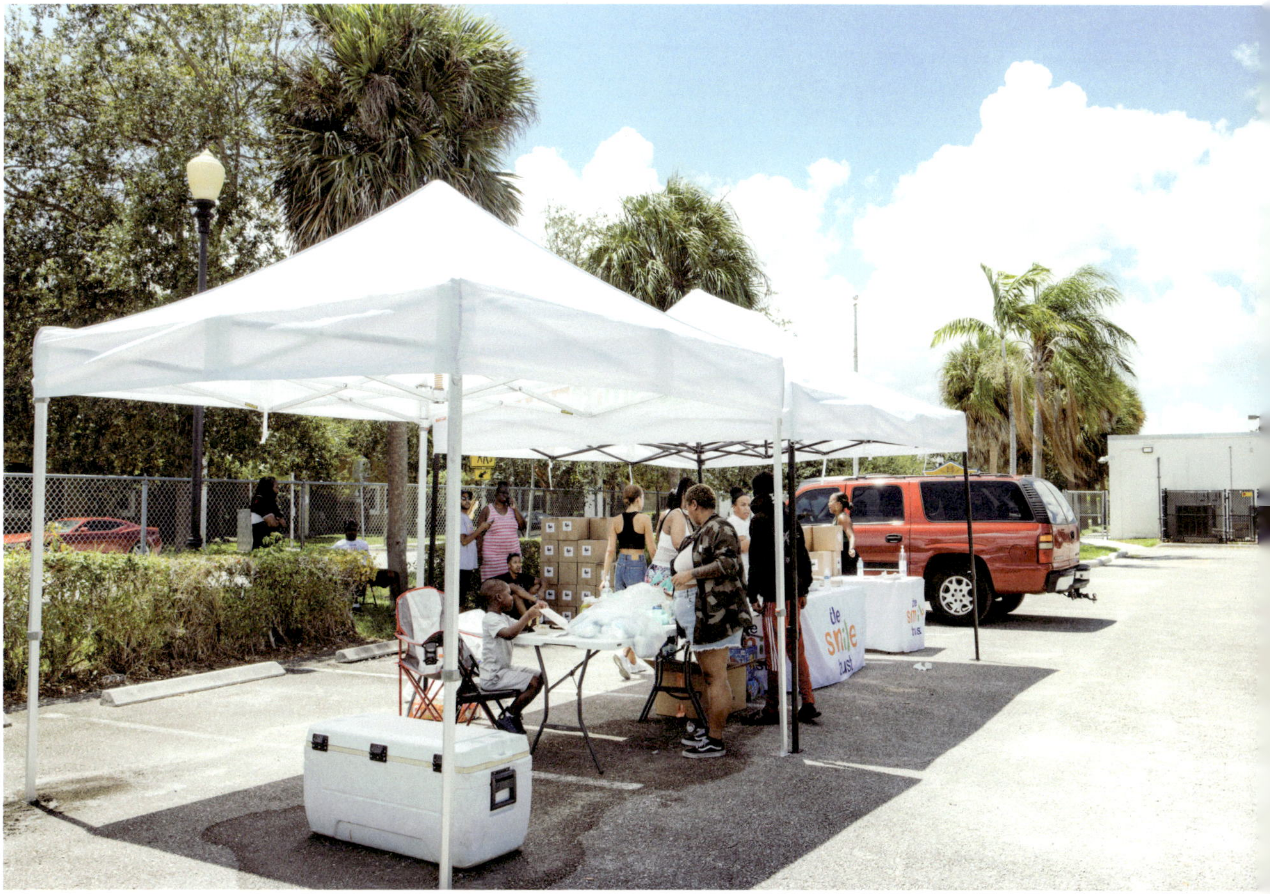

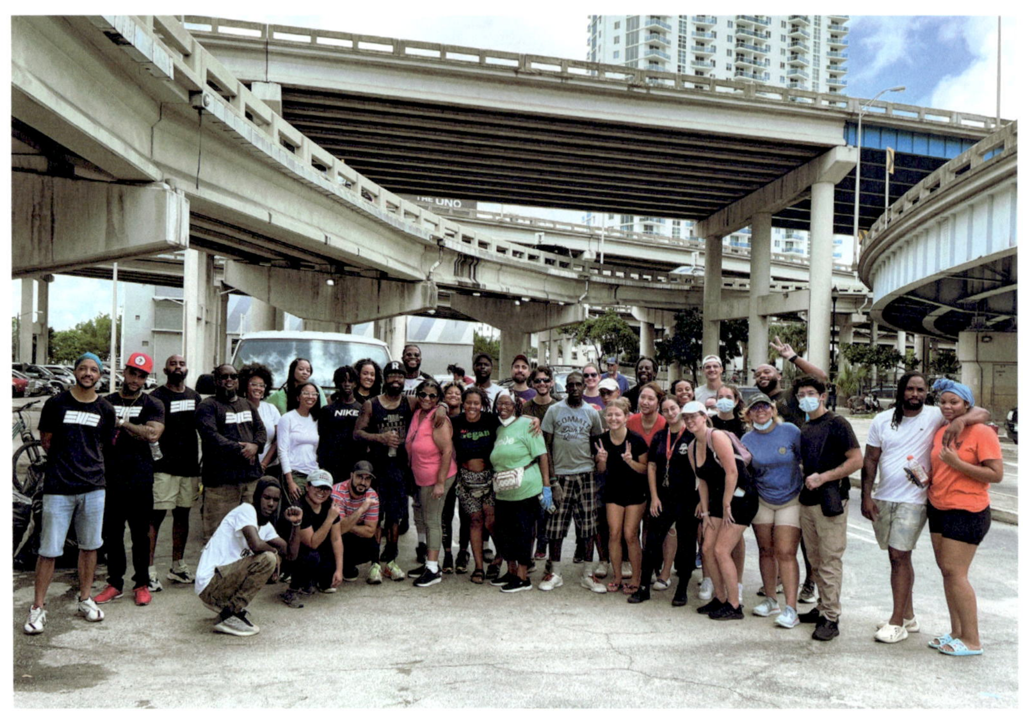

Volunteers gathered in Downtown Miami for Smile Day, August 2022. Courtesy of The Smile Trust Inc.

communities, we knock on doors, we get as many people's testimonies as we can. When we asked people how they felt about the effects of climate change on their neighborhoods, the response numbers we produced were overwhelming. Everyone said, "We're feeling it already. The rent is going up already. We're being harmed by law enforcement because of housing regulations. Taxes on our housing are going up." People who had lived in these communities for 40 or 50 years were having their property taken from them. You can't deny it when it's coming right from the people's mouths.

I'm also very grateful to the data scientists who took the time to listen and engage with us. While I was doing all this talking, I used to notice this little white man who would come sit in the back of my community climate conversations. He stuck out like a sore thumb, because he was literally the only white person in the space. It turned out he was Dr. Hugh Gladwin from Florida International University. He took all the testimonies he had heard and made us our first map. I gave a copy to every commissioner.

MS   Communication is such a crucial element of design, and you really get people to show up. This is especially important because climate is also a topic within which people of color often don't feel we have a voice. How have you made this work accessible, comprehensible, digestible?

VG   I teach people about climate the way I needed to be taught about climate. Somebody had to bring it to my front door. Think about everything under the climate umbrella—what are the few things people really give a damn about? Their light bill and their housing. That's where I start. I say, "Listen, let me tell you about these inflated electricity bills. Let me tell you about the toxic waste they're putting in our tap water. Let me tell you how they don't give us access to weatherizing." And when I teach climate science in communities, I do hundreds of workshops and I use household tools. When I teach about sea level rise, I use ice cubes, water, and two glasses. I break it down like that. I also set up spaces that are culturally fitting to the community I'm going to be in. Many people in Miami arrived recently from the Caribbean and Latin America. Many of them are also very familiar with natural disaster preparedness and have experienced disaster relief, which I am also part of. Bringing immigration into the conversation connects a lot of different voices. Because of sea level rise, 300 million people around the world will need to migrate. We need to be talking about that, too.

MS   What does preparedness look like for us now? Like I mentioned before, these storms are happening more frequently and are becoming more intense. Tell us about some of the work you're doing on both the policy level and the community level?

VG   Let's talk about the policy first. Then we'll get to the fun part. On a federal level, I work with the Black Hive at the Movement for Black Lives (formerly known as the Red, Black, and Green New Deal). I help lead that work. One of the things that we are focused on is addressing the Stafford Act. That has everything to do with preparedness and disaster response. Right now, the Stafford Act is everything that is racist, anti-Black, classist, and generally problematic. Poor people of color do not get served under the Stafford Act. This is representative of a structural issue that applies to many different concerns.

On a local level, a lot of the work that I've been doing is challenging. I'm literally always in the county's face, like, "Does your resiliency plan actually feel like a plan for everybody?" As a *place*, Miami is called the Magic City, but who feels the magic? Not the 60% of residents under the poverty line. You know what I'm saying? Through my organization, The Smile Trust, I've been working with people like the Miami Climate Alliance; it's also very important to me to make sure that Black voices are represented in the Green New Deal space, as I also sit in that on behalf of the Movement for Black Lives.

That's how I'm involved in the policy piece, but when it comes to preparedness through an alternative liberatory mindset, at The Smile Trust I created the Community Emergency Operation Center (CEOC). Usually, people see us at work after a storm, but we're activated all the time. We do trainings with organizations to teach them how to prepare their members, and education around hurricane and tornado season, because this is going to come up every year. It ain't never not going to come. Preparedness can be as simple as buying extra water for your home during the sales tax holiday, buying a portable heater, buying a tarp, storing power supplies at a local office or organization space, starting a phone bank and informing elders. I still think word of mouth is the best way. As of now I've worked with over 30 organizations in the US and 25 organizations in the Caribbean Islands, teaching them these strategies for resilience and communication.

MS   Do you feel a growing sense of urgency?

VG   I do feel it. I feel it because my phone rings nonstop. Actually, when I got on this call, I put my cell on do not disturb, because it don't stop ringing. I feel it when I see how communities are struggling to bounce back after these storms. I feel it when I see scarcity around certain supplies. It's making me very, very nervous. Climate change multiplies other threats. If you're already dealing with stress, if you're hungry, if you're already late on bills, if a storm hits—if anything extra happens, actually—you're wiped. Think about how many people on this earth are already strapped, already feeling the impact. I tell people, the climate crisis is not coming. It done came. It's been here.

MS   I'd like to end with a question about hope because I know you're not just doing this to stop the bleeding, you're doing it because you feel like there's a better way, and that we could get there.

VG   Even though sometimes I feel like I'm getting ready for doomsday, I have a lot of hope in community. Regardless of anything and everything negative that's said about our communities, I see the people stand up for each other every single time. It never fails. No matter what county or community I'm serving in, the people stand up with the little bit that they got and they try to hold on together. That's the hope that I need to see. That's why I don't complain. I get up and I do my part. And I also think that, well, the earth is going to take care of the earth. That's why all the stuff is happening. The earth is going to evolve, and we will have to also, one way or another, if we want to have a place here. I do feel that if we get together and really build networks of self-determination, we could sustain. The water is coming, the storms are coming, we know what's happening. But if I know the water is coming, do I teach my people how to swim? Absolutely. ●

Valencia Gunder, aka Vee, is a reputable, enthusiastic, self-motivated, driven, and inspiring community organizer and Miami native who has been branded "The Modern Day Fannie Lou Hamer." She is founder and codirector of The Smile Trust Inc., cofounder of the Black Collective, and coleader of the Black Hive at the Movement For Black Lives (formerly known as The Red, Black, and Green New Deal).

Photo of Valencia Gunder. Courtesy of The Smile Trust Inc.

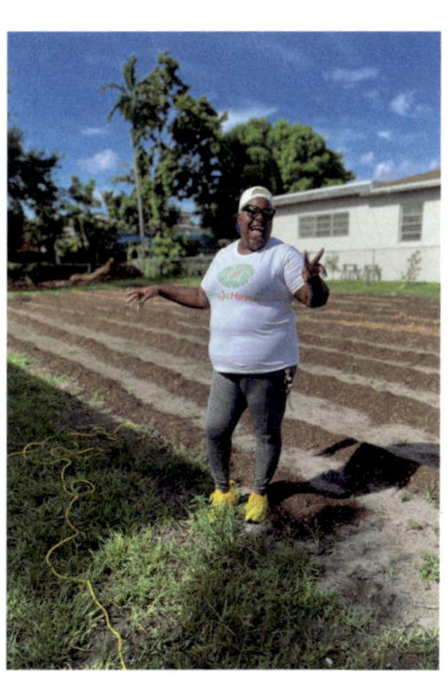

MYCELIUM YOUTH NETWORK: ARTIST TAKEOVER

Mycelium Youth Network—a Bay Area nonprofit organization founded in 2017—is dedicated to bridging the gap between increasing climate-related disasters and the abilities of young people to proactively respond, focusing in particular on the skills needed to survive and thrive while facing the uncertainty of a climate-challenged world. Their curriculum draws from ancestral and Indigenous traditions and practices, as well as the latest STEAM (Science, Technology, Engineering, Arts, and Mathematics) programming, to provide education that is free or low cost to low-income youth. For our pages, members of the MYN student community offered visual and verbal interpretations of what place means to them.

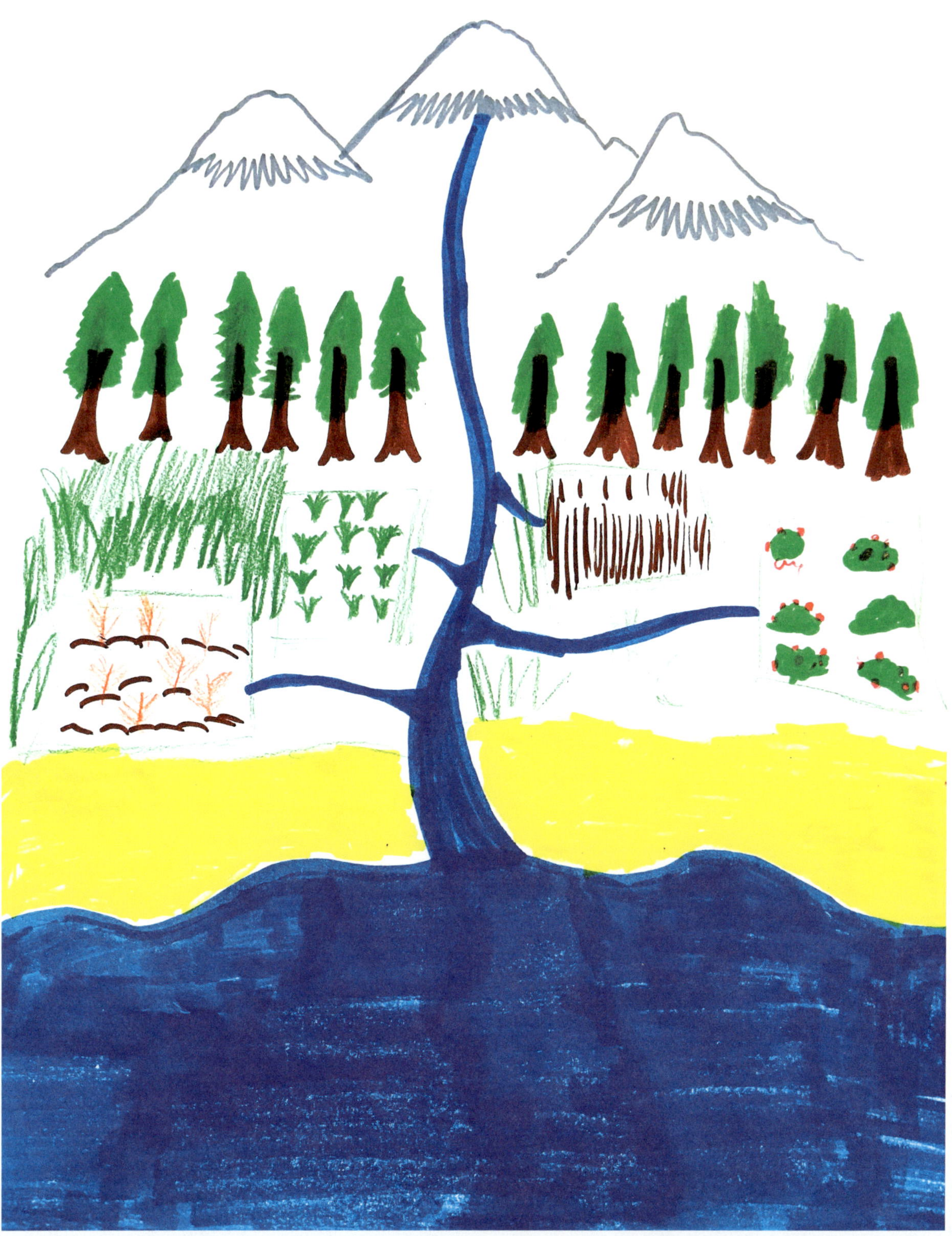

Illustration by Miguel G.

Tree   Tristán
                           Bernal

As I walked past aisle 8,
I saw saw some oak seeds,
I bought them...and took them home,
I planted them and waited care
-fully.
After a long time of rest,
I saw that the tree was making
progress.
After a decade of tending the
tree,

It grew to a size of 5 foot 3
After 3 decades, I checked on
it,

it was very tall,
and very unclimbable, if I tried
I would fall.

It grew to an mighty oak
tree,
It wouldnt have happened
without that little seed.

Illustration by Tristán B.

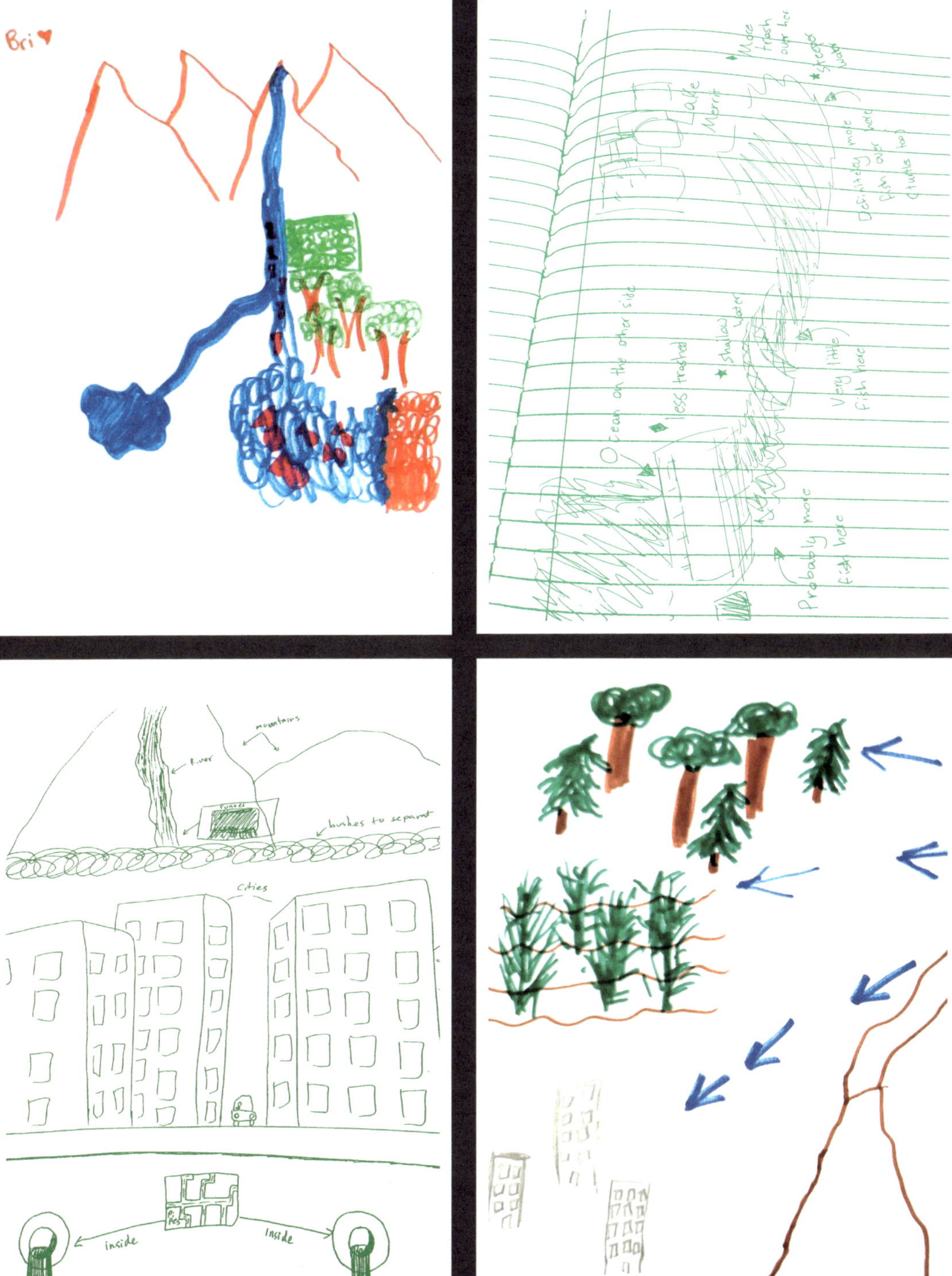

Clockwise from top left: Illustrations by Bri H., Jesus B., Jakob B., and Uzi J.

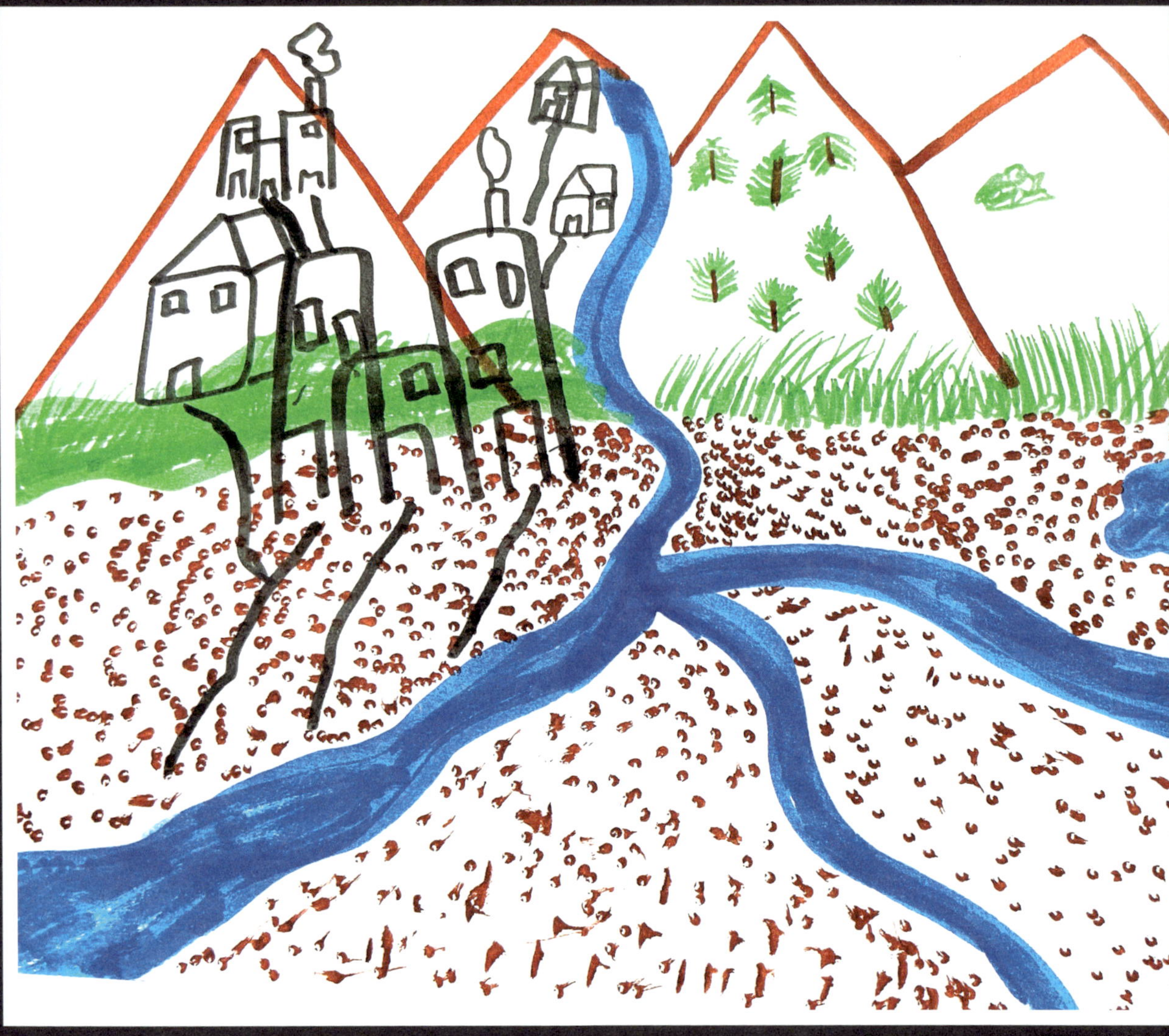

Illustration by Danai M.

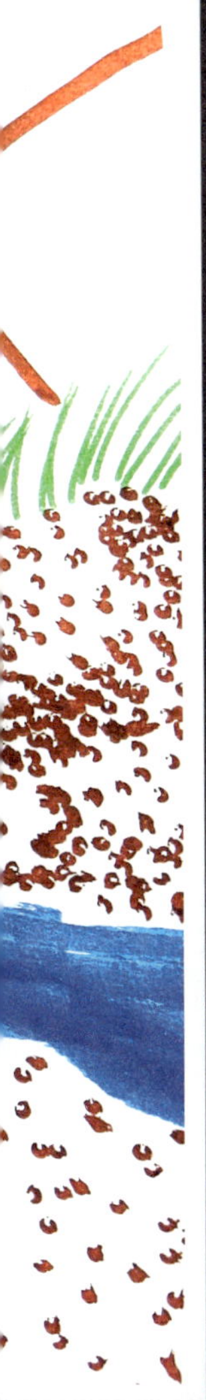

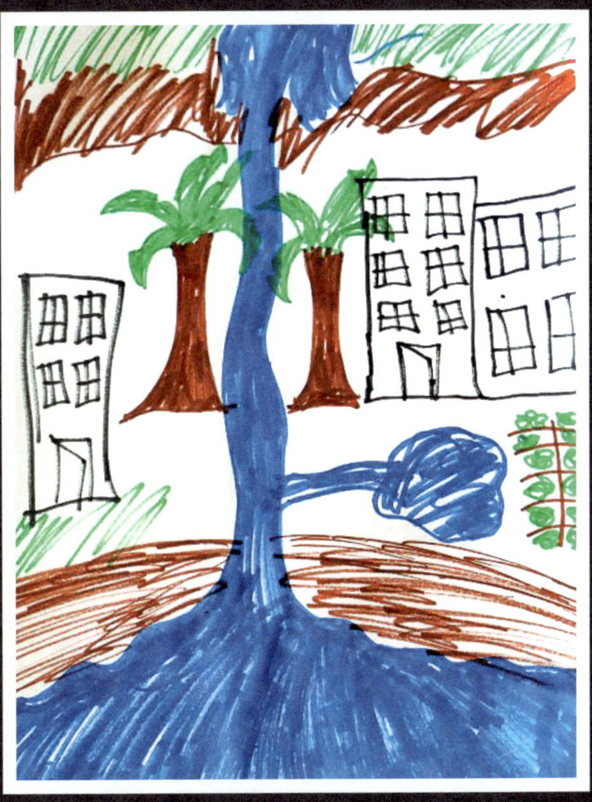

Anonymous illustrated contribution.

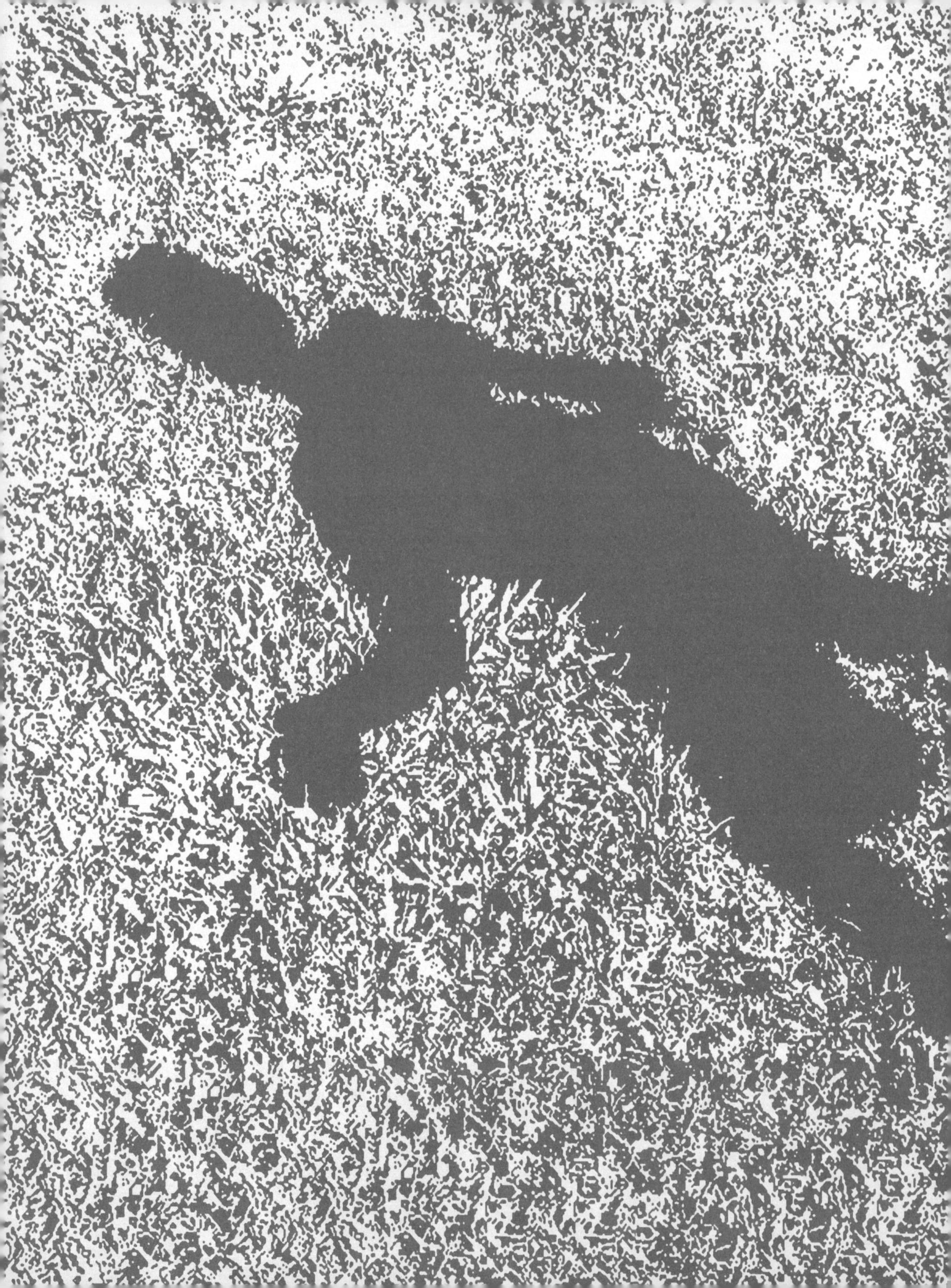

BEING WHERE WE ARE

Photography courtesy of
Prentis Hemphill

ALICE GRANDOIT-ŠUTKA I'd like to start this conversation by asking you to introduce yourself—whatever you feel called to share about yourself personally, and also a bit about your practice.

PRENTIS HEMPHILL I'm looking for a fun way to do this because I'm having a lot of fun most of the time, but I tend to introduce myself first with my work, which feels less fun. What's important to know about me? I'm from Texas. I'm a Black Texas queer. (There are many of us, and I find us to be extraordinary people.) I am a parent and a partner. I think that both temperament and circumstance made me curious about just what was going on inside me, and when I found the practice of somatics and embodiment work, it was a way to explore the things that I'd always had to steal away to think about. Embodiment work says we actually get to do that as the central way of engaging with being alive.

When I started studying embodiment, I wasn't thinking of it as something that would take over my life, but it did. I now have been doing embodiment work, as well as teaching and practitioning, for about a decade, especially in Black place where we experience life, change, and growth. It's also about recognizing that the body is inclusive of the brain and the mind, and that we can think of it as an expansive place where we are constantly learning, responding, adapting, creating, engaging, and feeling. The body is how we relate to everything around us. It is how we experience life.

I like to describe this work as turning the volume back up on sensations. They get so turned down in our current context. Our externalized attention economy puts us outside of our own experience all the time. There are reasons for this that are about commodification, and there are reasons that are about our culture of denial—about not wanting to experience pain or understand history. All of these things keep us focused on the external.

Somatics tell us that, actually, all sensations matter, and that trauma doesn't just disappear. Trauma isn't only a psychological experience. It shapes how we move through the world. It lives in our fascia and through the way we maintain or avoid relationships. It lingers in the system of the body. I use the term "embodiment" because I want

"The body is how we relate to everything around us. It is how we experience life."

movement spaces. I continue to teach through a project I co-founded called The Embodiment Institute. My podcast, *Finding Our Way*, sort of feels like an extension of that. I'm trying to have conversations—similar to what you're doing here—with people who I feel are asking questions about or experimenting with portal places: in other words, places that open up future dreaming. I'm also working on a writing project that will be a book about transitional characters, which is a family systems concept that thinks about our interpersonal capacities inside of every system that we are embedded in.

AGS Could you share a bit about the practices of somatics and embodiment, for any readers who might not be familiar with these concepts?

PH I started to use the word "embodiment" almost exclusively in the last few years. I wanted a word that was maybe a little more accessible. Because embodiment has the word "body" in it, people tend to have more of a sense of what I'm talking about. Technically the word "somatics" does too—*soma* signifies the body and its wholeness in Greek. The practice of somatics in the West has been about rediscovering the body as the primary to stretch that canon open even more, to understand that many of our cultures have always known that the body is a whole and full system, that our bodies have ways of digesting or responding or changing based on the environment, and that we build communal practices that sync up our nervous systems or support people to move things through their bodies. Embodiment is also a way that humans communicate and organize their cultural systems. It is the ways we share and care for each other, and ultimately become more aware of the fullness and quality of life through sharpening our ability *to* live.

AGS That was very generous. Thank you. Given that we are trying to frame up design as a social practice that seeks to add value to the ways in which we inhabit the planet and orient ourselves towards liberation, what can design learn from practices of embodiment as we move through this time?

PH That's a really cool question. Makes me wish I knew more about design. But what I can feel into is that embodiment—at least the way I'm trying to practice it—is really about the restoration of and practice of certain kinds of relationships. When we think about the way the world around us is designed, it shows certain values of relationality:

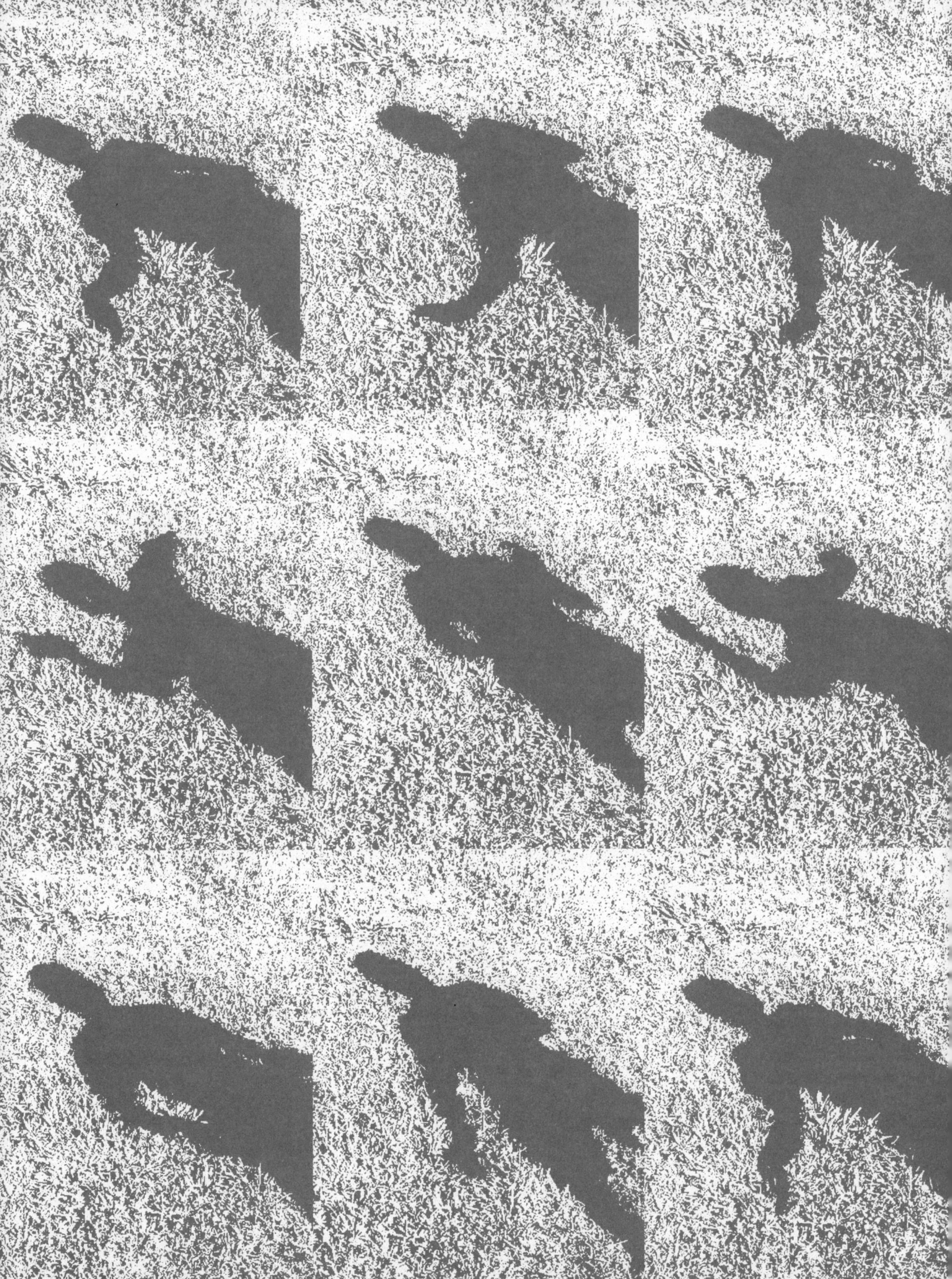

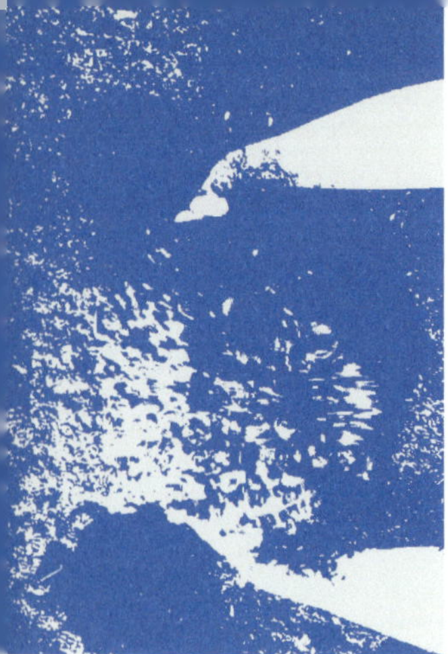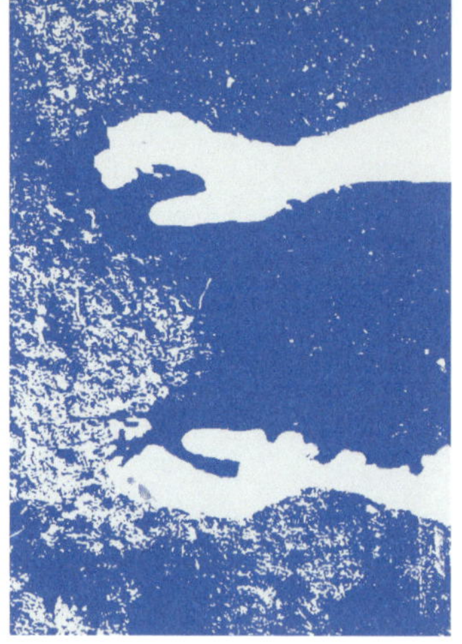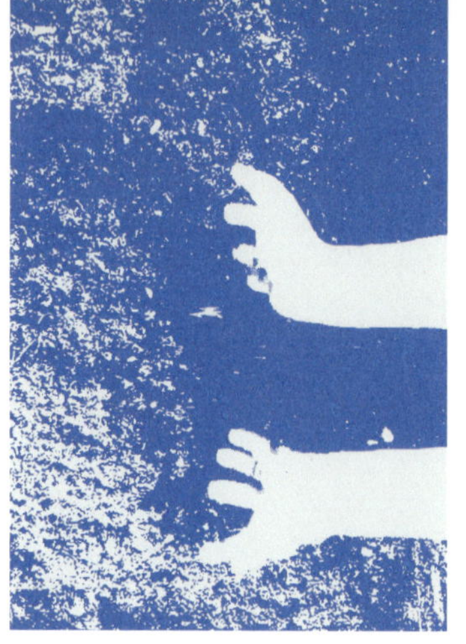

how we relate to each other; for what duration we relate to each other; whose relationships are meaningful; who we include in conversations or social and communal spaces. .

I think that embodiment helps us see that we have been shaped to prioritize or deprioritize particular relationships. I'm looking outside at the trees right now, for example. Just because we might not feel a relationship to the oak or the sycamore that is outside of our home doesn't mean that we're not in relationship to it. It just means that we're well-practiced in not feeling that relationship. We exist in an ecosystem and there's way more to those relationships than we are trained to recognize or experience. Embodiment is a way of reshaping and reprioritizing particular relationships, of letting them be felt and textured. And I think that design is an expression of those values, or could be.

AGS   You know much more about design than you believe yourself to!

PH   That's cool.

AGS   I also want to ask, what does place mean and/or represent to you? How do you differentiate space from place?

PH   I'm drawing on a couple examples. My partner is from Hawaiʻi and I lived there for about seven years. That experience was incredibly transformative for me—politically, emotionally, in every way. What I experienced that was so significant was that the place itself was full of stories. I lived in Kāneʻohe Bay. My friend Shelley's family had been there forever, for generations. I'm thinking about the kinds of stories she told me about the mountains, about the different kinds of rain, all the different words for it, depending on what speed it came in and how heavy. To me, place is full of stories and relationships. History gets to be there. Stories get to be there. Meaning gets to be there. And we get to be a part of and awash with that meaning. To me, that's what place is.

When I moved to North Carolina, one of my friends who lives here said, "The stories are here even if you don't know them. And they're shaping your life, even if you don't know them." I'll never know all the stories of this place, but for me there's an orientation to being in a place that is about listening for those stories, and what they contain about the people who are there, who they are, and what their values are. Place is inhabited with that.

AGS   How did you make North Carolina home? When did it become a place for you?

PH   That's interesting. I guess I didn't really answer the second part of your question, about space and place, but what I think I was trying to imply is that space could be both the absence and potential of those stories. When I move to a space, I could keep engaging with it as if it were just that—a space. But I want it to become a place. I want it to become haunted by stories.

I came here to be close to certain people. I don't want to say rural, but I'm from a non-urban South. That's how I grew up. As I moved around in my adult life, I think I was always pretending that wasn't true. I was like, "I can blend in like I'm from the city," but I'm actually not. I'm not from that pace or those stories. The stories are different in North Carolina than in Texas, of course, though there's some relationship. But I think overall I wanted to be back in the South. I wanted to be around more Black humans than I had been around in Hawaiʻi. I wanted proximity to those stories. Also, it's lush here. It's green. There's still so much land that it's easy to get lost. I've felt called here, and that relationship deepens every year as I learn more about where I am.

AGS   In the Embodiment Basics Course that you offer through The Embodiment Institute, I was moved by your emphasis on how landscape shapes us. I was curious if you could provide some reflections on the interrelationship between our bodies and the landscape.

PH   We are shaped by our experiences—the ones we categorize as positive and the ones we categorize as negative. We are shaped by other human beings. We are shaped by trees and plants, even if we don't acknowledge that. And we are shaped by the absence of them as well. I grew up in a town called Grand Prairie. It's literally on a prairie, meaning that it's a wide expanse. When you sit outside, there's not a lot obstructing your view. What I got from that was a wide, long breath. A capacity to settle and sit still. I breathe differently when I'm in the city. How we breathe is shaped really deeply by the landscape around us. I'm so grateful to have learned to breathe that way just by sitting in the grass, and to have had that place as a teacher.

AGS   In this issue, we're also reexamining, or recovering, the idea of placemaking. Do you think that the somatic theory of the arc of transformation—in which you change shape through commitment, regeneration, opening, connection, and embodiment—might also be a relational framework for how place is made?

PH   That's a smart-ass question. Let me see if I know how to get into that! I don't know the term "placemaking"…

AGS   It's okay that you're not familiar with it. We've learned that many people feel many very different ways about it. I think what we're witnessing with this word is the commodification of language, and in this case it maybe even perpetuates a further disassociation from the land. But if we come back to relationality, I wonder how this arc of transformation might relate to making place as a circular, cyclical process? Is it a kind of placemaking?

PH   I really like that. This is interesting, because I have thought through that arc as a way of coming home to the next layer of self, of you. It's about allowing what is, or what is longing to be. That's what growing is. When something grows out of the ground, it's what longs to be that blossoms. It's al-ways changing, from a seed to a bloom to the fruit it bears, yet at every stage there's still something very fundamental about it.

The arc of transformation is about figuring out how we allow ourselves to be and to become. It's about longing. With a longing for change comes a commitment to that change and to the practice of it, as well as understanding what is getting in the way: what blocks, tricks, lies, and habits we have within ourselves that undermine growth. We often don't realize how practiced we are at certain ways of being, certain ways of thinking, certain ways of relating, certain limitations on our vulnerability. And it's about creating the experience of safety that allows for something new to be experienced. Then there will also be disorder, disorganization, and discomfort. When we are allowing something new to happen, it won't always feel welcome if we have previously felt safe in another form. There's a spiritual component to understanding that there are things that you haven't yet felt that are possible to you. I love how somatics opened me up to that possibility. How do we join, within the practice of living, elements of both protection and of unraveling?

In terms of placemaking, this requires reactivating relationships inside of you and between you and the world. So yes, embodiment is a way of making place. It's saying, "My body is a complete place from which I have relationships with myself and others. It is where I am."

AGS   I want to again express my sincere gratitude for this conversation, because I think that one of the things that we think about with *Deem* is, "What if design could help us feel more?" So much about design focuses on innovation and disruption, but what if design could alter or enhance our capacity to feel? For this issue in particular, your practice has helped us be receptive to the variety of ways in which we can sense interrelation and belonging.●

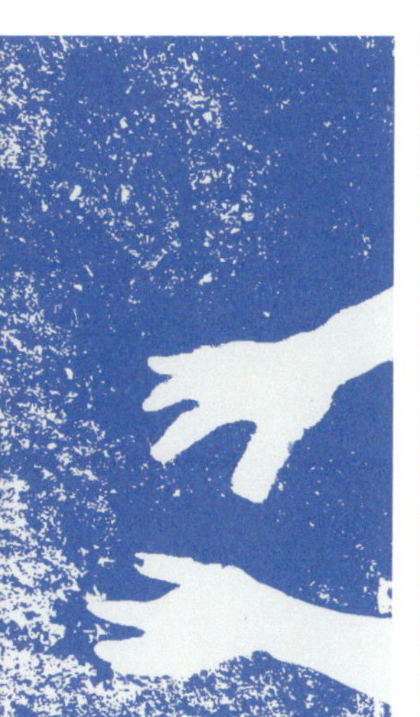
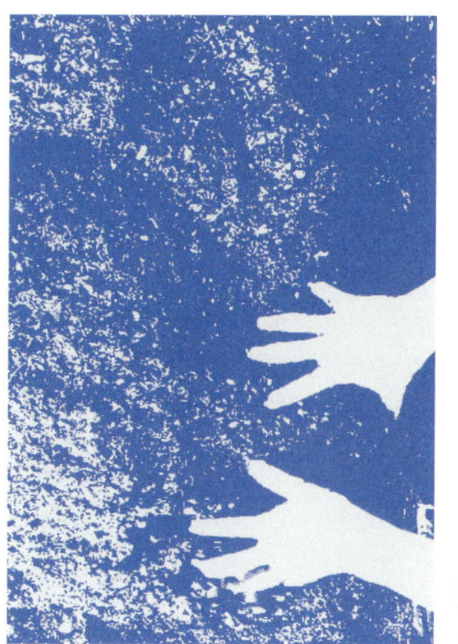
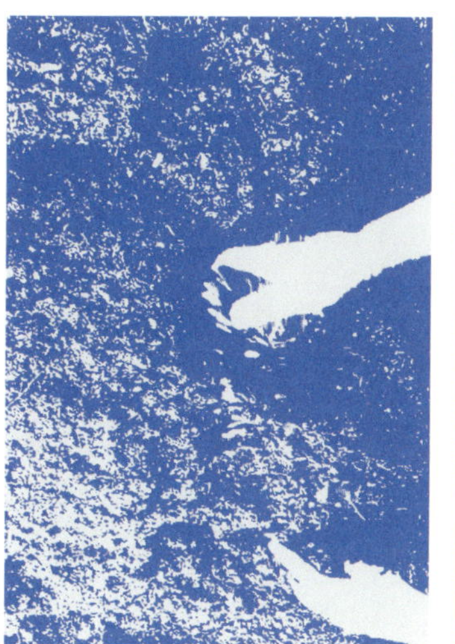
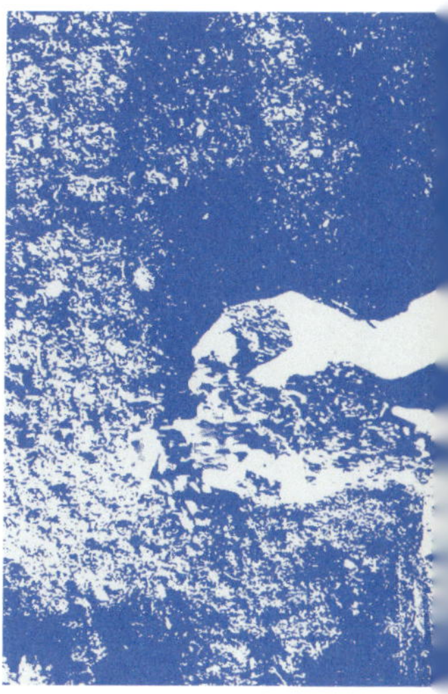

PRENTIS HEMPHILL

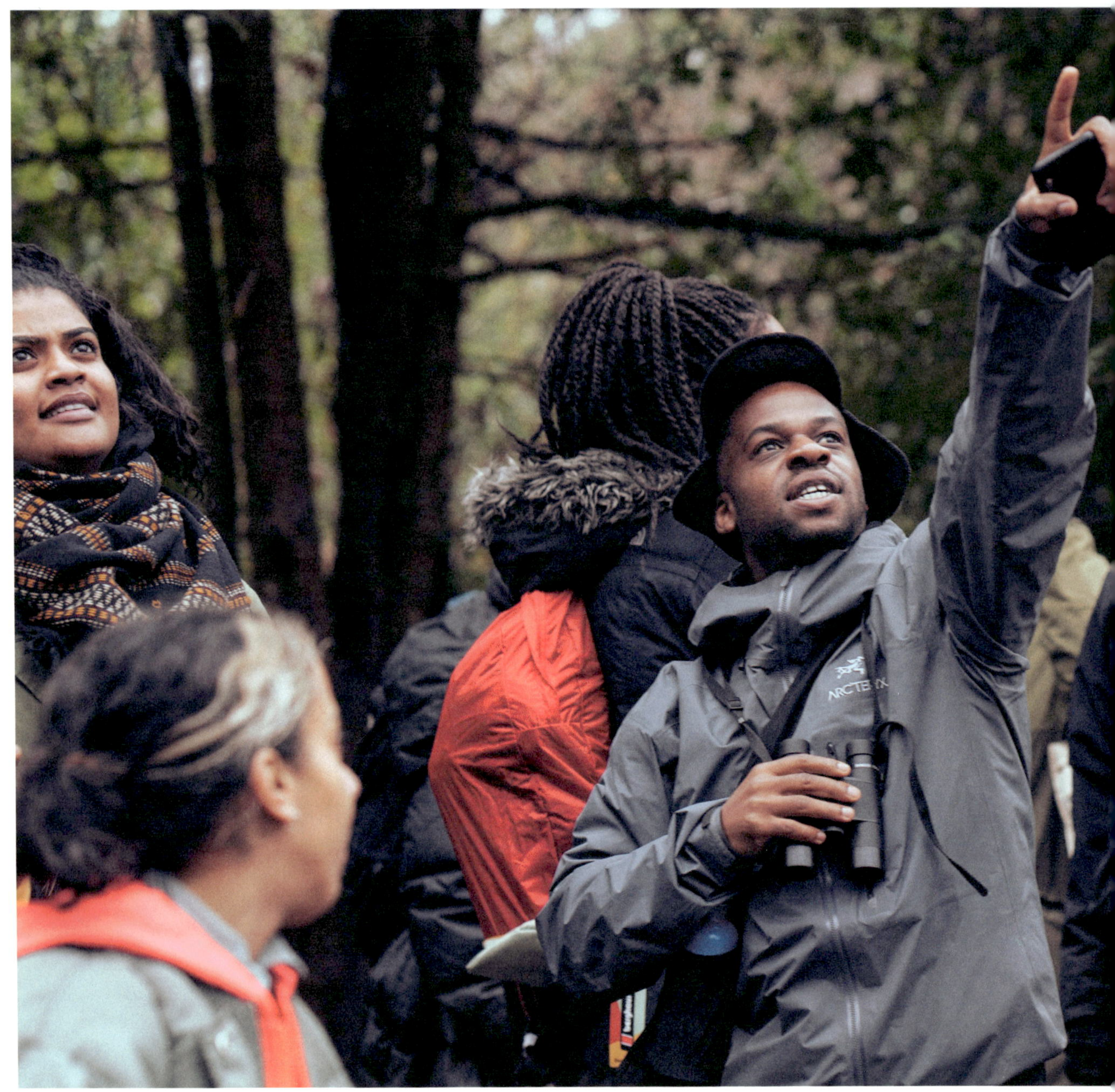

Looking Up:

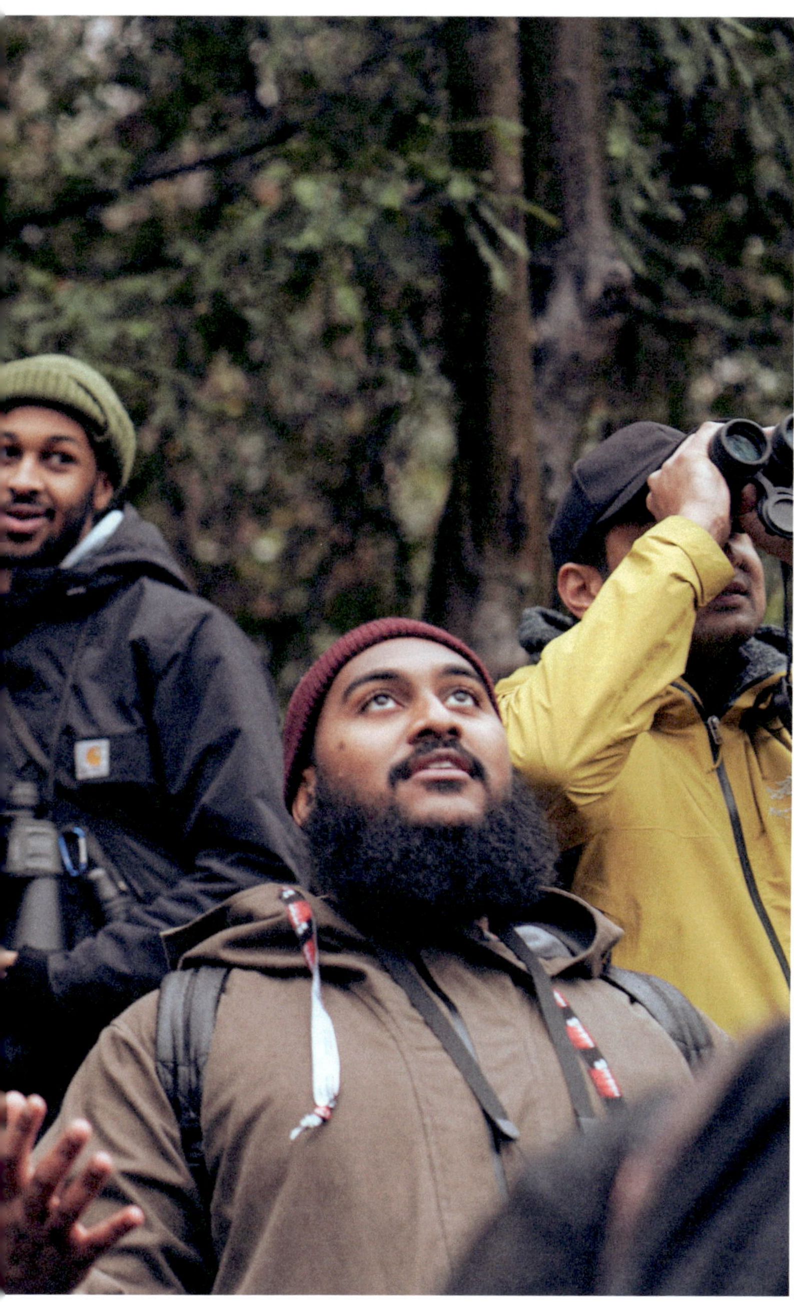

Interview by
Alice Grandoit-Šutka

Finding Place
with Flock Together

91

OLLIE OLANIPEKUN   My name is Ollie Olanipekun, also known as Olaolu. That's my real name. I do quite a few things. By "day," I am the creative director of an agency I own called Futurimpose. I'm also cofounder of Flock Together, which is a birdwatching collective with big ideas.

ALICE GRANDOIT-ŠUTKA   Can you tell us more about Flock Together and how it came together?

OO   Flock Together was born in May 2020 from a serendipitous encounter with a now very good friend of mine named Nadeem Perera. I've been birdwatching for the last 10 years on my own and it's done a lot for my mental health, among many other benefits. Nadeem was the first person of color I ever met who was also passionate about that activity. Straight away, I said to him, "We have to set something up that is more directed towards people like us." A few weeks later, we had our first Flock Together walk, which was attended by 15 people. And then, from there, the rest is history. It exploded, and it's still exploding.

AGS   How would you describe some of the experiences Flock Together has created so far?

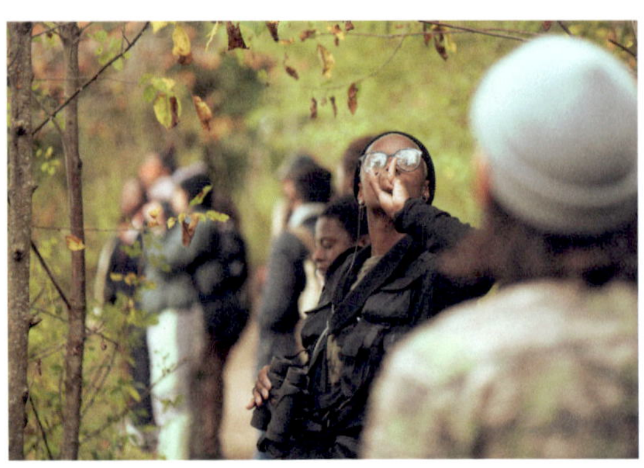

gone through and are going through similar experiences to you and are there to do nothing but spend time with and support you—that is unique. I don't think these spaces exist. Imagine group therapy for your family and friends, but outside. Again, it's hard to describe, but believe me that it's a truly magical environment.

"You know, it's hard for me to talk about Flock because, more than anything, it's an experience."

OO   Magical. You know, it's hard for me to talk about Flock because, more than anything, it's an experience. As much as I can tell you about what I take away from it personally, as well as testimonies from people who've attended, it's truly, especially for people of color, a unique experience. I don't think we've ever been afforded a space like this. To be in the great outdoors, that openness, to look to your left and to your right and see people who have

AGS   Sometimes things don't need to be overly described. Maybe they just need to be felt. Not everything fits into verbal language.

OO   Of course.

AGS   Maybe you didn't have any set expectations or plans when you first started, but if you did, do you feel those intentions still align with how Flock Together has grown and evolved over the past couple of years?

OO   I want to return again to the serendipity of how Nadeem and I met. I posted some birds on Instagram and he named them all. I was like, "How do you know this?" and he was like, "I'm an avid birdwatcher." I asked, "Where do you live? This is crazy." I expected him to say Scotland or something, but it turned out he lived five minutes from my house.

I'd had an idea for a long time about the outdoors and bringing people together there. And this was in 2020, when we were all being forced to face and address how our minds operate within this strange concept of lockdown. I think we were all struggling, and still are. In the Black community, this is sometimes still a taboo. Therapy might

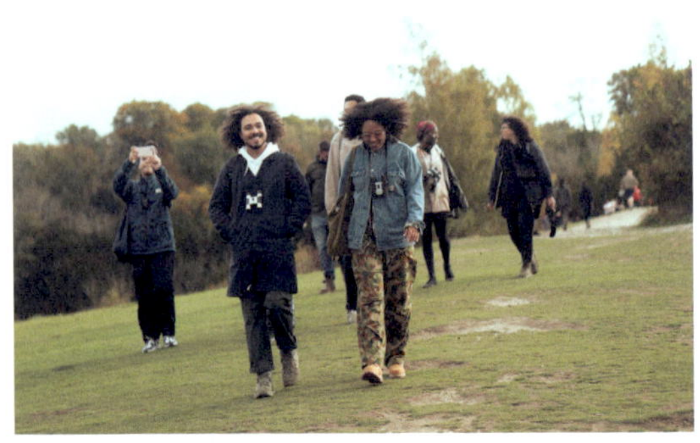

not be something you can discuss with your parents. At that particular moment, I knew that the benefits I'd received from birdwatching might actually be applicable to supporting my friends.

When Nadeem and I met in person, we talked for hours about our upbringings, our struggles with school, our struggles with careers, our struggles with society. We both realized that we've used nature to get through some really difficult times. This reinforced the idea that maybe we could share that experience with our wider community.

AGS   As you know, this issue is centered around the idea of place, as well as interrogating the newer concept of placemaking. What does place mean and/or represent to you? What makes place different from space?

OO   When I hear the word "place," it holds a slight negative connotation. Growing up in white-dominated spaces, and struggling with authority and bad experiences in school, the idea of a place makes me think about being told where I have to be. That reminder of my freedom being limited creates my negative connotation around the word, but that's purely personal.

AGS   To you, place represents authority?

OO   Yeah.

AGS   Do you feel like the word "space" also contains that feeling of authority, or does it offer more possibility?

OO   Definitely more possibility. Possibility is a really nice word. Opportunity, creativity, a platform—that's what I think when I hear "space." I can voluntarily see myself in a space. I think I have a choice in space.

AGS   I can give you some context around how we're framing up the concept of place. Placemaking thinks a lot about consistency, about routine, about maintenance, about ritual. How these things could become negative, in your interpretation, is extremely valid to me. I'm interested to know if and how you consider Flock Together as a way of making space, or potentially making place?

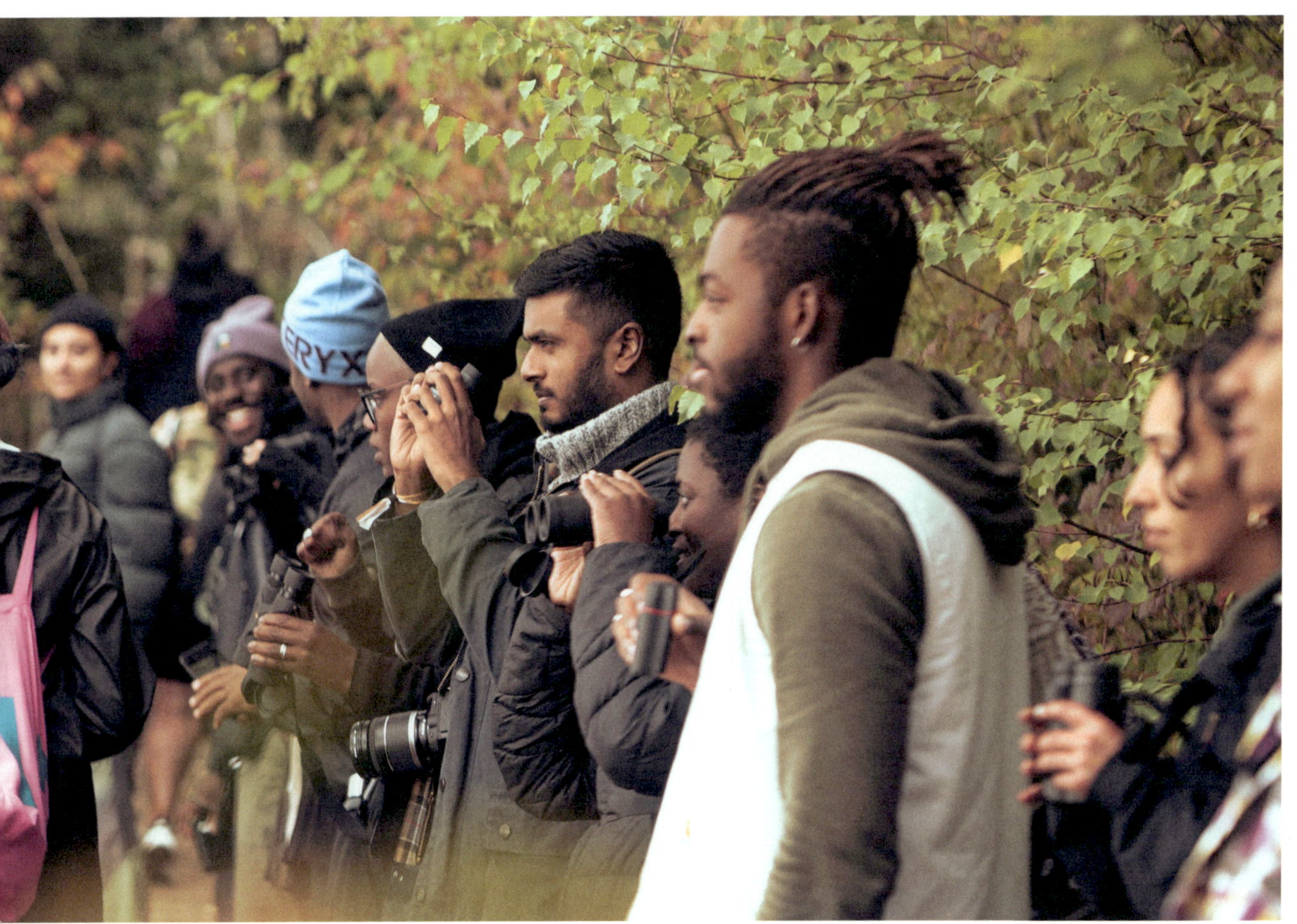

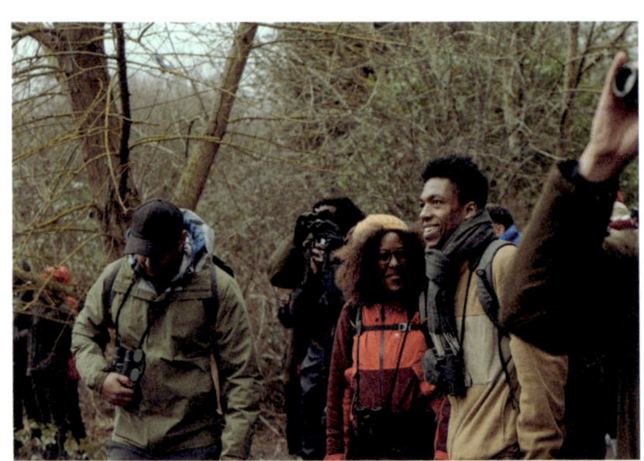

Early last year, I got diagnosed with ADHD, which I've always known was there somewhere. I always struggled with focus and with meditation. I tried and tried, but my brain is constantly overreacting. I'm distracted by everything. Even now, you see my head just going all over the place. Yet the first time I looked through my binoculars and locked in on a bird, my mind was completely clear. Nothing else in life gives me that. Nothing. So naturally when I understood, felt, and experienced that clarity I'd been searching for, I was addicted.

That is the kind of space we want to share with people, and the kind of place we want to make for them. I think when we talk about connecting with nature and feeling grounded, that goes over a lot of people's heads. A lot of us have no idea what it actually means to be present in a world where we're always distracted, always on our phones, always walking to get somewhere. It's nearly impossible to be present now, and that's why having this space to think and to be inspired is what we all truly need more than ever. Unlike your work, or your personal life, or your commitments in general, the outdoors doesn't require anything from you. For once, you can just be.

> **AGS** I love that you relate the practice of birdwatching to a medicine for how we hold our attention, because these days it feels like everything is designed to steal our attention. I also think that a lot of us are finding that we are neurodivergent in a variety of ways. The idea of reclaiming your attention through practices that sustain it, like birdwatching, is so important.

OO We all have an issue with attention. I work in one of the most aggressively attention-capturing-focused industries. When we're cramming as much as we can in six seconds, what does that do to us? What does it do to creativity?

What's also important about Flock Together is accessibility. There is no barrier to entry or skill set needed for this. All you need to do is step outside your house and look up. Now you're a birdwatcher. We don't want to dictate people's experience. We're inviting you into a space and allowing you to create your own experience there. What you take away from that is completely up to you. But we're giving you that invitation that you didn't know you needed.

OO There are many layers to this but, to start, people of color have not felt welcome in these spaces and activities—politically, historically, socially, all of that—and we could go on forever about why. For me, there is also the idea that sometimes we are most comfortable in a world with many guard rails, where many areas are off limits. Yet the outdoors became a place where I could feel free, and through birdwatching and Flock, it also became an environment to collaborate, create, and feel empowered by each other.

> **AGS** Can I ask you a question about your personal birdwatching practice? You mentioned earlier you've been doing it for 10 years—how did you find your way?

OO I realized the importance of birdwatching for me when I was working at a very stressful desk job. When I was struggling with a brief and just couldn't get through it, or if I was struggling with something personal like my relationship, I was always drawn to go outdoors. I'd go on long walks, and by the time I came back, I'd have a much better perspective on that issue or challenge.

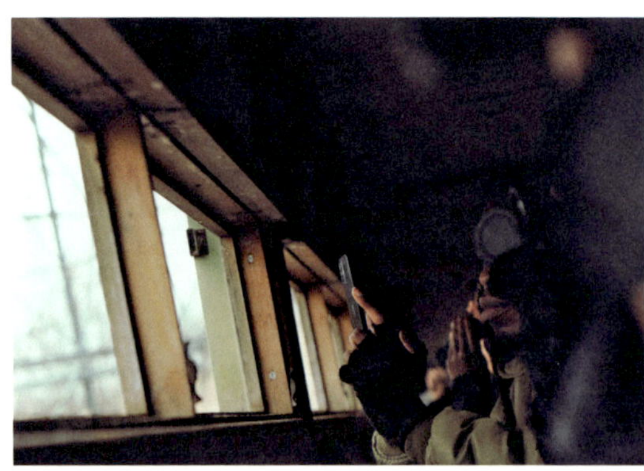

94

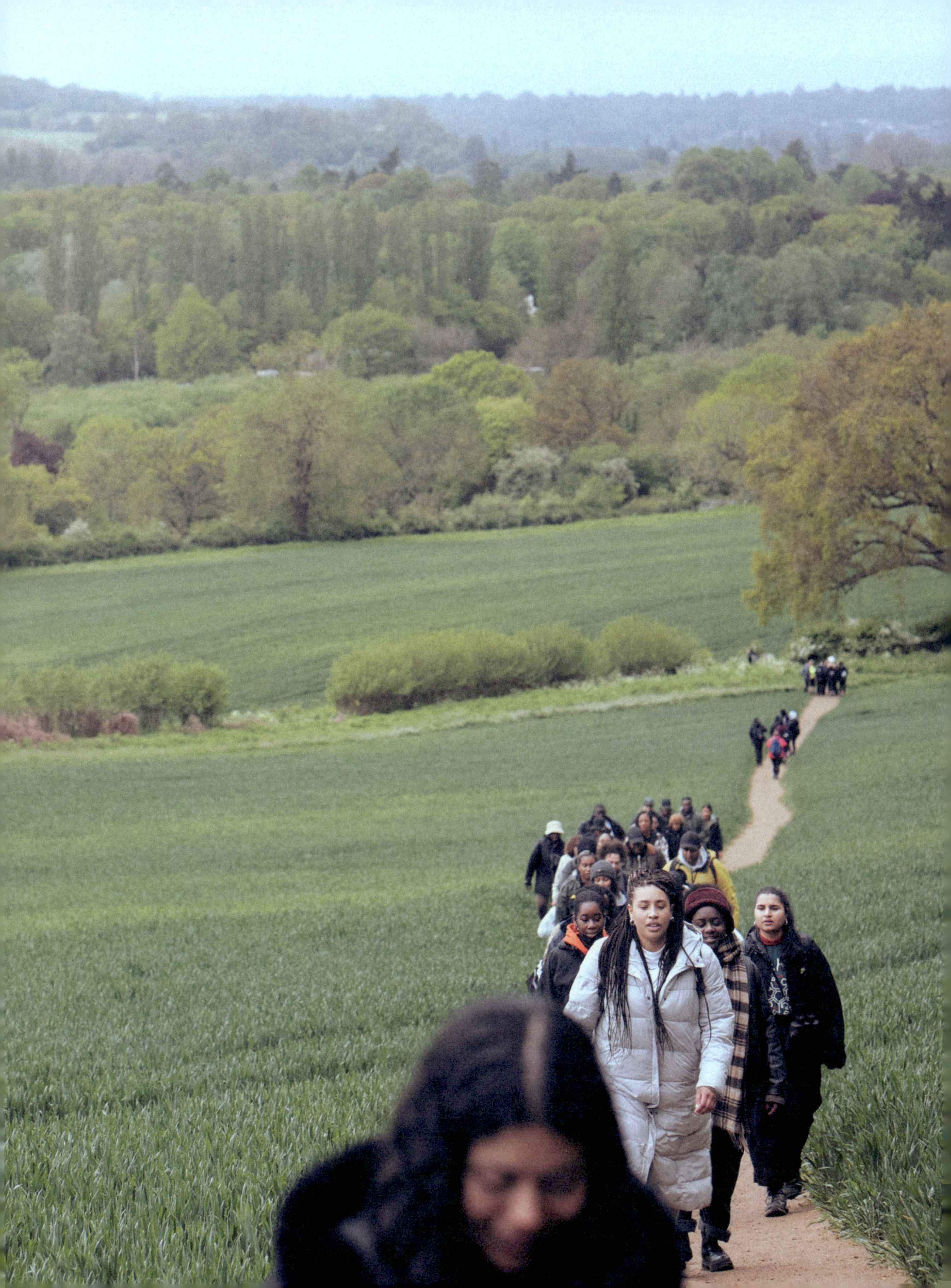

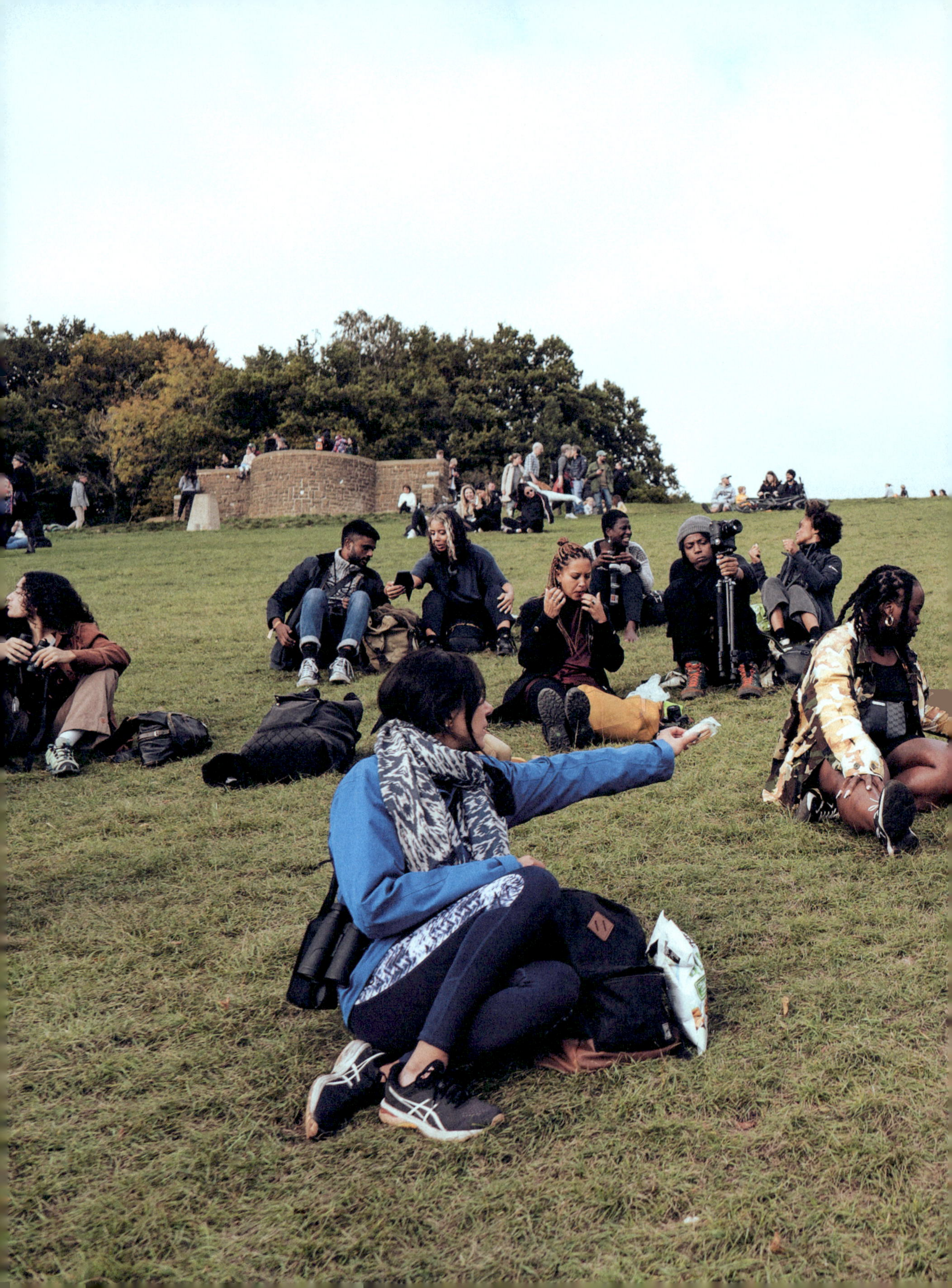

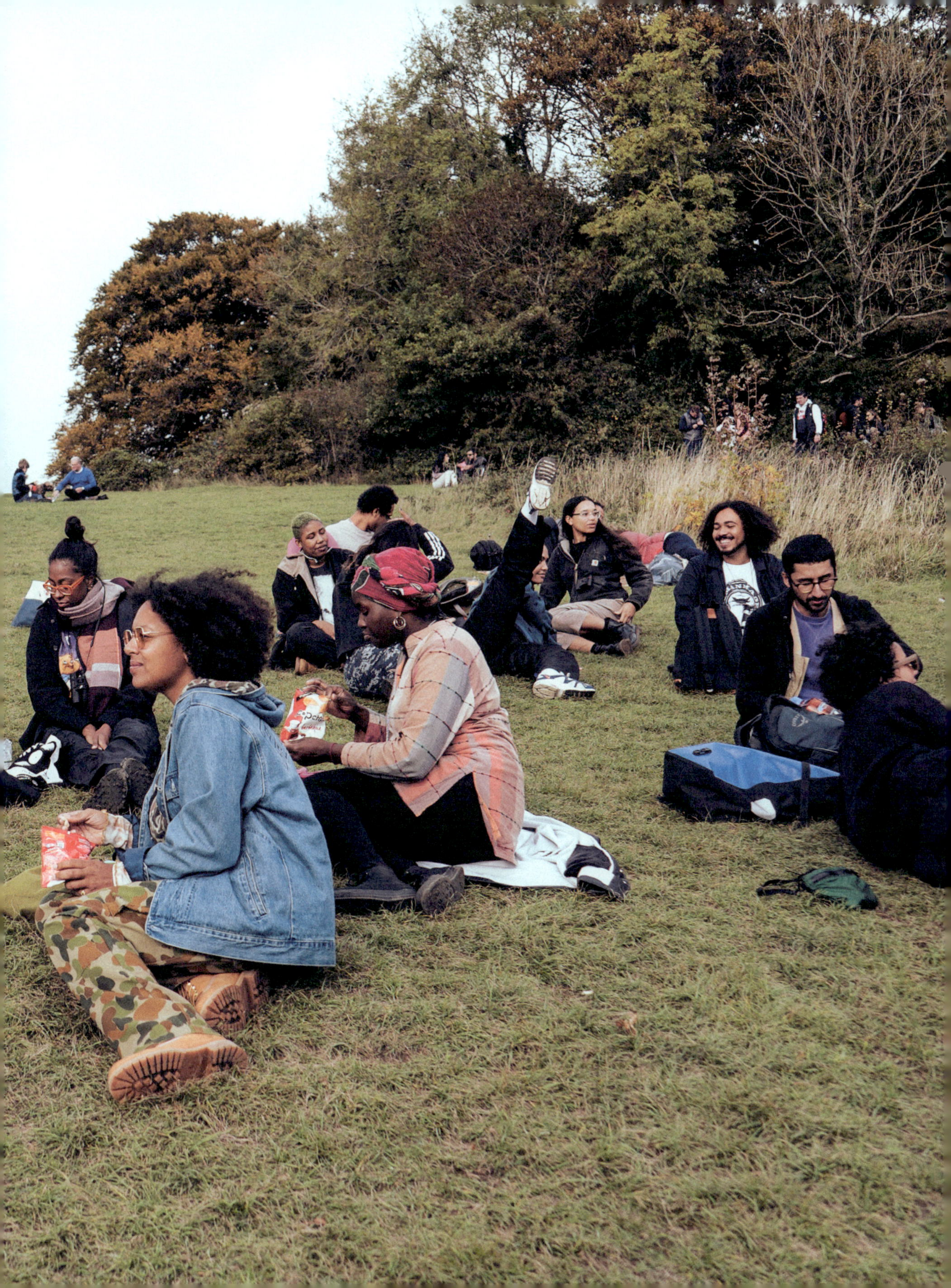

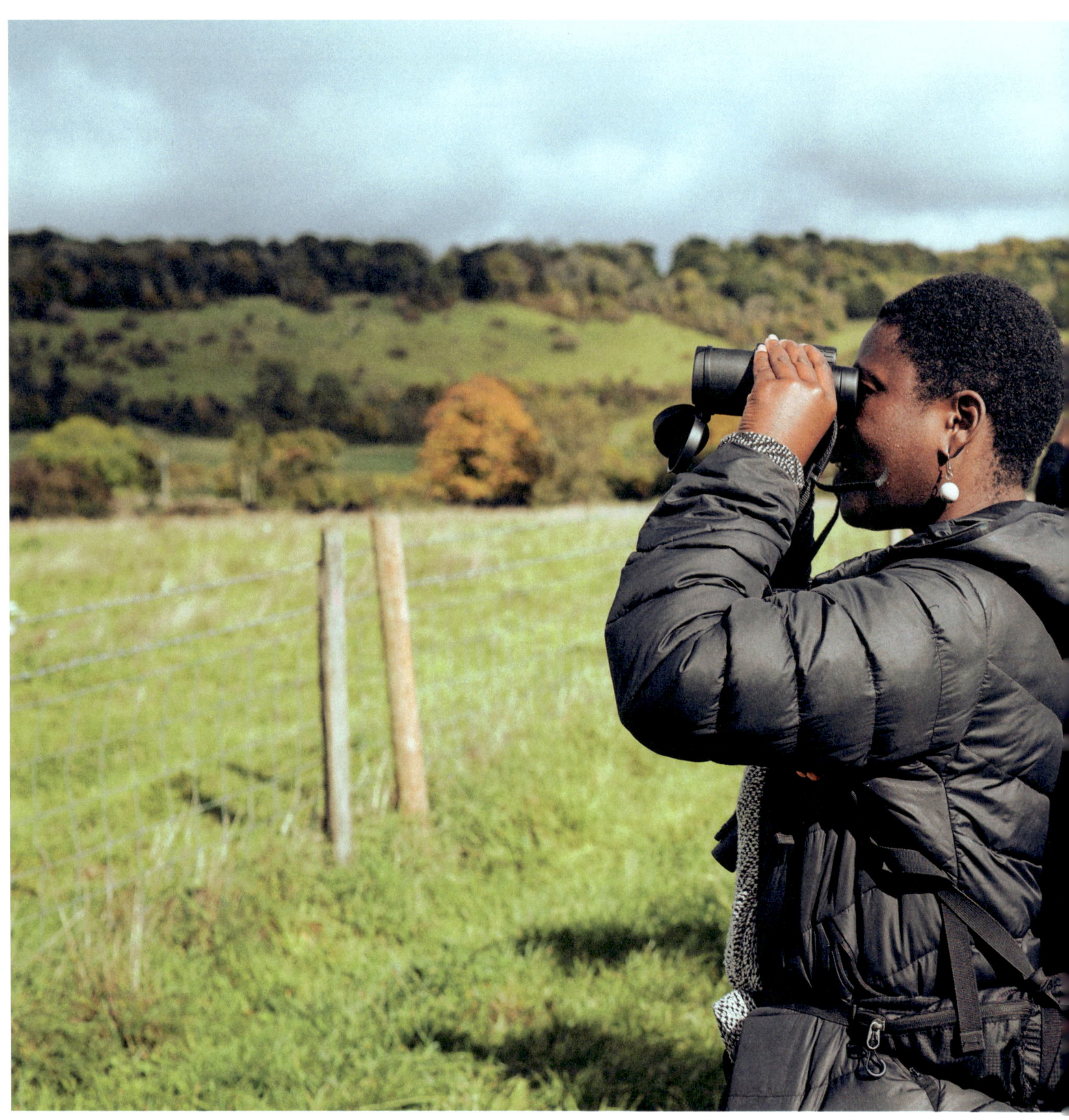

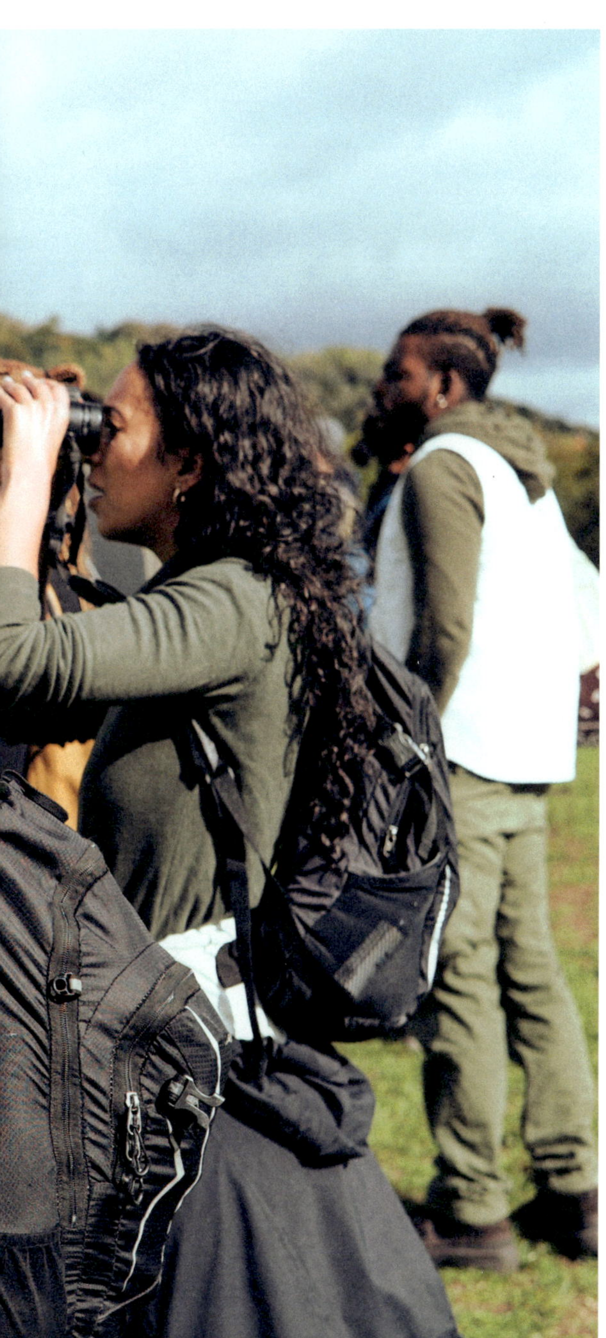

Nadeem and I are also on our own journey. It's a work in progress. We don't know exactly where we're going, but believing that we can open up people's imagination, in a world designed to prevent that, is incredibly powerful. But for me to sit here and say what that means for everyone and where it's going to go would be a disservice to Flock.

> AGS   I think that's something that design, as a discipline, struggles with: making space to be limitless, not being bound to output. There could be an intention, but that doesn't have to translate to a specific or measurable goal. Like you said, it's not really something that can even be described in words. It's a felt experience. I think it's important to have more spaces where there is no output. Are there any skills you think you've brought from your creative studio practice into Flock Together?

OO   Honestly, just knowing how to make it cool. From our messaging to how we photograph people to the vibe in person—it's in the energy we bring to everything. Bird-watching is considered by some to be a tired activity with an aging demographic. We wanted to bring a fresh take and engage new and younger people. Veteran birdwatchers are also super excited by our passion. They're like, "Oh my God, finally."

> AGS   I'm very interested in the types of intergenerational bridges Flock Together might open up. That's so important for us at *Deem*, to have spaces not just for intergenerational dialogue, but even simply to coexist.

OO   When we first started, Flock was naturally more focused on people around our age. Then, a lot of people would come with their parents, their aunties. Imagine we meet at a local train station and there are 100 Brown faces waiting there. It's insane. We make our way to the local green space and the line just goes on and on and on. We walk for the first hour or so then we break. We call our break "the communion," because we bring and share food, and Nadeem and I stand up and present any updates or news.

Then we ask people to share personal stories from the last month. Someone might explain how they recently quit their job because they weren't happy, or someone else might tell us about an idea for a project they want to work on. Someone else might present spoken word poetry. Everyone's there to support whatever it is you're doing or dealing with. Having people of different generations present broadens the perspectives, knowledge, and stories, as so often those ties are severed by modern life.

> AGS   I think this is such a testament to what happens when you design experiences that are open-ended. They are generative. They keep giving you more.●

Placemaking when "freedom is a place": Tracing liberatory infrastructures from queer Riis Beach

Text by
jah elyse sayers

Illustrations by
Acacia Rodriguez

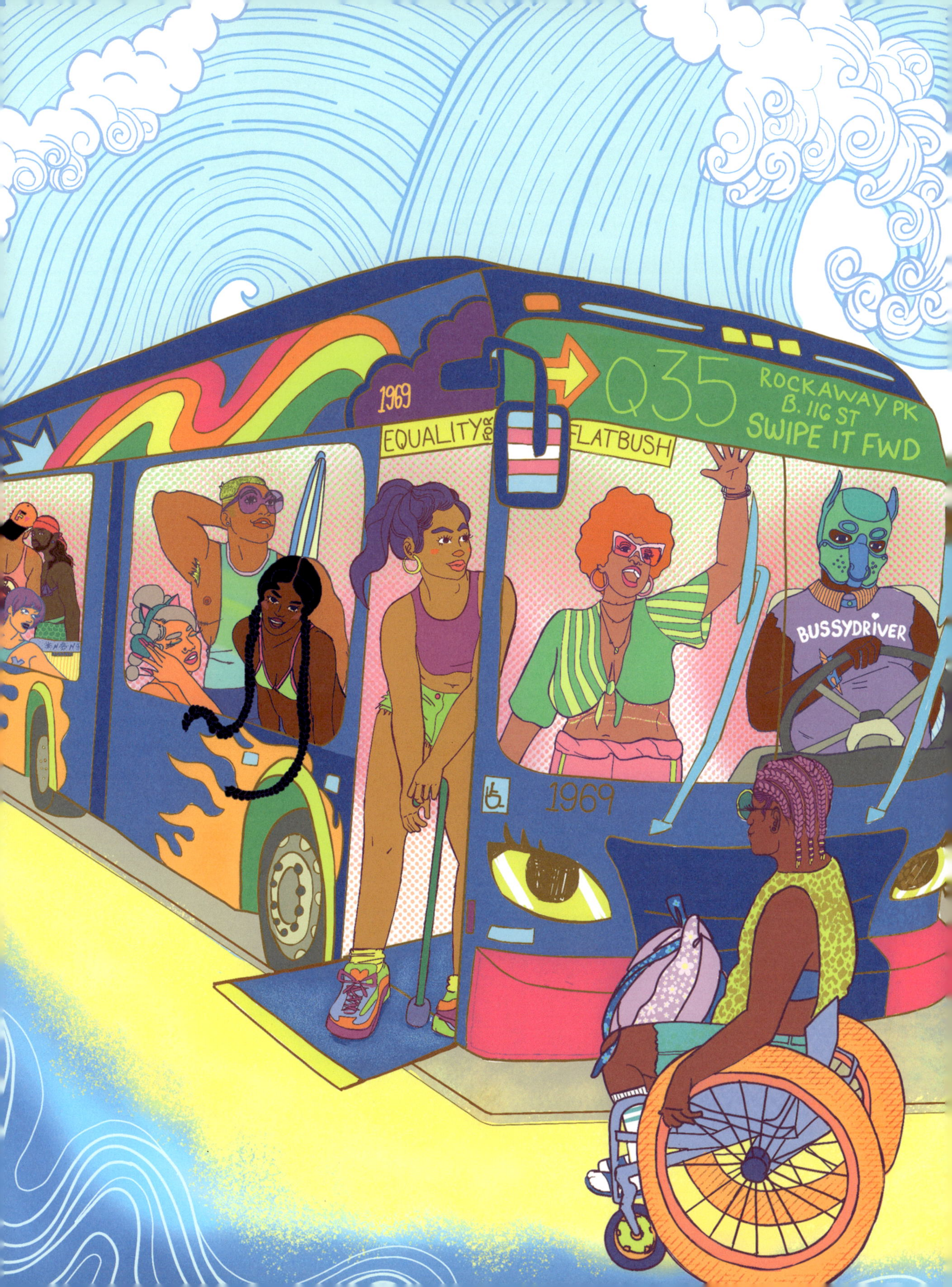

1969
EQUALITY FOR
FLATBUSH
Q35
ROCKAWAY PK
B. 116 ST
SWIPE IT FWD
1969
BUSSYDRIVER

In 2018, I began intentionally gathering stories of Bay 1 of People's Beach at Jacob Riis Park in Neponsit, Queens, New York City. The area is generally referred to as "Riis" and has served as a queer gathering place since at least the 1940s, facilitated by the beach's proximity to Neponsit Beach Hospital. The hospital's buildings provide a sense of cover to the beach by blocking sightlines from the boardwalk, bus stop, and sidewalk. The hospital buildings, however, face demolition.[1] The sense of safety they provide is at risk of displacement.

1 "Neponsit Home Set For Wrecking Ball," *Rockaway Times*, February 11, 2021, https://rockawaytimes.com/index.php/columns/7443-neponsit-home-set-for-wrecking-ball

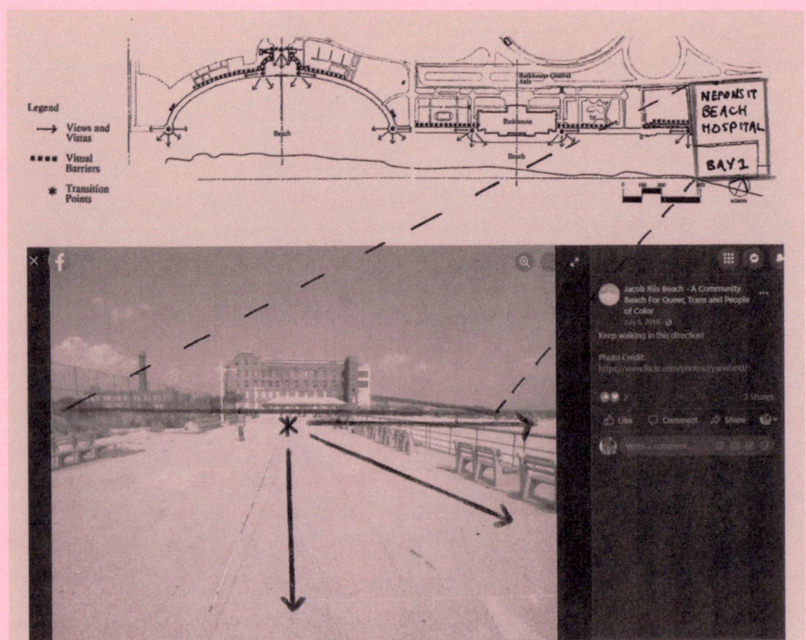

Adapted from pages 4-8 and 4-9 of Lane, Frenchman and Associates, "Jacob Riis Park: Cultural Landscape Report," 1992.; Screenshot of "Jacob Riis Beach - A Community Beach for Queer, Trans and People of Color," Facebook.; Annotations by author.

Notice the Facebook profile photo is not of the beach itself and is instead of one of the hospital buildings marking the end of the boardwalk. The elevated seawall, fencing, and building obscure views of Bay 1's beach. This choice of photo for the page embraces and helps beachgoers navigate obstructions of visibility.

2 Katherine McKittrick, *Dear Science and Other Stories* (Durham and London; Duke University Press, 2020), 9; Ruth Wilson Gilmore, "Abolition Geography and the Problem of Innocence," in *Futures of Black Radicalism* (London; New York: Verso, 2017), 227.

3 Informed by the concept of countertopography; see: Cindi Katz, "Accumulation, Excess, Childhood: Toward a Countertopography of Risk and Waste," *Doc. Anal. Geogr.* 57, no. 1 (2011): 47–60.

4 see: Brenna Bhandar, *Colonial Lives of Property: Law, Land, and Racial Regimes of Ownership* (Durham and London: Duke University Press, 2018); Sara Clarke Kaplan, *The Black Reproductive: Unfree Labor and Insurgent Motherhood* (Minneapolis: University Of Minnesota Press, 2021).

5 The National Park Service hosts the National Register of Historic Places and is manager of Jacob Riis Park.

As I conduct surveys and interviews, comb archives, participate in community organizing, and share conversations, I notice that Black queer and other queer-of-color stories that begin with or move through Riis often travel elsewhere. They challenge the idea that the *place* in placemaking might be limited to urban public and shared spaces like blocks, parks, gardens. They move me toward Katherine McKittrick's assertion that "stories make place" and Ruth Wilson Gilmore's assertion that "freedom is a place" to reflect on storytelling as placemaking and placemaking as, potentially, freedom-making.[2] Black queer storytelling's insistence on embodied mobility demands method-making that seeks threads between seemingly disconnected time-spaces and ephemeral experiences of freedom and safety. These threads potentially trace out existing alternatives to racial capitalism's illusions of inevitability, against and beyond reliance on private property.[3] I am specifically interested in how Black queer and trans people, as well as other queer and trans people of color, draw these connecting lines and, through this, choose and make liberatory ecosystems that offer possibilities of belonging that defy ownership and its racialized and gendered constructions of significance.[4] Can we recognize blocks, parks, and gardens as infrastructure for making a larger place: freedom?

On paper, a story about significance appears to protect Jacob Riis Park via the Jacob Riis Park Historic District. However, preservation extends only to "historically significant" features. Despite the beach's role as a refuge for queer placemaking, the National Park Service defines significance within a tight spatiotemporal context.[5] The period of significance here is confined to 1932-37 (related to Works Progress Administration [WPA] construction of Art Deco architectural styles). Spatial significance is confined within the "scope of work/limit" demarcated below by a thick (but porous) line:

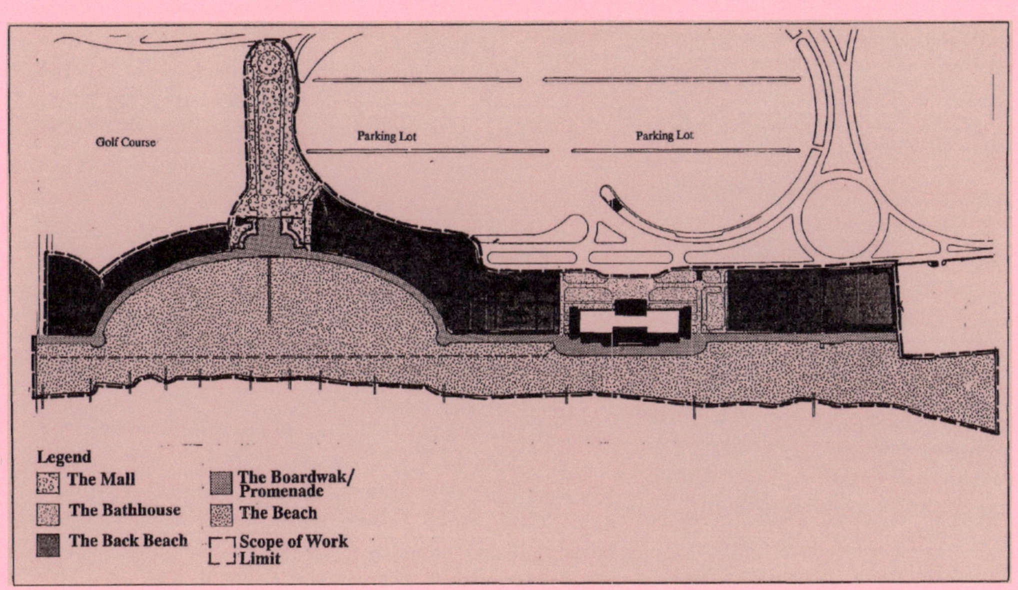

From p. 1-6 of Lane, Frenchman and Associates (1992)

But despite Neponsit Beach Hospital's shared history of elements of WPA-funded 1932-37 construction and Art Deco architecture, the hospital is outside the historic district's spatial limit, and documented queer use of the beach falls outside the period's temporal limit, rendering both queer use of Bay 1 and the buildings that provide its visual cover beyond the scope of worthiness for preservation.

In Black queer and trans storytelling about Riis, the porosity of the scope of significance is undeniable. Audre Lorde writes about 1950s Riis in *Zami*, but she does not discuss her time at the beach beyond "split[ting...] early." Instead, she writes of its traces sticking to her skin far beyond the beach's boundaries. Long after the ocean water dried from their bodies, Lorde and her partner were "full of sun and sand," and they "loved with the salt still on [their] skins." She writes that her time at the beach graced her with a certain "raunchy(ness) and restless(ness)," how she knew—more consciously and pridefully now than before—that she was "fat and Black and very fine," and later challenged an expression of anti-Blackness that she would typically "let[...] go."[6] Her experience of Riis followed her well beyond park boundaries to impact the ways she moved.

Similar ruptures animate contemporary tellings of Riis as I hear stories about last night's parties, at-home preparations, subway transfers and bus rides, bodega and chicken-spot stops, musings about neighboring residents and the Black trans*Atlantic, tales of stubborn sand in apartment floors and bedsheets. Beachgoers often mention the hospital as a landmark and protective feature, and I'm sometimes gifted a popular, though grim, fiction of the hospital's history: that it was a psychiatric facility where queer and trans people were tortured.

In reality, Neponsit Beach Hospital initially opened in 1915, following advocacy by the Association for Improving the Condition of the Poor as a beachfront tuberculosis sanitorium for children.[7] Riis was initially part of the hospital grounds in order to offer patients the "fresh air cure."[8]

6 Audre Lorde, *Zami: A New Spelling of My Name* (Berkeley: Crossing Press, 1982), 222–23.

7 The AICP was led by Jacob Riis. The park was posthumously named after Riis.

8 Before the 1940s introduction of antibiotics to treat tuberculosis, open air was the leading treatment for the disease, but traveling to and staying in the resort-like sanitoria built most often in mountainous western states was costly. AICP advocated for a tuberculosis treatment facility that might offer fresh air to city dwellers; see: "$250,000 Raised by a Sick Boy's Smile," *New York Times*, May 2, 1909.

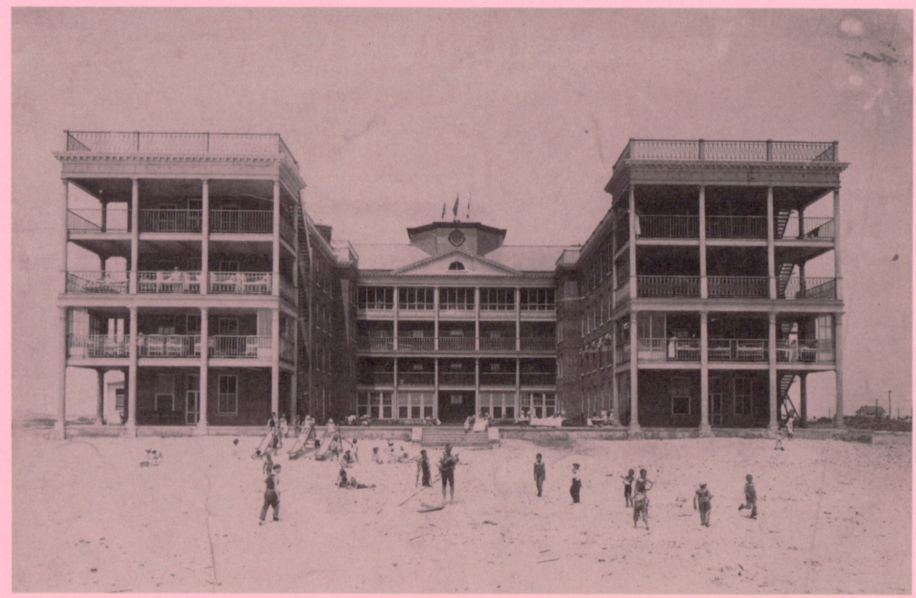

"Neponsit Beach Hospital for Convalescent Tubercular Children. Children on beach in front of 4-story building with wings." Department of Health, Accessed from NYC Department of Records & Information Services, Collection: "DPC: Public charities & hospitals."

Vulnerable to shifts in the military industrial complex, Neponsit Beach Hospital underwent multiple closures during the 1940s. Changes in tuberculosis treatment protocols and a land-use dispute between City Planning Commissioner Robert Moses and the city comptroller led to another closure in 1956 until 1961, when the hospital reopened as a nursing home and its beachfront was reallocated to park grounds. Queers filled

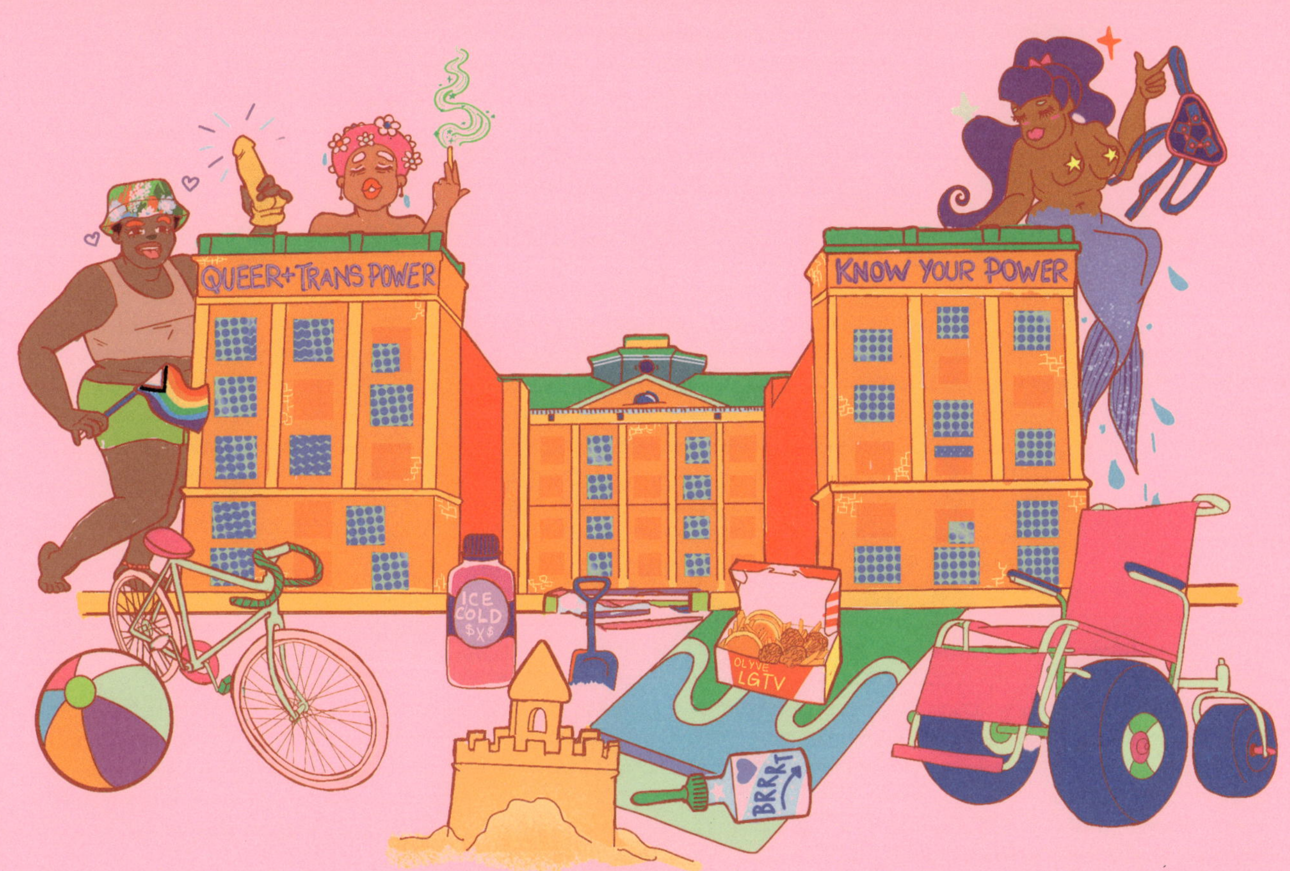

9 "See: sanatorium," in *APA Dictionary of Psychology* (American Psychological Association, 2022), https://dictionary.apa.org/.sana

10 Lew Simon, "Lew Fights Back," *The Wave*, November 25, 2000, https://www.rocka-wave.com/articles/lew-fights-back/; James Colgrove, *Epidemic City: The Politics of Public Health in New York* (Russell Sage Foundation, 2011).

the gaps, both through cuts in chainlink fences and in years between court decisions, taking advantage of the buildings' concrete disruption of policing gazes. I suspect that the fiction of an anti-queer psychiatric facility originates in the occasional application of the term sanatorium to describe psychiatric institutions.[9] Rather than focus on this erosion of public memory, we can locate an impulse toward connection across an otherwise divisive property line and preservation boundary, as most of these imaginings place historical beachgoers in conversation and solidarity with patients. As fleeting pleasures in the 1940s accumulated into a consistent presence on the beach by the mid-1950s, it is more feasible that it was nursing-home residents—from which queer-assumed HIV/AIDS patients were explicitly excluded—that beachgoers interacted with across jurisdictional lines.[10]

The imagined and actual connections between sites is a potentially liberatory thread worth reinforcing through the hospital's story of abandonment. Around two in the morning on September 11, 1998, then-mayor Rudy Giuliani ordered the nearly three hundred residents of Neponsit Beach Hospital to be transferred to other NYC public hospitals. Given no prior notice, residents were promised they would return pending renovations. Renovations never came, and the residents never returned. The abandonment of patients' safety was handled out of court, with the city giving patients or their estates settlements of $18,000 each and agreeing to provide advance notice before future mass patient transfers. Although an

JAH ELYSE SAYERS

assessment in the year 2000 estimated hospital repairs at about $600,000, millions of dollars have been spent since to maintain the hospital buildings' abandonment through fines for mismanagement, contracting of security personnel, maintenance of security infrastructure such as fences and a guardhouse, piecemeal repairs, and clean-up of debris; another $5 million is marked for demolition.[11] In the wake of governmental neglect of patients and property—what we might call *organized abandonment*, or governance by neglect[12]—queers have maintained the buildings' utility from a distance by utilizing their sightline-blocking functions toward safety.

As demolition looms, can we model the rupturing of an edge after the embodied mobilities of Black queer life and storytelling? In their reliance on and deferral to property logics, dominant systems for allegedly protecting and preserving place(s) or placemaking fail to acknowledge placemaking as living. They instead render some lives (and the socialities amongst them) surplus and appropriate for abandonment and displacement. They render lives unworthy of preservation. We need to embrace approaches to preservation that disrupt rigid divides and risk change by nurturing life itself in order to enable continued placemaking. The organization Gays and Lesbians Living in a Transgender Society (GLITS) proposes a community land trust on the Neponsit Hospital site dedicated to providing trans-centering holistic healthcare with Black trans leadership. Even in its navigation of property systems, this proposed intervention has the potential to loosen the stranglehold of private property logics on public-space preservation by supporting the embodied health of beachgoers. This approach takes seriously the necessity of living to placemaking and the necessity of care to living. It embraces Riis as a crucial site for making life and freedom, at and beyond the shoreline.

No one saw a crucial site of Black queer gathering emerging from a tuberculosis hospital for children. However, a commitment to life means risk, surprise and, to follow Barbara Christian, "tuned sensitivity to that which is alive and therefore cannot be known until it is known."[13] This means reaching beyond scopes spatially, as occurs in the acknowledgement of Neponsit Hospital's impacts and in the ways beachgoers' stories of bus rides and bedrooms might carry us to consider public transit accessibility and tenant organizing as preservation methods. It means, too, reaching beyond temporal scopes by expanding the 1930s period of significance not only into the queer gathering of the 1940s and subsequent decades, but also toward our futures. We can build up the infrastructures and nourish the ecosystems of the freedom ephemerally emplaced at Riis if only we support our living all over.●

jah elyse sayers (they/them) works through research, writing, farming, building, teaching, organizing, and art-making to further Black queer and trans liberatory placemaking. jah is currently a PhD candidate in environmental psychology at The Graduate Center, CUNY. Their writing has appeared in Wagadu: A Journal of Transnational Women's and Gender Studies *and BRICLab Essays; they have performed at Brooklyn Arts Exchange (BAX) and exhibited sculptural work at metaDEN. jah is grateful to Diane Enobabor and Simone Lee Sobers for shaping this article with their listening, reading, questions, encouragement, and thorough generosity.*

11 Brendan Brosh, "Abandoned Neponsit Health Center Fixed," *NY Daily News*, April 21, 2008, https://www.nydailynews.com/new-york/queens/abandoned-neponsit-health-center-fixed-article-1.280481; Katie McFadden, "Neponsit Money Pit - The Wave," *The Wave*, March 7, 2014, https://www.rockawave.com/articles/neponsit-money-pit/; "Neponsit Home Set For Wrecking Ball."

12 Ruth Wilson Gilmore, "Organized Abandonment and Organized Violence: Devolution and the Police" (The Humanities Institute at UCSC, November 9, 2015), https://vimeo.com/146450686.

13 Barbara Christian, "The Race for Theory," *Cultural Critique* no. 6, Spring 1987: 358.

deem

Deem's partner pages highlight like-minded organizations, businesses, and initiatives whose work models ways in which design can add value to communities.

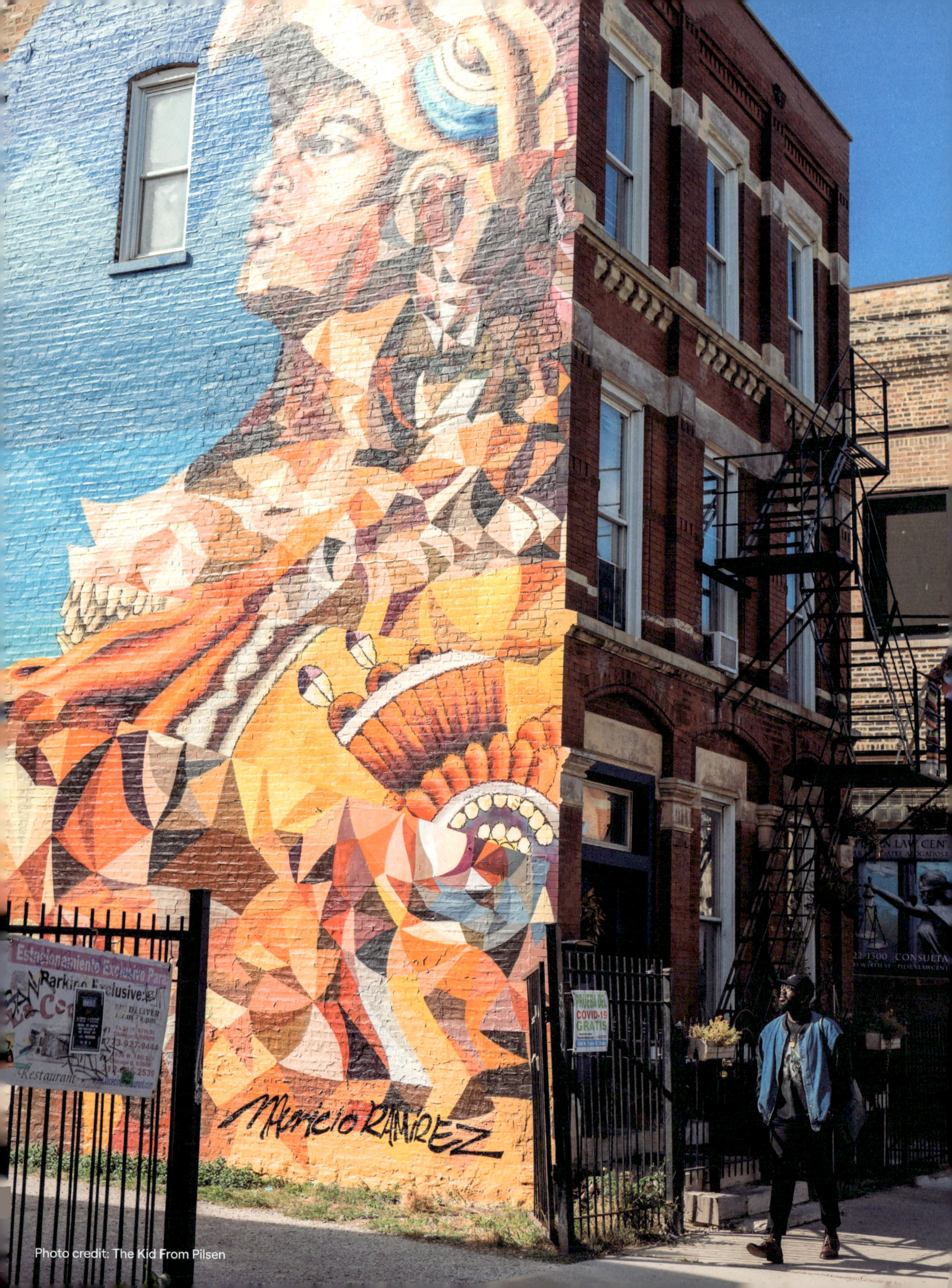

Mauricio RAMIREZ

Cultivating Chicago

Bridge-building is something that comes easily to Otez Gary.

As the Museum of Contemporary Art Chicago's Community Engagement Manager, Gary is out and about locally in Chicago's many neighborhoods, cultivating healthy, sustainable, and impactful collaborations with community partners. These relationships are critical to fulfilling the MCA's mission to be a place of dialogue and co-creation with community members.

Learn more about who we are, the museum's commitments, and our Community Partnerships and Engagement program at mcachicago.org/community.

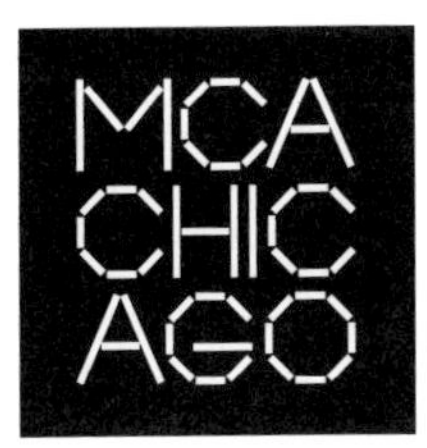

The MCA is deeply committed to supporting the community that we live in and serve, and we are constantly working to create space for dialogue, learning, and growth.

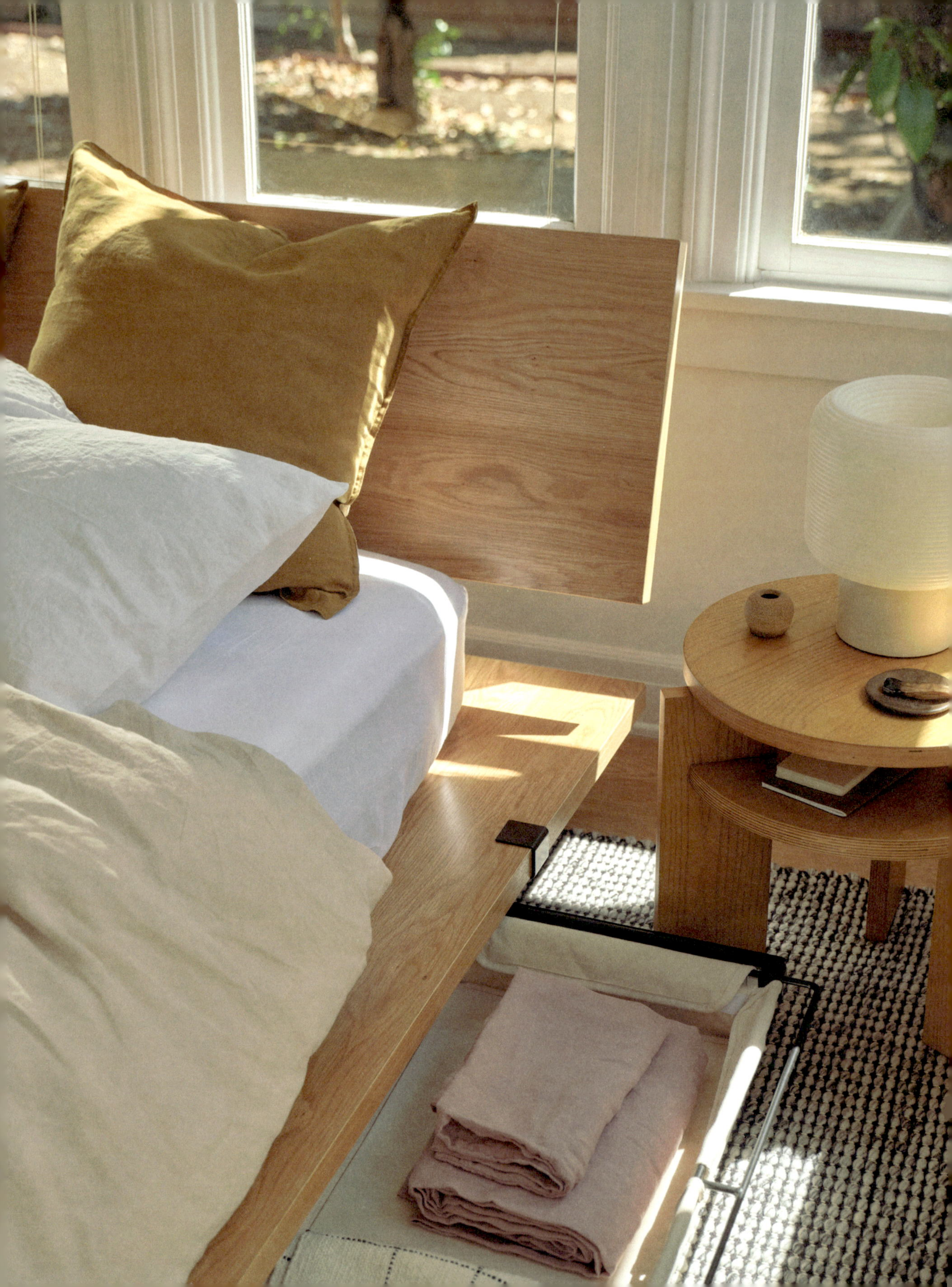

Rethinking Sustainability Means Buying Less

Just because something is made from recycled materials doesn't mean it's sustainable. As a consumer, the most sustainable thing you can do is not to buy anything at all. The next best thing is to buy something that is designed to adapt and last over time, rather than to wear out, go out of style, or become obsolete and end up in a landfill.

Life changes, so our furniture should too. That's why we designed our bed frame to grow with your needs. Start small, and choose a sustainably sourced material such as oak grown in US forests, or a bold color created with 50% recycled wood waste. Expand its size later by adding an additional panel, or make it smaller by storing a panel away. Add practical features with sliding underbed storage, or an upholstered headboard made with all-natural fabric. A bed frame you love is one that you'll keep. That's what sustainability means to us.

See how we make homes more sustainable at floydhome.com

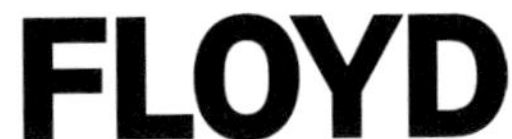

Floyd was founded in 2013 with a single product, The Floyd Leg, as a reaction to disposable furniture. In this spirit, our Design Principles are centered around solving problems & being more thoughtful about the home.

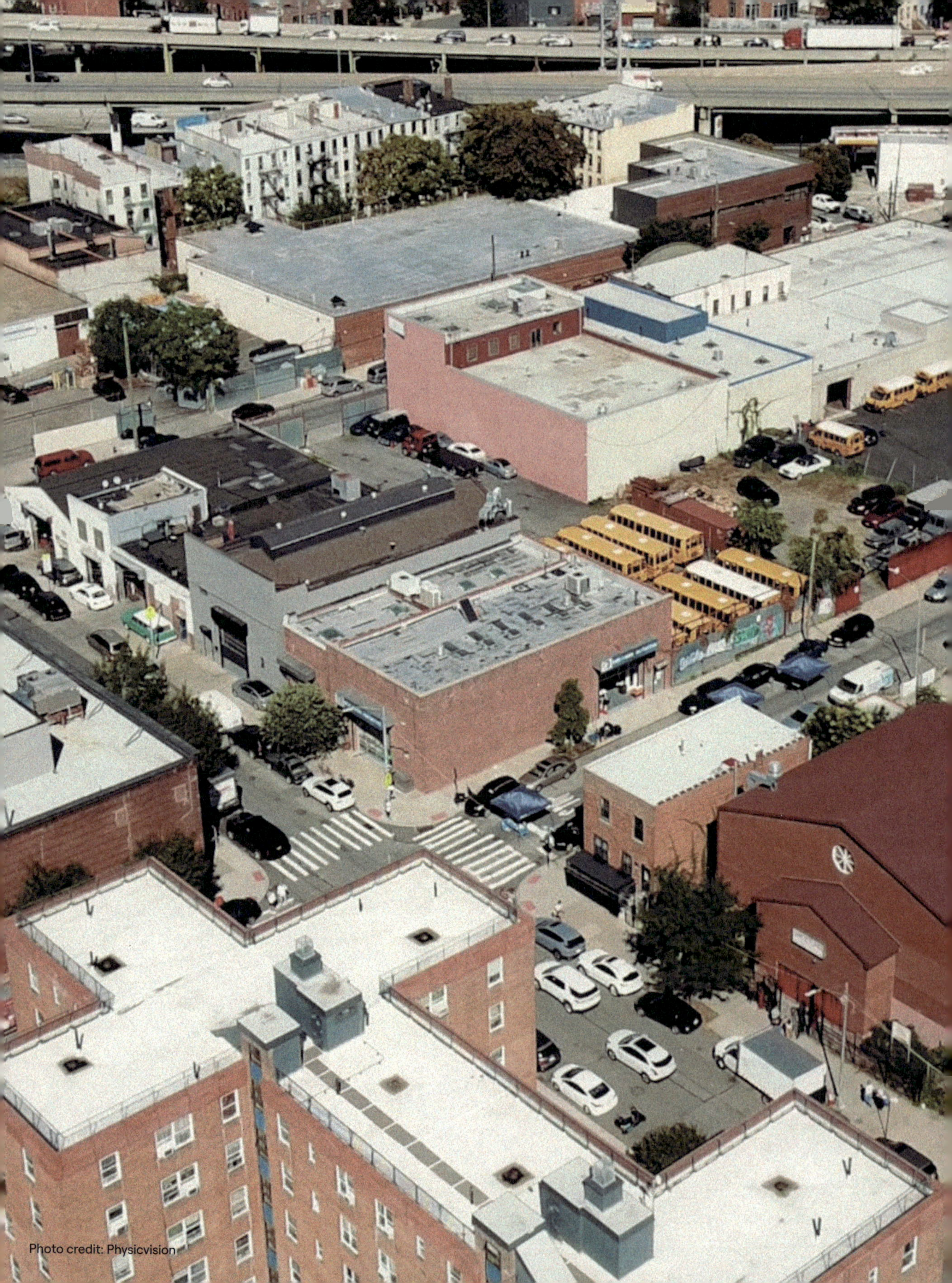
Photo credit: Physicvision

Creating Change from Within

In 2002, a program from a local hospital provided aid to a group of young mothers from Red Hook, Brooklyn. These mothers brought their children to our doors and, as they grew up, Red Hook Initiative was formed to provide programming that adapted to their needs. Today, on the corner of West 9th and Hicks Street, a converted warehouse serves as a safe haven in this community for resources, opportunities, and connectivity.

Youth development, community building, and community hiring are at the core of our approach, giving young people and residents the tools, resources, and opportunities to interrupt the systems and barriers that perpetuate historic inequities in the Red Hook community. Our nationally recognized model for place-based social change serves over 6,500 BIPOC residents, and the children who grew up with us are members of our staff today.

To learn more about Red Hook Initiative and get involved, please visit: rhicenter.org

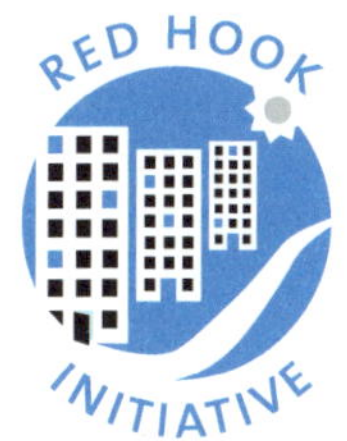

Red Hook Initiative (RHI) believes that *social change to overcome systemic inequities begins with empowered youth*. In partnership with community adults, we nurture young people in Red Hook to be inspired, resilient, and healthy, and to envision themselves as co-creators of their lives, community, and society.

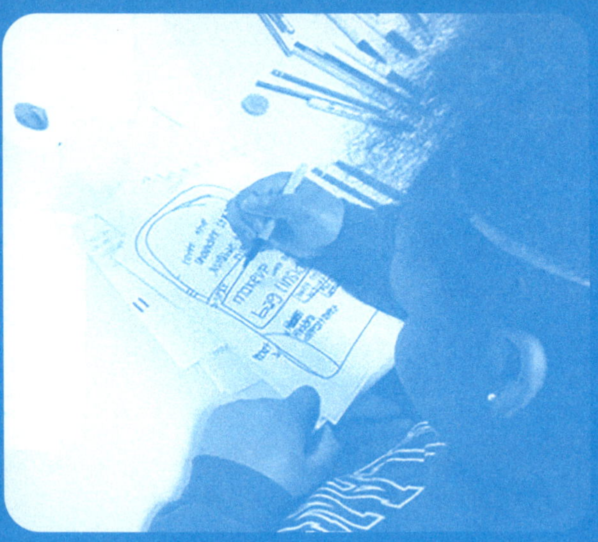

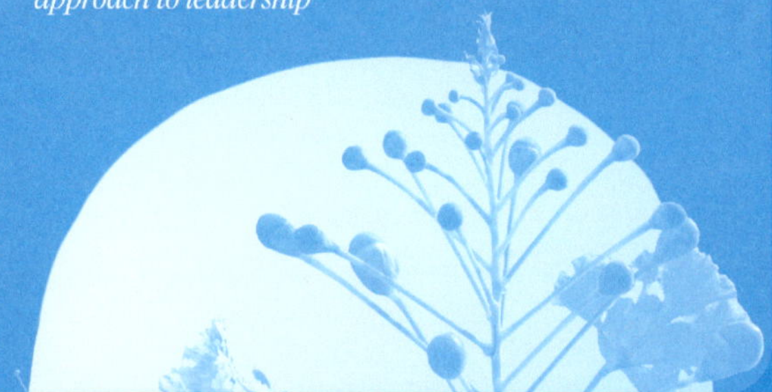

Claim Your Space

*with an intentional
approach to leadership*

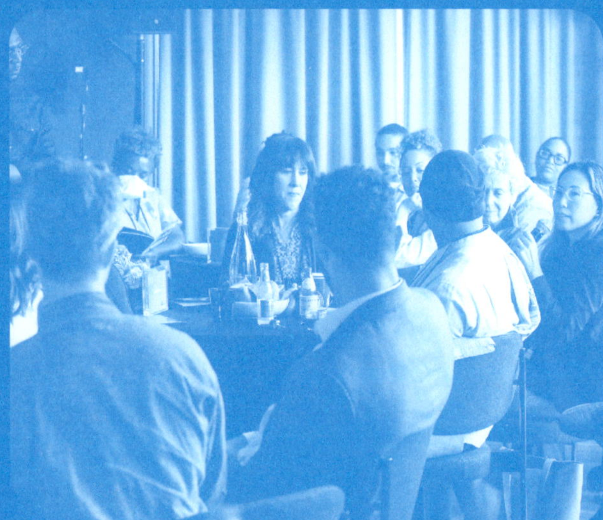

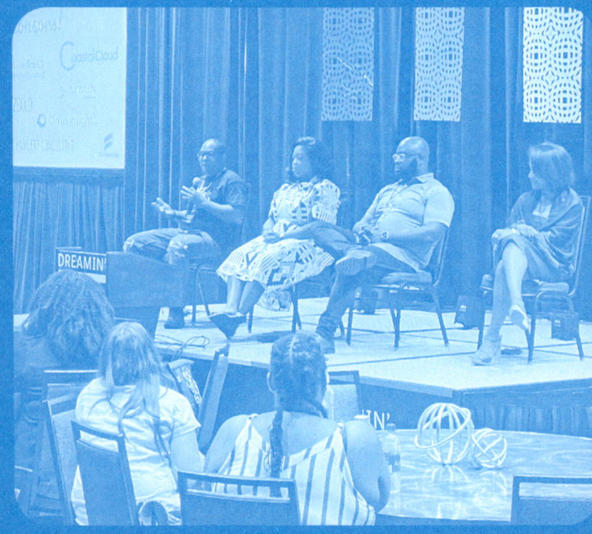

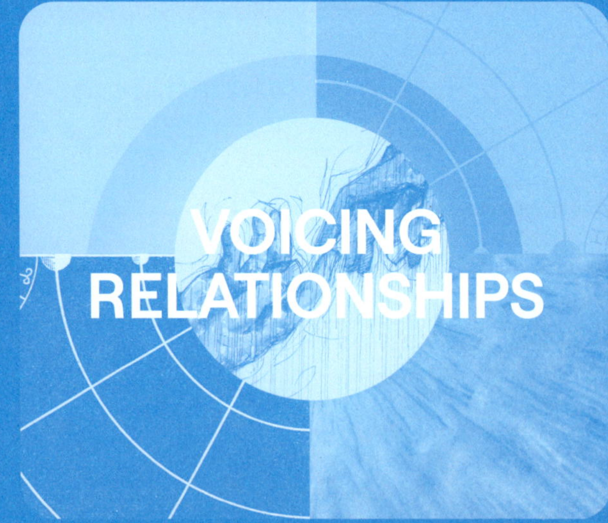

Clockwise from top left: Inneract Project, Salesforce Medium Blog, Àròko Cooperative, Dreamin' in Color, Voicing Relationships

Building Relationships by Design

Relationships are at the core of our company's philosophy, design practice, and product. In an issue dedicated to giving meaning to space through making place, we want to share some partners and people who inspire our work.

Àròko Cooperative — A Black-led creative organization dedicated to cultivating a future of Black Liberation, care, and wellbeing for Earth and all of her inhabitants.

Dreamin' in Color — A community-created conference at which current and aspiring Black Salesforce professionals discuss how to build thriving careers and businesses.

Inneract Project — A nonprofit that empowers students of color through design education.

Voicing Relationships — A podcast made in collaboration with the House of Beautiful Business.

Our Medium Blog — A platform for stories about the development of relationship design through philosophy, process, and pursued outcomes.

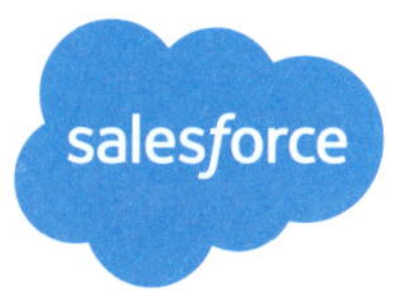

design.salesforce.com
Scan to learn more about our partners

DALEEN SAAH: ARTIST TAKEOVER

Palestine is a place. Nonetheless, Western media outlets and institutions influenced by Zionism have created a climate in which saying so is taboo and often avoided. Referencing Palestine as a place is now considered a political act and a controversey, leading to Palestinian censorship and, subsequently, Palestinian erasure.

My father's 2020 US passport has "Palestine" written as the country of birth. I've always thought this was incredible. My dad was born in 1944, before the establishment of an Israeli state. To see "Palestine" written on American paperwork is comforting and exciting for me. I dug into other official paperwork in my family, finding my grandfather's 1984 naturalization certificate and my great-grandfather's 1939 British-issued identity card, all documenting these men from the country of "Palestine." What could be better proof, or more damning, than a lineage of official documents that report Palestine as a place?

"Keep Your Identity Card," reads my great-grandfather's ID carrying case. Continuing the Palestinian exile into today, Israel systemically confiscates Palestinian ID cards, revokes citizenships, and refuses renewals. My family and community try to conceal their Jerusalem or Palestine IDs when crossing Israeli-manned borders, because these cards are often taken and never returned. Keeping our old, expired IDs might be one way we can come home when Palestine is free. The photo on the left in the final spread shows my dad and his friends at a party in Ramallah, sometime in the 1950s. They were forced into exile in 1967, and we are their descendants. We (all) want to come home.

Identification cards, certificates, and photographs from my family give us one lens with which to show that Palestine is a place. While erasure and exile aim to make Palestine abnormalized and hidden, Palestine *is* a place; it always has been and it always will be. —*Daleen Saah*

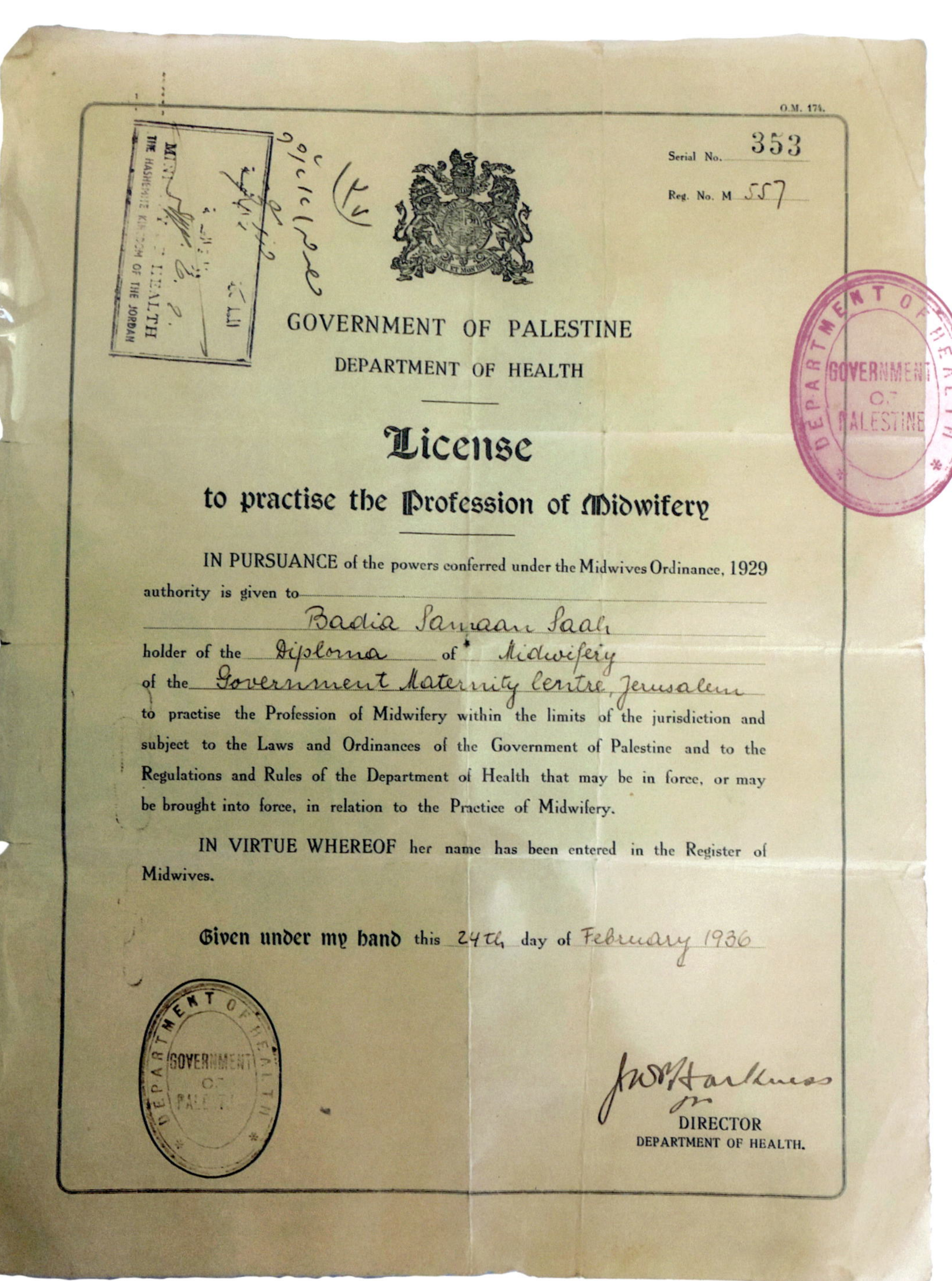

O.M. 174.
Serial No. 353
Reg. No. M 557
GOVERNMENT OF PALESTINE
DEPARTMENT OF HEALTH
License
to practise the Profession of Midwifery
IN PURSUANCE of the powers conferred under the Midwives Ordinance, 1929
authority is given to
Badia Samaan Saah
holder of the Diploma of Midwifery
of the Government Maternity Centre, Jerusalem
to practise the Profession of Midwifery within the limits of the jurisdiction and
subject to the Laws and Ordinances of the Government of Palestine and to the
Regulations and Rules of the Department of Health that may be in force, or may
be brought into force, in relation to the Practice of Midwifery.
IN VIRTUE WHEREOF her name has been entered in the Register of
Midwives.
Given under my hand this 24th day of February 1936
DIRECTOR
DEPARTMENT OF HEALTH.

KEEP YOUR I.D. CARD

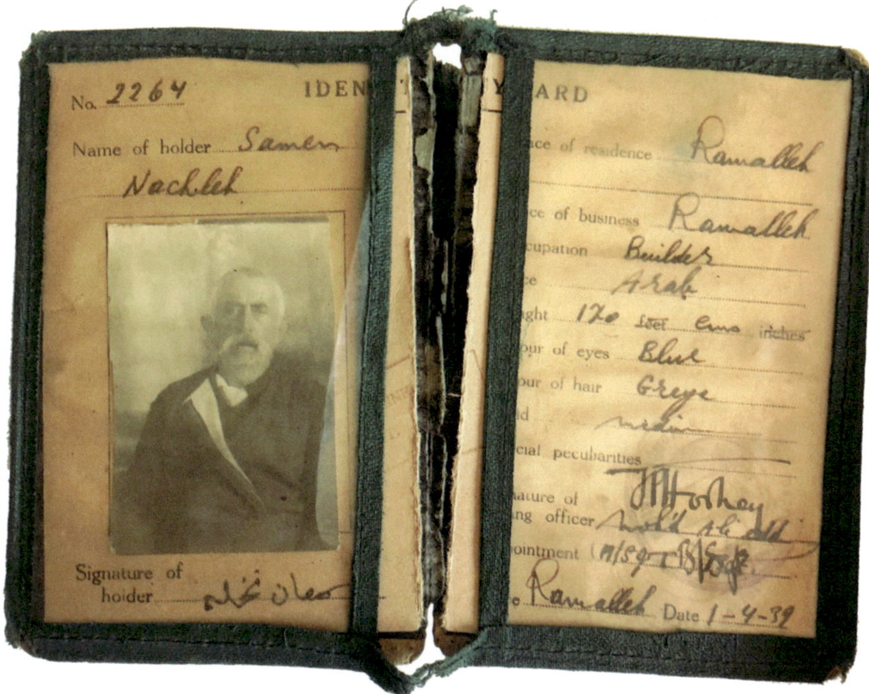

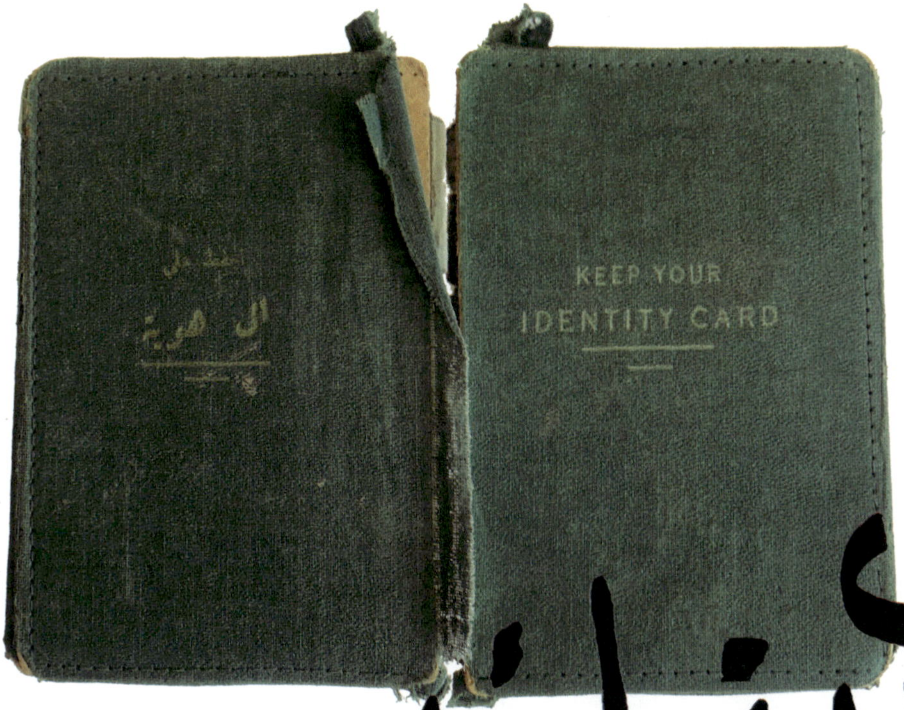

DALEEN SAAH: ARTIST TAKEOVER

FREE PALESTINE

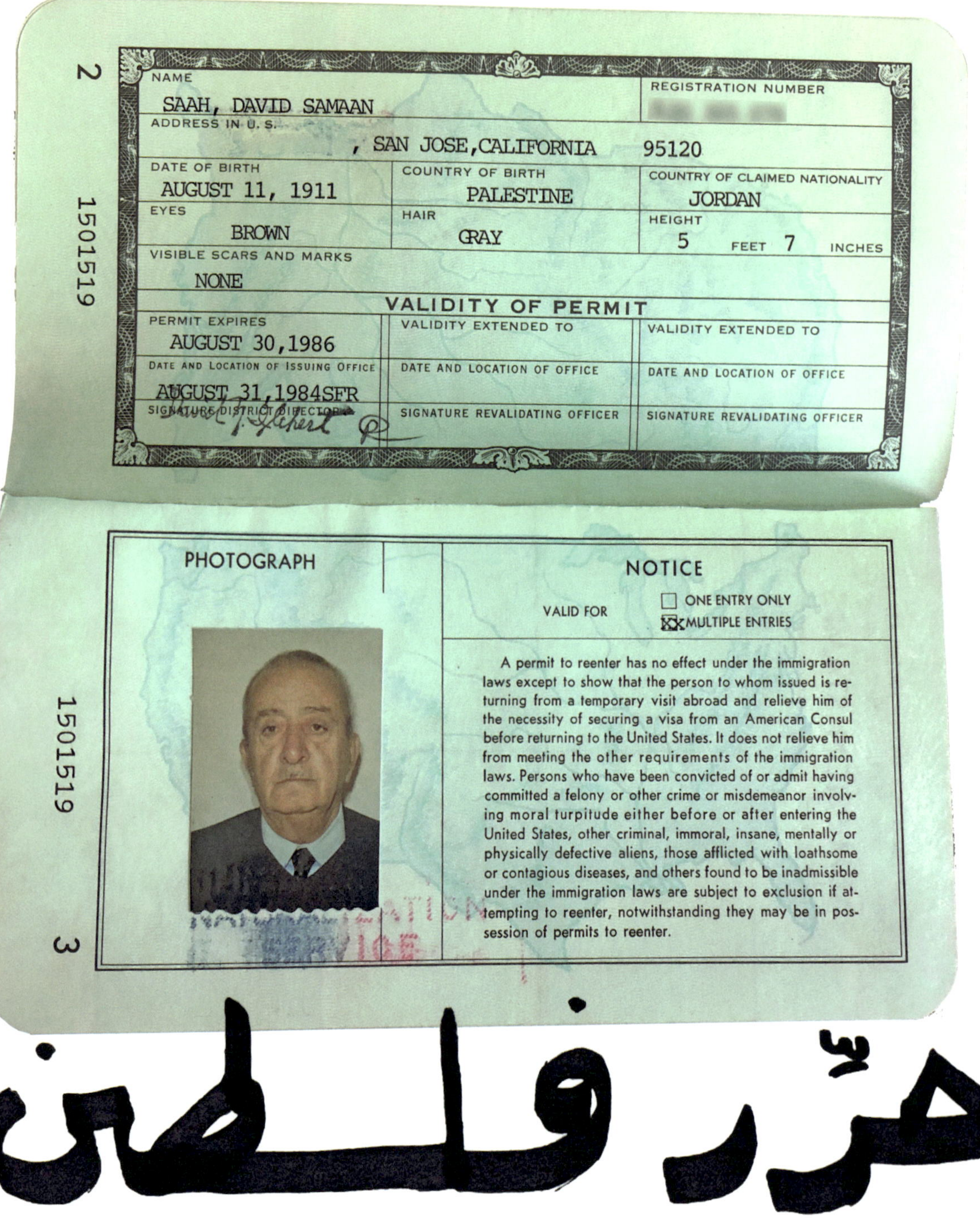

NAME

SAAH, DAVID SAMAAN

ADDRESS IN U. S.

, SAN JOSE, CALIFORNIA   95120

REGISTRATION NUMBER

DATE OF BIRTH	COUNTRY OF BIRTH	COUNTRY OF CLAIMED NATIONALITY
AUGUST 11, 1911	PALESTINE	JORDAN

EYES	HAIR	HEIGHT
BROWN	GRAY	5 FEET 7 INCHES

VISIBLE SCARS AND MARKS

NONE

VALIDITY OF PERMIT

PERMIT EXPIRES	VALIDITY EXTENDED TO	VALIDITY EXTENDED TO
AUGUST 30, 1986		
DATE AND LOCATION OF ISSUING OFFICE	DATE AND LOCATION OF OFFICE	DATE AND LOCATION OF OFFICE
AUGUST 31, 1984 SFR		
SIGNATURE DISTRICT DIRECTOR	SIGNATURE REVALIDATING OFFICER	SIGNATURE REVALIDATING OFFICER

PHOTOGRAPH

NOTICE

VALID FOR   ☐ ONE ENTRY ONLY   ☒ MULTIPLE ENTRIES

A permit to reenter has no effect under the immigration laws except to show that the person to whom issued is returning from a temporary visit abroad and relieve him of the necessity of securing a visa from an American Consul before returning to the United States. It does not relieve him from meeting the other requirements of the immigration laws. Persons who have been convicted of or admit having committed a felony or other crime or misdemeanor involving moral turpitude either before or after entering the United States, other criminal, immoral, insane, mentally or physically defective aliens, those afflicted with loathsome or contagious diseases, and others found to be inadmissible under the immigration laws are subject to exclusion if attempting to reenter, notwithstanding they may be in possession of permits to reenter.

حرّروا فلسطين

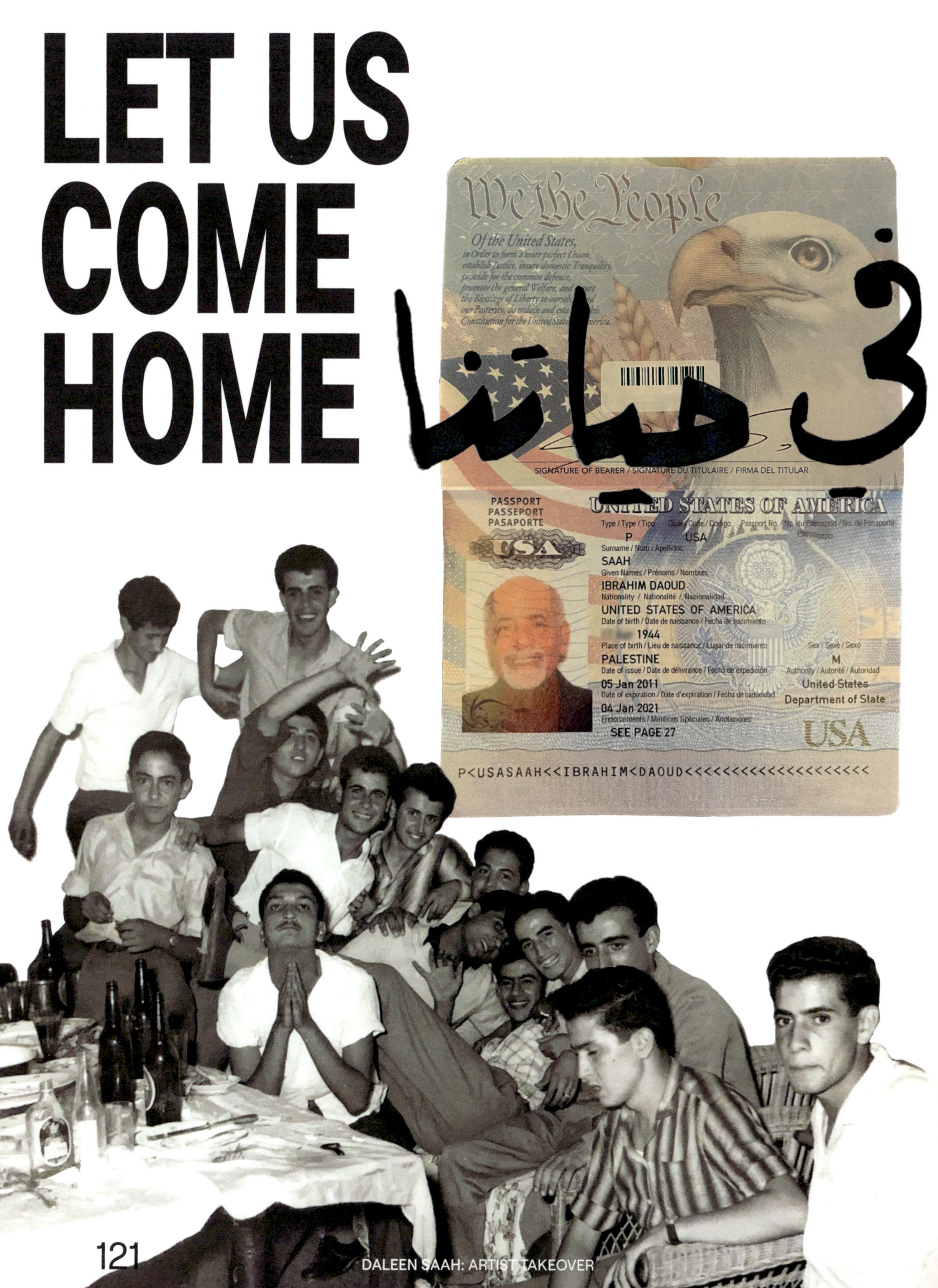

121

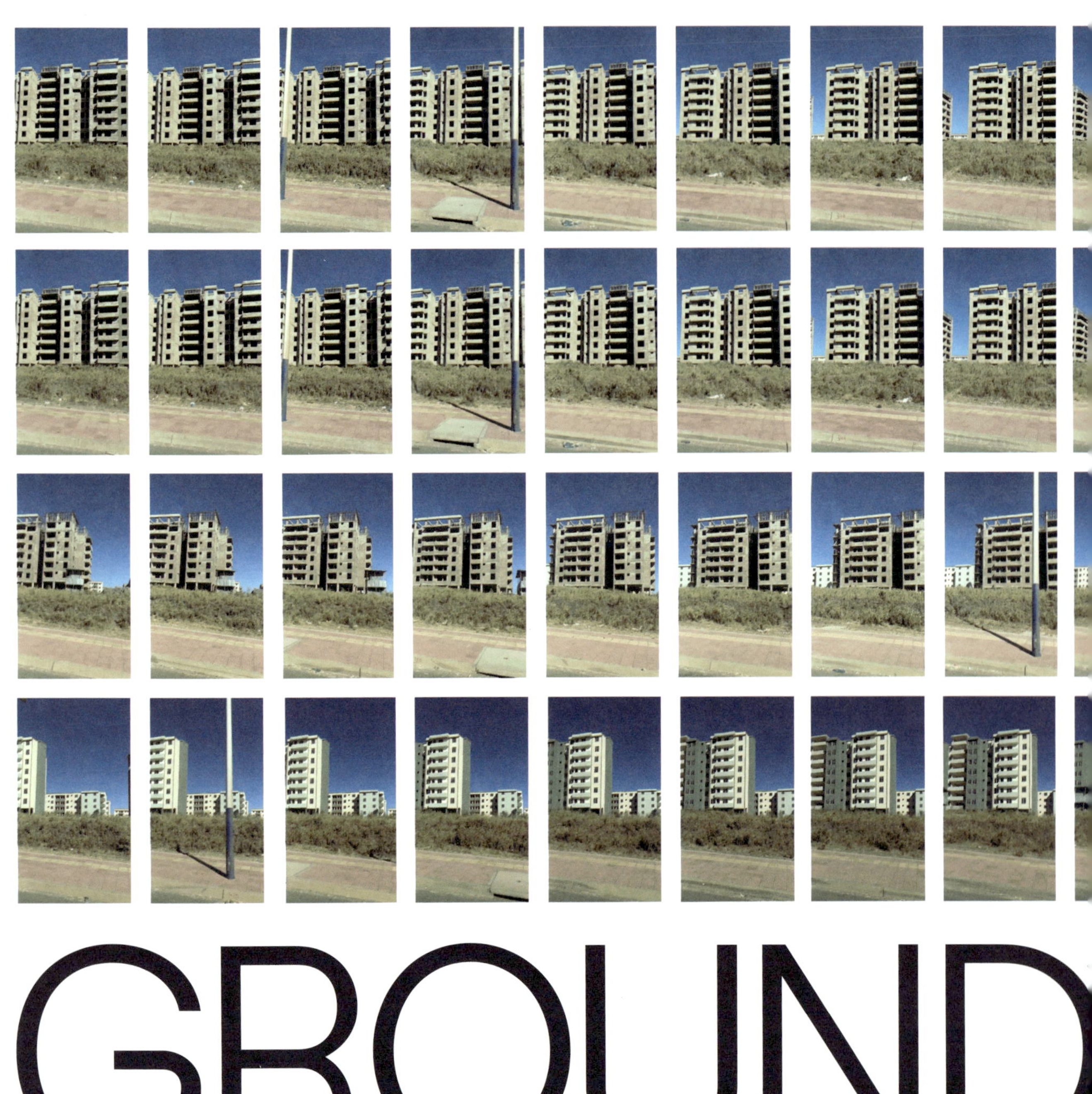

GROUND

Text and photography by
Ruth Gebreyesus

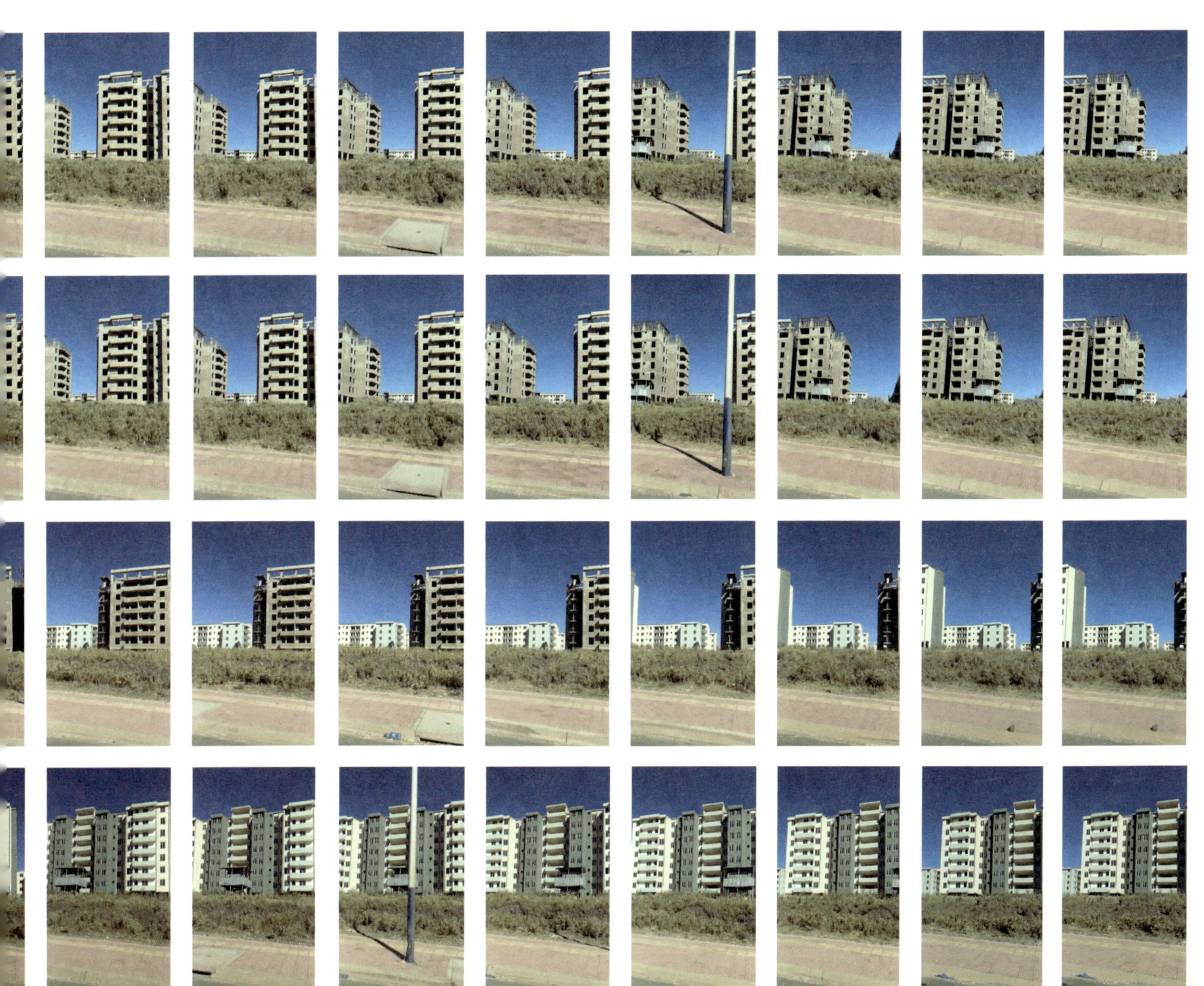

PLUS EMPTY

RUTH GEBREYESUS

Last spring, I was in Addis Abeba obsessing over vacancy taxes. I was staying with a close friend in a mostly untenanted building in a desirable neighborhood. The bottom floor housed a bank, like many Addis buildings in central locations. The second floor's two units were vacant. The building's guard sometimes slept on a mattress in one apartment on the third floor. The other unit was leased as an office by a sports association. And then there was us, on the fourth, facing an empty apartment across the hall. The top floor right above us was built for an unrealized rooftop cafe, but its unfinished walls and windows made it an ideally breezy place to dry our clothes.

Previous spread: On the outskirts of Addis, I stared at these developments, upright and dense, wondering where people would dry their berbere. Where would clothes be hung? What trees would provide enough shade for gossip and children's play?

Right: The view from my friend's apartment where I found no use in counting all the empty buildings after a while. I even lost track of how I felt about the city itself.

A month after she arrived, my friend encouraged two other friends looking for a place to move into her under-occupied building. The owners lived in the US, but they relayed through their local consigliere that there was a monthly increase of 2,000 birr for new tenants. Since most African currencies are dollarized and many landlords themselves are dollarized, it's better to characterize this as an additional $40 monthly. They refused to budge, so the units remained vacant.

In 2002, two years after I left Addis, my hometown decided that urbanization meant vertical growth. Every main and sub-arterial road was zoned to erect five-story buildings, or "ground plus four" by the local count. The building height mandate for the city has been updated twice since. The most recent, in 2015, orders that new buildings in my friend's neighborhood climb up to ground plus 19 stories. The city's plan is to accommodate a swelling population of at least five million, many flowing in from rural areas towards commercial activity—which is to say, livelihood. And so developers plot on, cement is mixed, and skinny young eucalyptus trees are culled to serve as scaffolding to grow the city up. But somehow, Addis all grown up has only replaced big empty skies with empty buildings and the city's bottom floor is more congested than ever.

One day, in impossible traffic at Megenagna, a roundabout moving as slow as an ungreased wheel bearing, I wondered out loud in my phone—

the streets are full of people on foot they go
on the bus they sit and stand fill the bus full
in minibuses they sit packed glowing faces against their phones
the cars are full of people and the street is full of cars
if everyone is here, where is it empty?

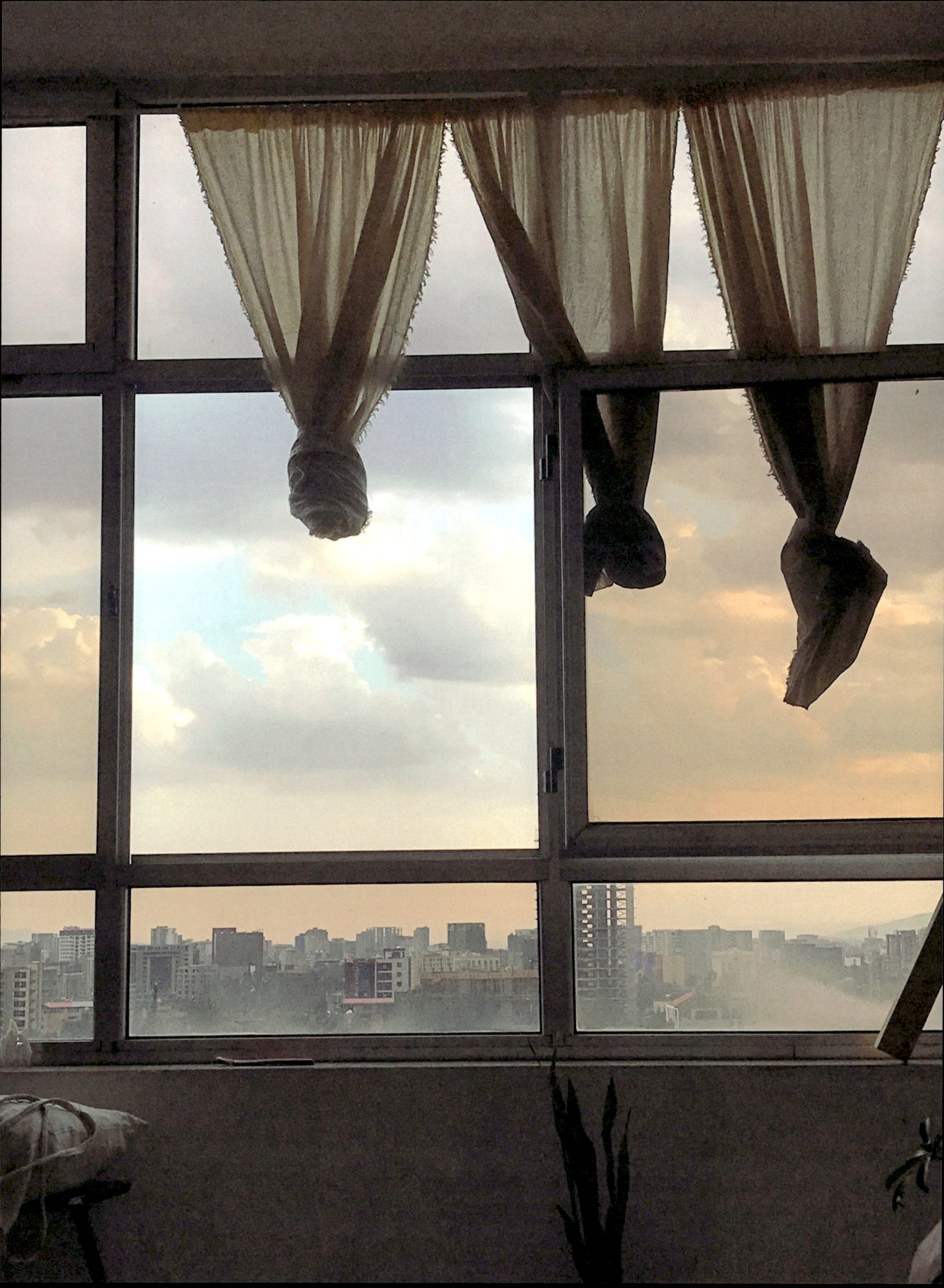

The truth is Addis didn't just grow tall. It also sprawled, expanding its outskirts and swallowing farmland and small towns along the way. Those new margins were now dense with tall government-subsidized housing projects. Those displaced by zoning ordinances for new developments were sent there. And these buildings have high occupancy and were built with the intention to be so. Their residents, geographically segregated based on their economic capacity, traveled towards the center of the city for work and back again at night.

From my friend's balcony, I could see across the street to another sparsely habited five-story building. We noticed activity on the top floor and the bottom. The rest were dormant. Our parallel mostly-hollow build-ings hugged a busy road that, if followed up and to the left, would take you to sprawling embassy grounds given to nations during Ethiopia's empire. To the right, the road leads to Shola Gebeya, a major and densely packed open-air market in town. Before Shola became the market we know it as today, I wonder what harvests it held. At my grandmother's house over lunch once, she casually mentioned how the best teff used to come from Bole. It seemed unimaginable now, but within her memory's reach, a now-posh neighborhood adjacent to the city's international airport had cows plowing fields to prepare for tiny teff seeds to be dispersed. Addis's density is full of historic and contemporary betrayals.

"WHERE WE USED TO BUY CORN ON THE COB FROM CHARCOAL VENDORS AND BUNDLES OF GRASS FOR HOLIDAY DECOR NOW LIVE ROW AFTER ROW OF SHOPS SELLING LOUD FENDI KNOCK-OFFS AND POLYESTER DRESSES PRINTED WITH TRADITIONAL MOTIFS ON GOLD PLASTIC MANNEQUINS."

Followed south, the road leads to my childhood home after three turns. Maybe four. In my youth, the neighborhood was a low-humming transportation and school hub from which residential rows bled out. In the last decade, it has successfully managed to exterminate all sense of intima-cy. The neighborhood had decidedly become a place to make and spend money. Night and day it blared sonic and visual cues for this consumption. Where we used to buy corn on the cob from charcoal vendors and bundles of grass for holiday decor now live row after row of shops selling loud Fendi knock-offs and polyester dresses printed with traditional motifs on gold plas-tic mannequins.

When night fell, blue fluorescent lights blared until late for the af-ter-work crowd of shoppers. People also faded into informal honey wine, khat, and liquor spots where dim lights twinkled over loud conversations. This cacophonous activity all lived on either the ground floor of tall build-ings or in former residential homes adapted to integrate into a new economic productivity. The top floors of tall buildings remained unoccupied or under construction.

The concept of a vacancy tax was fresh in my mind from back in the Bay Area, where I've spent most of my years since leaving Addis. Va-cancy and houselessness are inescapable contradictions there. In 2019, as a housing crisis that displaced thousands from their homes into faraway

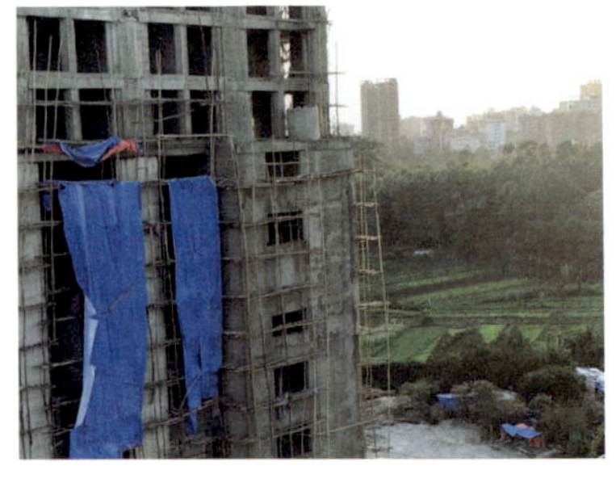

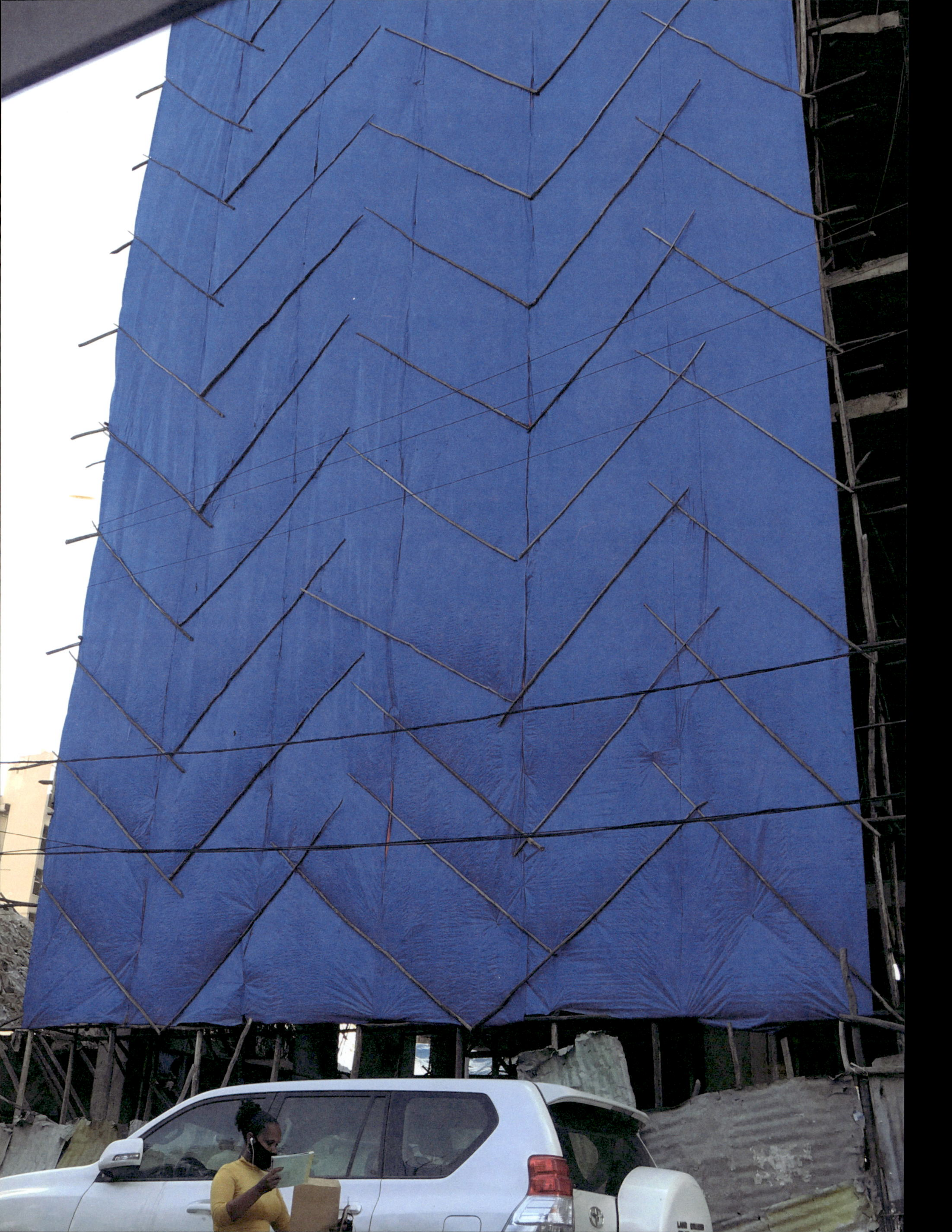

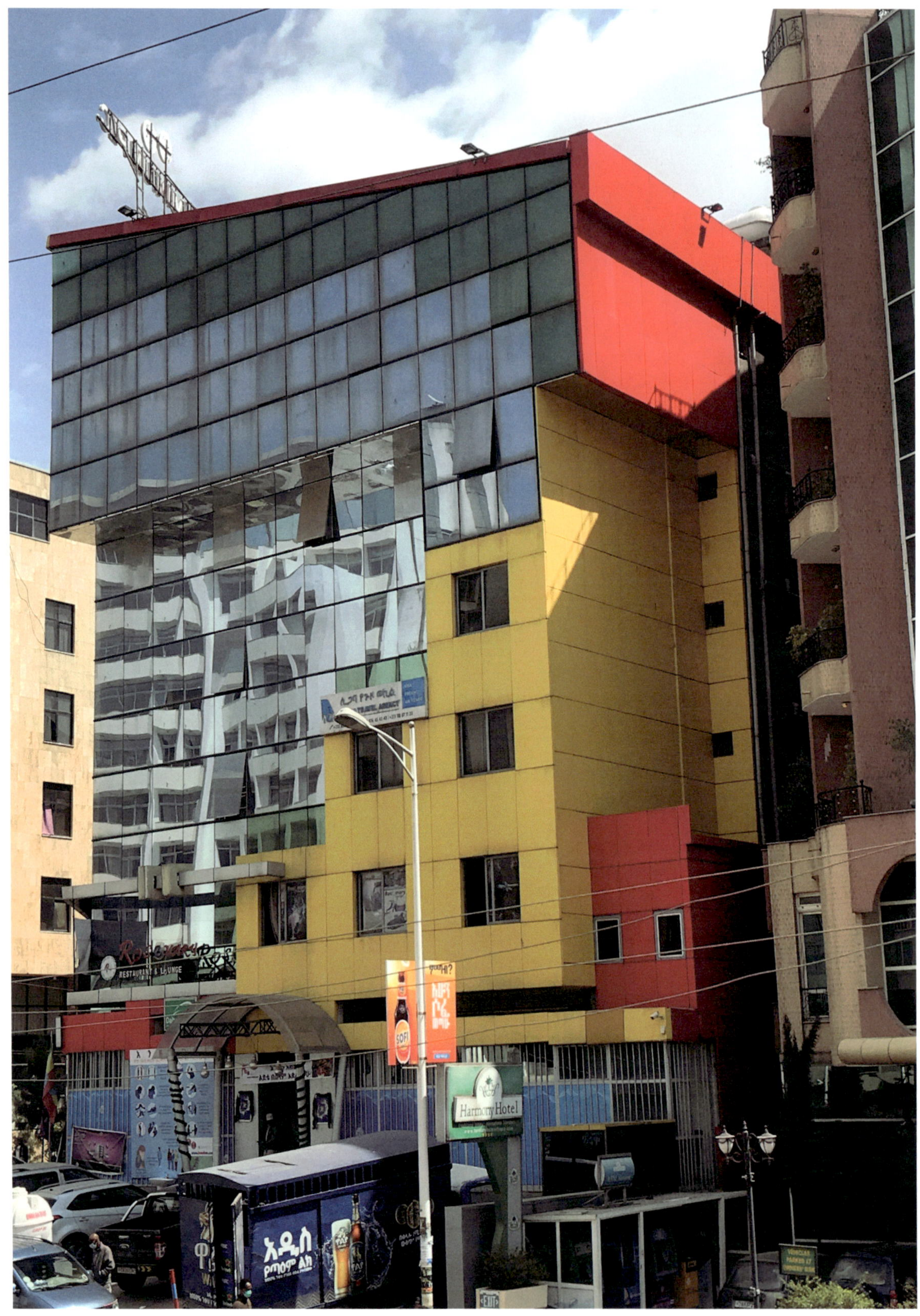

Left: Beyond the frantic energy that construction and high-rises create, there's the aesthetic betrayal of their look. On rare occasions, I spot a newer building that looks distinctly African and Ethiopian and, naturally, I cherish it.

Below and right: The intense commercialization of my childhood neighborhood no longer stings. On my last trip home, I allowed myself to revel in characters and details.

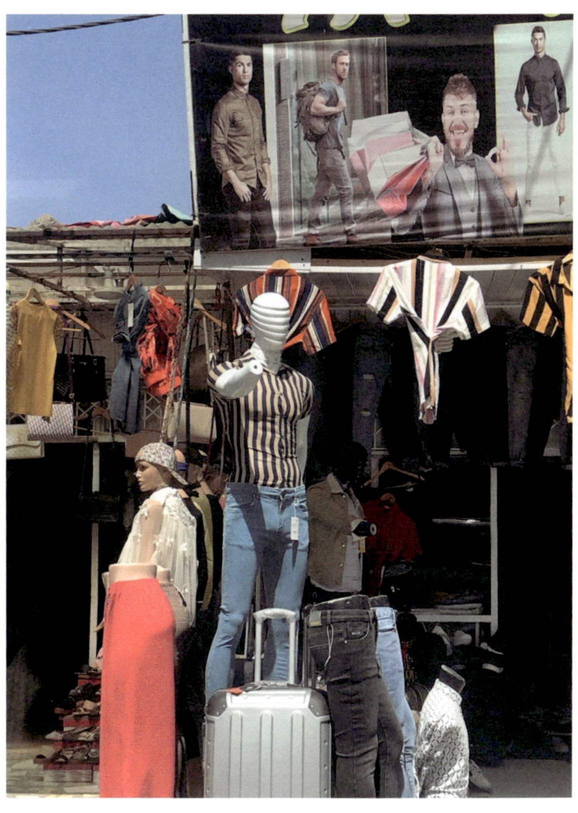

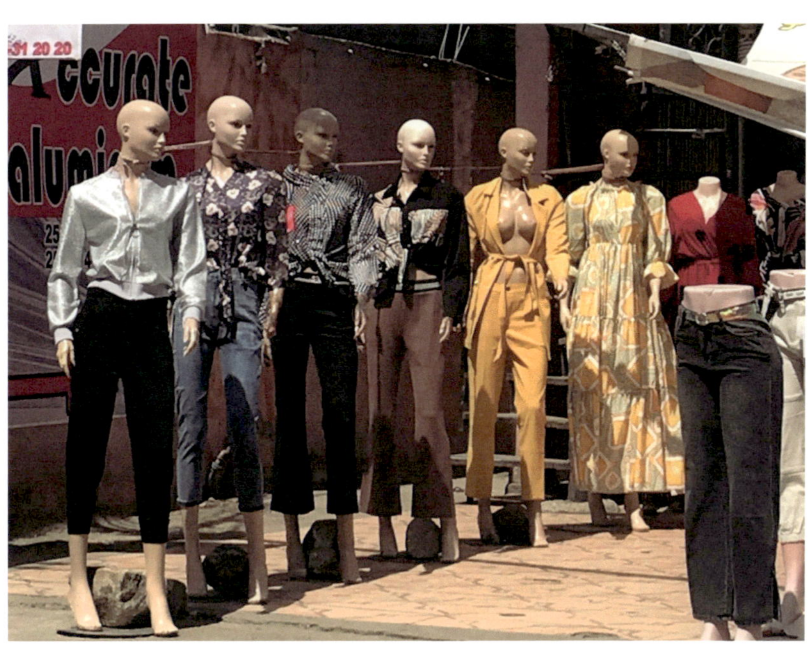

RUTH GEBREYESUS

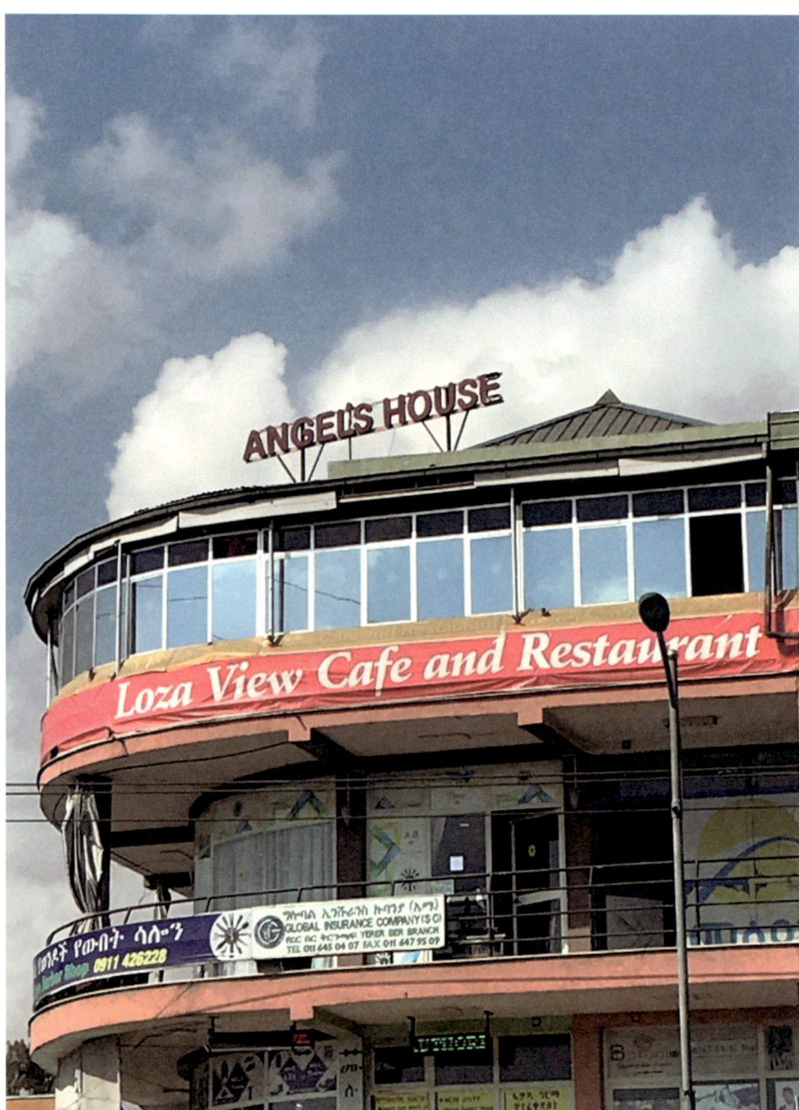

Left: I sometimes think maybe Addis is as good as a city could be, given the municipal, national, and global forces at play. When I'm ready to dismiss that thought as overly optimistic, a building will charm me with its names. Another will soon send me down a fiery spiral.

cities and tents under freeway overpasses raged, a law went into effect in Oakland taxing vacant residential, commercial, and undeveloped lots. The tax would go towards affordable housing as decided by the city. Landowners who didn't want to pay would ostensibly have to rent or develop units at a rate that would encourage tenancy. It's nearly impossible to measure empty apartments and houses in Oakland but Moms 4 Housing, a housing advocacy group led by a group of mothers, estimated that there were four times as many empty homes as there were people without homes. A study by UC Berkeley's Terner Center estimates there are 4,000 empty lots in Oakland. All these numbers amount to some value but the simplest way to un-abstract those figures is Moms 4 Housing's refrain: housing is a human right.

In Addis, vacancy is even slippier to measure, but is itself an impossible fact to miss. Its blatancy makes every building mandate feel deeply insincere. I dream about a vacancy tax to confront that insincerity. A vacancy tax would trouble the frantic pace of development—the architects rendering one glassy building after another perched in thin elevated air, the importers of construction materials who've not missed a beat in two decades, the mines left as hollow as the buildings their minerals would go on to raise.

For now, Addis taxes its citizens' memory. Memories of childhood homes, eateries, and parks. Even the grievers can't catch a break. Cemeteries are upturned to build roads to lead to more tall roadside buildings. One day while riding with my cousin, I saw him signing a cross like many Orthodox Christians do at the sight of a church. Only this time, I couldn't see the church he was gesturing towards. He was signing to a memory of a church eaten by new buildings.

After a month at my friend's place, I left Addis like I usually do, promising a return to my loved ones. My friend—she ended up leaving Addis for good. Just last month, she got word that a new tenant finally moved into the building.●

Ruth Gebreyesus is a writer based in the Bay Area. Her work centers cultural production and consumption across physical and digital margins. She also serves as a co-curator of Black Life, a multidisciplinary art and film series at the Berkeley Art Museum & Pacific Film Archive.

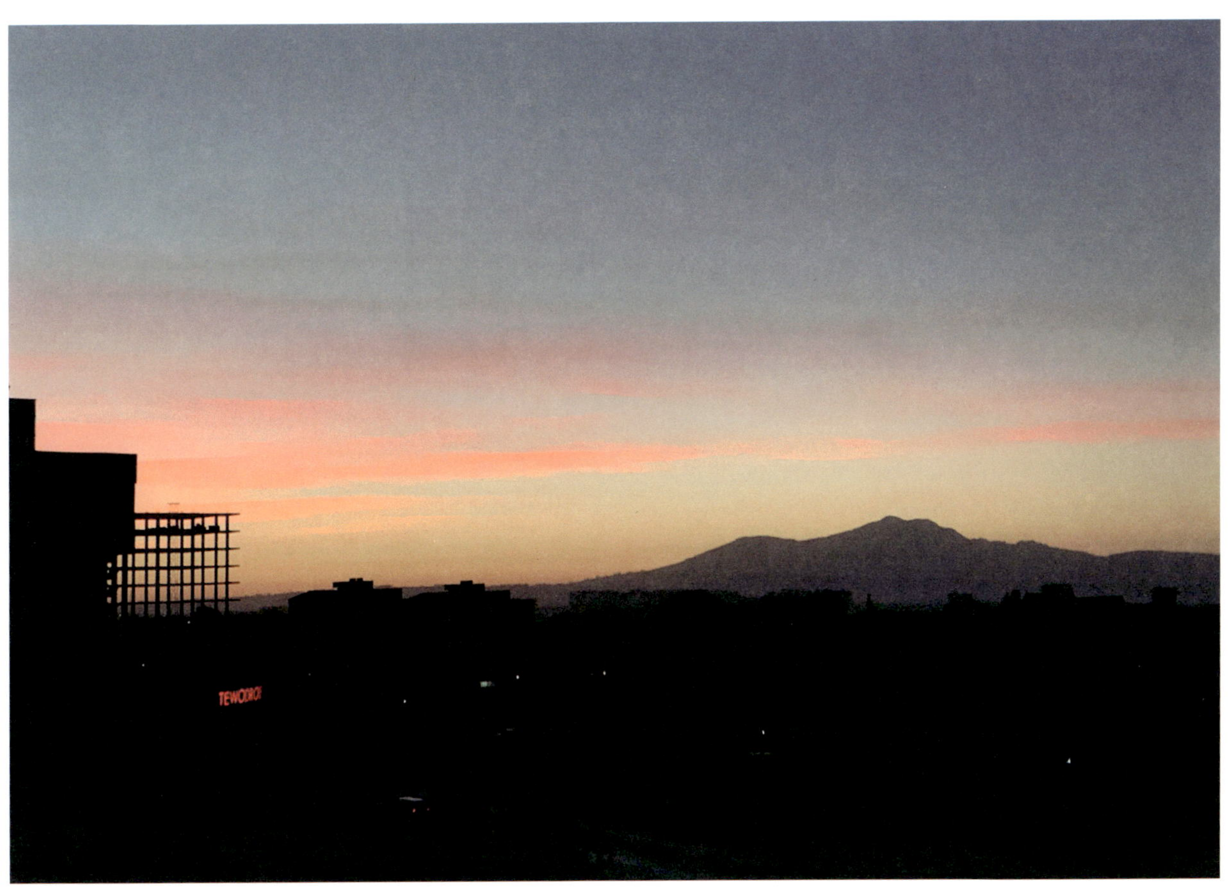

RUTH GEBREYESUS

The Kambule Light Carnival's Path

By Cherry-Ann Davis

Photography by Warren Le Platte

*Inspired by the work of
Eintou Springer, Idakeda Group,
and Joan Yuille-Williams*

In the Caribbean, Carnival is the celebration of freedom that goes beyond the street parade; its roots run deeper than the pretty costumes and its impact grows wider than the Queen's Park Savannah. Destra Garcia's 2004 Soca hit, "It's Carnival," encapsulates the sentiment of those who've experienced it: "Carnival in T&T [Trinidad and Tobago] is so special to all of we / Like we need blood in we vein, that's how we feel about Port of Spain." If you've ever crossed the <u>Grand Stand</u>, you feel those lyrics deeply, and probably sang them instead of reading. Port of Spain is home to the heart of Caribbean carnivals and diasporic celebrations, but there is a vein which keeps the heart beating that seems to be often forgotten.

When Christmas and the <u>parang</u> songs have faded, the new year appears and the spirit of <u>Kambule</u> descends. Kambule is the blood to the heart of Carnival; it is the warrior spirit of <u>mas</u>, which radiates from 'round the bridge, moving through Besson, Duke, Picton, and Nelson Street. The blood started pumping because of <u>commess</u>, when Captain Baker and his constabulary pressured the freed Africans to "<u>play ah mas</u>," but respectfully. How yuh go tell free people how to <u>fête</u>? How you go say behave, to a <u>bois man</u> and a <u>jammette</u>?

During enslavement, Africans on the sugar estates created their own version of French and British masquerade balls that mocked the antics and dress of the enslavers. The mas of the Africans wasn't the adoption of a European festivity, but an act of sustaining their own traditions of masquerade. Freedom came in 1834 and the emancipated Africans, who settled in the city and neighbouring villages, continued their celebrations on August 1st, Emancipation Day. The revelry and jubilation from then on were excessive, and rightly so—freedom from the inhumane conditions of slavery warranted a grand celebration, which the Europeans always found to be vulgar.

Carnival is not only a celebration of freedom but a release of explosive energy, which builds for a year, through dancing and music. Denying or stifling that release is <u>bacchanal</u>, as the government learnt. Laws were made to suppress prominent African culture and Captain

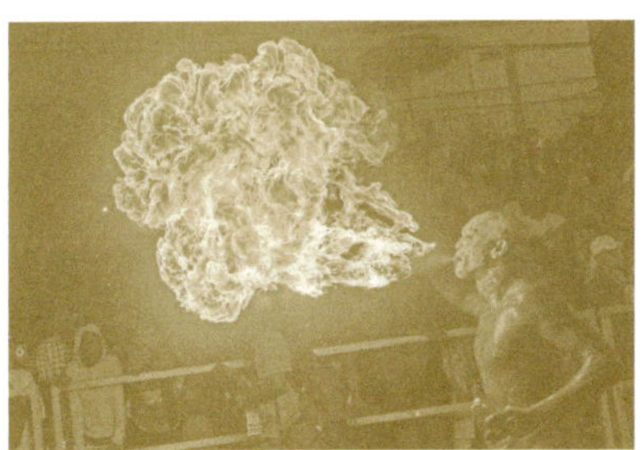

A blue devil blows fire during the annual Canboulay reenactment along Picadilly Street in east Port of Spain, Trinidad. Carnival 2020

Baker was to put them into effect. In 1881, the Africans faced off with the police in the <u>Bois Bataille</u>, and the bois men and jammettes picked up their sticks and held their ground. Dem bois man and jammette beat dem police bad and they retreated. The cultural saviours from 'round the bridge led the charge to preserve our right to expression and masking traditions, which gave Trinbagonians the freedom to fête.

Today, Kambule is a low steady hum, an ever-present bass line that crescendos in anticipation of the bacchanal that is Carnival. The <u>riddim</u> of Carnival is rooted in its African traditions but is also as colourful a kaleidoscope as its costumes, drawing inspiration from everything and everywhere. This is evident in the varied sounds of <u>kaiso</u>, <u>calypso</u>, <u>chutney</u>, and <u>soca</u>, genres birthed in Trinidad and Tobago; when they hit you, you get that feeling. The music fills you, making your body move effortlessly to the groove, floating through meandering parade routes and <u>chipping</u> to rhythmic ancestral memories.

A deep rumbling embedded into the sound of carnival is resistance, heard through the drums which crossed the Atlantic and were eventually banned for fear of inciting rebellion. Music is crucial for the mas and yuh can't stop the riddim, so innovation stepped in. The Africans invented new instruments to recreate the sound of drums, turning bamboo tubes into a rhythm section called <u>tamboo bamboo</u> and eventually making discarded steel drums into the <u>steel pan</u>. The pan was forged from the love of liberty in the ghettos of Laventille by hammering steel drums to create indentations and tuning them into an incomparable instrument that can be its own orchestra.

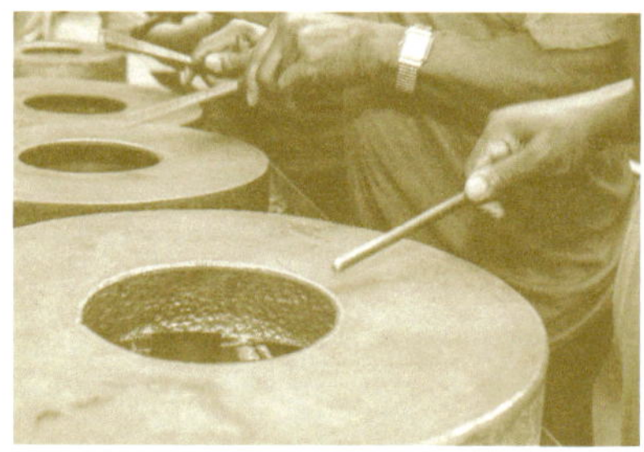

A row of iron men form part of the riddim section of the Curepe Scherzando Steel Orchestra during their performance at the Panorama semifinals held in the Queen's Park Savannah, Port of Spain, Trinidad.

Steel pan plays a pivotal role in Carnival, with <u>pansides</u> gathering for the clash of bands that is <u>Panorama</u>. Family and friends convene to support their favourite bands, which they may have all played with at one time or another, meeting up to lime with food and drinks. The smell of <u>pelau</u> and <u>bake and shark</u> fills the air with rum, white and dark, flowing freely, and your choice of chasers abound. The perfect medley of green seasoning, pumpkin, and split peas wafts your way and leads you to a new liming spot in a winding line, for the best <u>corn soup</u> to grace your tongue.

The panside takes the stage. You're so close you can feel the vibration as the tune starts to rage and the crowd dances along. Stripped-away vibrant melodies give new life to popular songs arranged on sweet sweet percussion. The music engulfs you into a sea of memories of your first Panorama, as a young child spellbound by the flag woman waving and leading the charge of her band. The music seems to follow her as she <u>wines</u> low in sync with the beat of the pan. The gust from the flag woman's standard prickles against your skin, jerking you to reality and getting you attuned to how Carnival feels. The drone of the music caresses your skin and you realise every aspect of Carnival is an experience to behold, to be held, to be cherished.

Much of Carnival owes a debt to the bravery of the men and women of the barrack yards of East Dry River—Kambule fighters—and because of them Carnival is what it is today. I imagine that without them, it might have died a slow, polite death. We would never be able to cross a stage at Piccadilly Greens, Victoria Square, South Quay, or the Savannah. There would be no Miami Carnival, Houston Carifest, West Indian Day [Labor Day] Parade in New York, Notting Hill Carnival in London, nor Toronto's Caribana. They carved the path on the parade route you walk by enduring ridicule and slander; they paid the price for you to fête. Pay homage to the makers and creators who settled in what was known as Yorubatown [Belmont, Morvant, and Laventille], when you sing along to kaiso, calypso, chutney, and soca or hear a popular rendition on the steel pan. For without them there would be no place for the sound of Carnival—the beating of the pan, bamboo, and drum. The heart would be missing a beat.●

Cherry-Ann Davis is a Trinbagonian professional macco and bacchanalist (i.e., a decolonial, pan-African hybrid ethnographic storytelling creator from Trinidad and Tobago.)

GLOSSARY

Grand Stand, *noun*
A building and raised seating on the south side stage of the Queen's Park Savannah, used during Panorama and Carinval.

Parang, *noun*
A traditional Venezuelan-derived type of singing, sometimes improvisational, on religious themes, usually entirely in Spanish and performed around Christmas in house-to-house caroling or while visiting friends.

Kambule/Canboulay/Camboulay/Cannes Brulèes, *noun*
A celebration of the emancipation from slavery on August 1, 1838, involving bands with torches and drums; later these celebrations were incorporated into those of Carnival. The Kambule was a flambeau (torchlight) procession which took place from midnight on Carnival Sunday. It is currently re-enacted in part at dawn on Carnival Friday morning in Port of Spain on the Piccadilly Greens.

Mas'/marse/mask/masque, *adjective*
as a street parade.

Commess/comess, *noun*
A situation of confusion, commotion, scandal.

Play ah mas'/play mas, *phrase*
To participate in Carnival by dressing and parading through the streets in a masquerade costume as part of a band or solo masquerade.

Fête, *noun*
A major festival most often around Carnival, usually observed with music, food, dancing.

Bois man, *noun*
A man who fights with a traditional stick (bois: a long supple wooden stick usually from the Poui tree used in Kalinda/stickfighting); a stickfighter.

Jammette/jammet/diametre/jamet/jammaitre, *noun*
Generally refers to the "underclass" of people, mainly women, whose public behaviour is considered vulgar, obscene, loud, violent, etc.

Bacchanal/bakanal/bacchannale, *noun*
1. A wild party or fête, enjoyable and vigorous dancing, drinking etc. Usually an admiring or positive term. 2. An event that gets out of control, argumentative behaviour.

Bois Bataille, *noun*
A type of competitive combat between two stickfighters.

Riddim, *noun*
Creole pronunciation of the English word "rhythm," referring to percussion accompaniment which might include, but is not limited to, a drum set, conga drum, bàta drum, güiro, claves, cow bells, brake drum Crix tins.

Kaiso, calypso, chutney, and soca, *nouns*
Indigenous musics of Trinidad and Tobago, created within the context of Carnival.

Chip, *noun*
A small shuffling step used especially for moving through the streets to music during Carnival.

Tamboo bamboo/tambour bamboo, *noun*
A musical instrument made from bamboo of various lengths and diameters, each producing a different note or pitch when struck with sticks or stamped on the ground.

Steel pan, *noun*
An instrument made from the 55-gallon steel oil drum, with one end hammered in to make different notes. Types of steel pans include the tenor, double tenor, double seconds, guitar, cello, quadraphonics, and bass.

Panside, *noun*
An orchestra of any size comprising a variety of steel pans and percussion, better known as the Engine Room.

Panorama, *noun*
The annual Steelband competition held during the Carnival season, with finals on Carnival Saturday. The competition began in 1950 but was incorporated into Carnival officially in 1963, as part of the Independence celebration from British colonial rule.

Lime, *noun*
1. An informal gathering characterized by semi-ritualized talking and socializing, drinking, and eating. 2. A group formed and loosely maintained for a specific purpose, frequenting a usual location or associated with a specific activity.

Pelau/peleau/pilau, *noun*
A dish of brown stewed meat, usually chicken or beef, with rice and pigeon peas.

Bake and shark, *noun*
A popular snack food consisting of a fry bake (puffy fried bread) and fried seasoned shark, especially well-known from Maracas Beach in Northern Trinidad.

Wine, *verb*
To make a rhythmic, gyrating pelvic dancing movement.

Corn soup, *noun*
A hot soup made with pieces of corn along with meat (usually chicken), vegetables, and provisions such as yam, potato, dasheen (taro root), and cassava (yucca root).

ESSAY AS SCULPTURE #2

Text and photography by Shirt

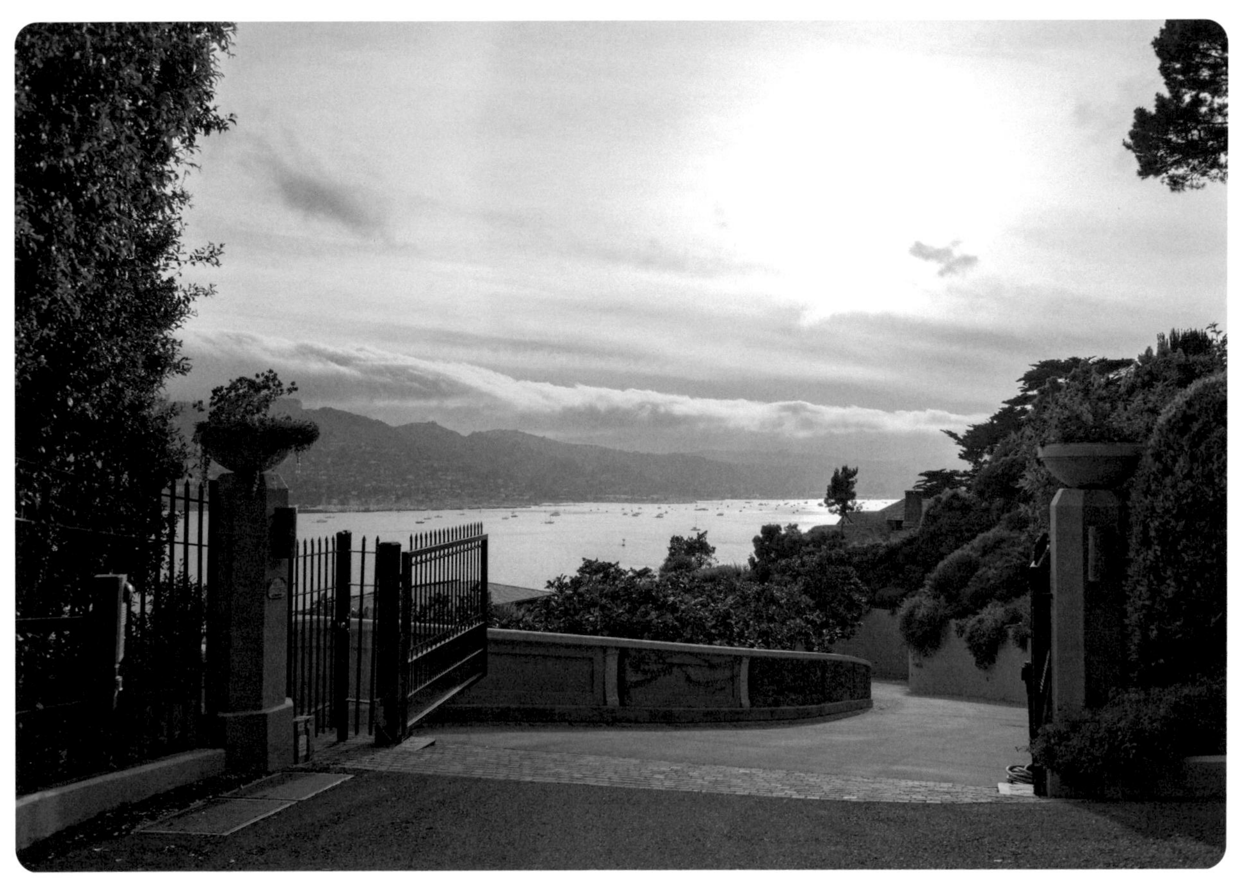

137

The poet Evie Shockley writes, "Vocabulary takes us under its wing." It's the kind of idea that sticks to my ribs. Sentences help lead the way forward—not just the ones we learn to string together or get to utter if we're lucky, but the ones we live and experience, whether we have the audible language for them or not. When I began writing this work, the E key on my Mac stopped working. For some time I had to copy and paste the "E" in every word that needed one. You do what you can to trudge forward and you must always remember, most stories don't come out.

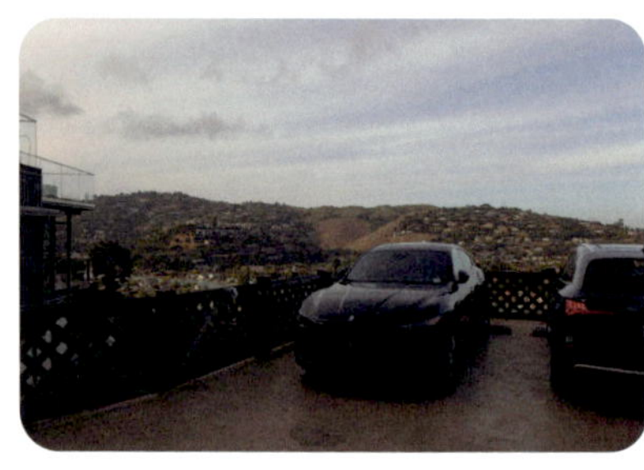

I was writing about this distance. There was a day last summer when we drove through an area in Marin County in Northern California, where it seems like every house is an elaborate compound built into the hills. I was in the backseat, where it's nice to be sometimes. We'd bend corners on the road and slowly I'd get glimpses of these properties through garden entrances, lush hedges trimmed with matte-painted sports cars and Benz trucks peeking from open garages out front. It felt like a scene from a Bond film. The cherry blossoms, my god! These didn't feel like NYC cherry blossoms. There was something about these winding roads opening up to these cliff views and maze grounds. I kept thinking, "These are the streets that the people who live here take to the supermarket." It became that tactile for me. I started tracing the steps. These are the houses people come back to at night, and invite their friends to for dinner. This is where kids do their homework and play video games and ride their bikes.

I became uncomfortably aware of, like, this big distance. What felt like too big of a distance. How far it is from what me and so many people know. I grew up in Queens, New York, on the farthest tip of the island you can drive to, by the Con Edison plant. Because just a block away we were on the water, it was picturesque. The buildings were that Section 8 brown brick in the '80s and '90s. They might have painted over the bricks now. They might have closed off the garbage cellar you used to be able to walk through under the buildings. My memory takes me to the dirty lobbies and rundown courtyards. The dry cleaners and Johnny's place. Fucked up neighbors on my block who I'm sure thought the same or worse about us. My dad put my mom in the hospital on a bad night. Bad nights, my mom beat me up and kicked me out of the apartment, naked. Cops knew our address well off the bad nights. My mom did her best but she had been abused herself, grown up through her own bad nights. And still, she loved me more than anything and taught me to love. She took me to parks across the city just to show me my world was bigger than my block.

I know enough to know that people in nice houses are not spared fucked up nights. I know horrific things happen in nice houses and behind lily-white fences. I know the opposite is true, too; tender, beautiful nights can and will happen in the harshest fucked up reality. And I personally didn't grow up in the harshest reality by any means. We had Hell's Gate and the strip. But driving around that day, I thought, postcards are the same everywhere, right? I've never seen a postcard of an asbestos-laced apartment in the projects. What happens when your home and neighborhood feel rogue and abandoned? What is the net effect on people born into environments so far from what I was seeing on this day? What are the effects on kids who wake up in bedrooms with the paint chipping off the walls, mice running around in the ceilings, broken windows and doors and floors, a fucked up fridge? Psychologically, it fucks with me. I hate a fucked up fridge. God, I hate a shit Queens apartment, my bad. Those orange wood floors they all have and the gates on the window. Ambulances all night, random screaming. Interacting with police who treat you like shit daily. How does it affect a kid who has to walk past the rundown check-cashing spots, and the liquor and dollar stores on their way to school everyday? Or steppng over neighbors you've known your whole life to get into your building? People make it out of things, but who are they on the other side?

This distance was too glaring. It felt like more than money—like money alone wouldn't do it. People where I'm from might get money and go buy a big ugly house in New Jersey, or some fake nice condo wherever. Unless you've seen and know about some shit. In New York City, rich and poor people all walk the same dirty ass sidewalks, damn near. But here was this realization, for me, that it wasn't just money that got you to a neighborhood like this, in these homes fucking built into the side of the earth. Here was this other, palpable distance I was being forced to reckon with: how fucking slim-next-to-impossible it is for someone where I'm from to see this shit, let alone end up living in this postcard world. Who tells you about places like this? Places you don't hear no one rap about! I was shown this place on this day. I thought I'd seen some nice places around the world—leaving America is a different conversation altogether—but this was just some place we drove in California.

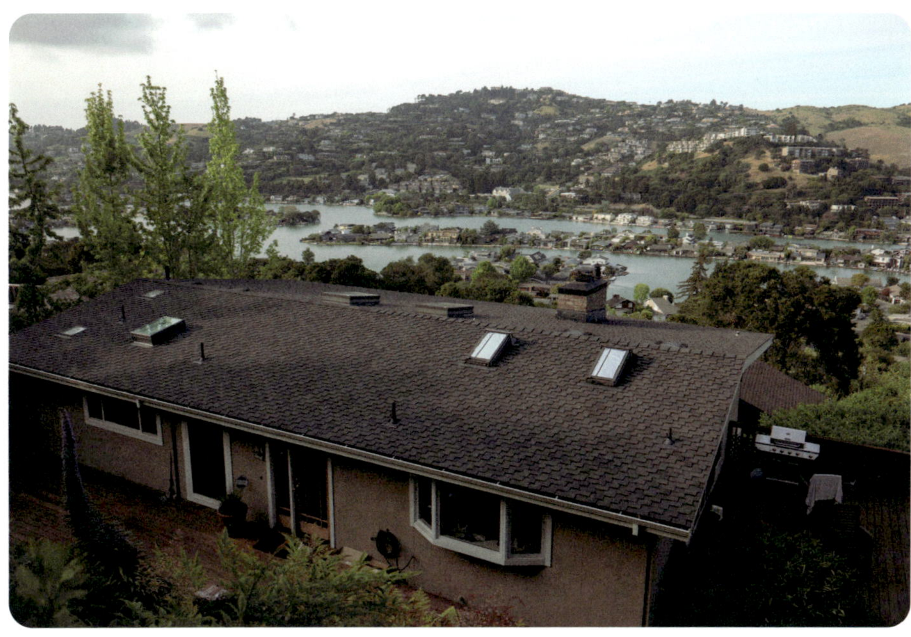

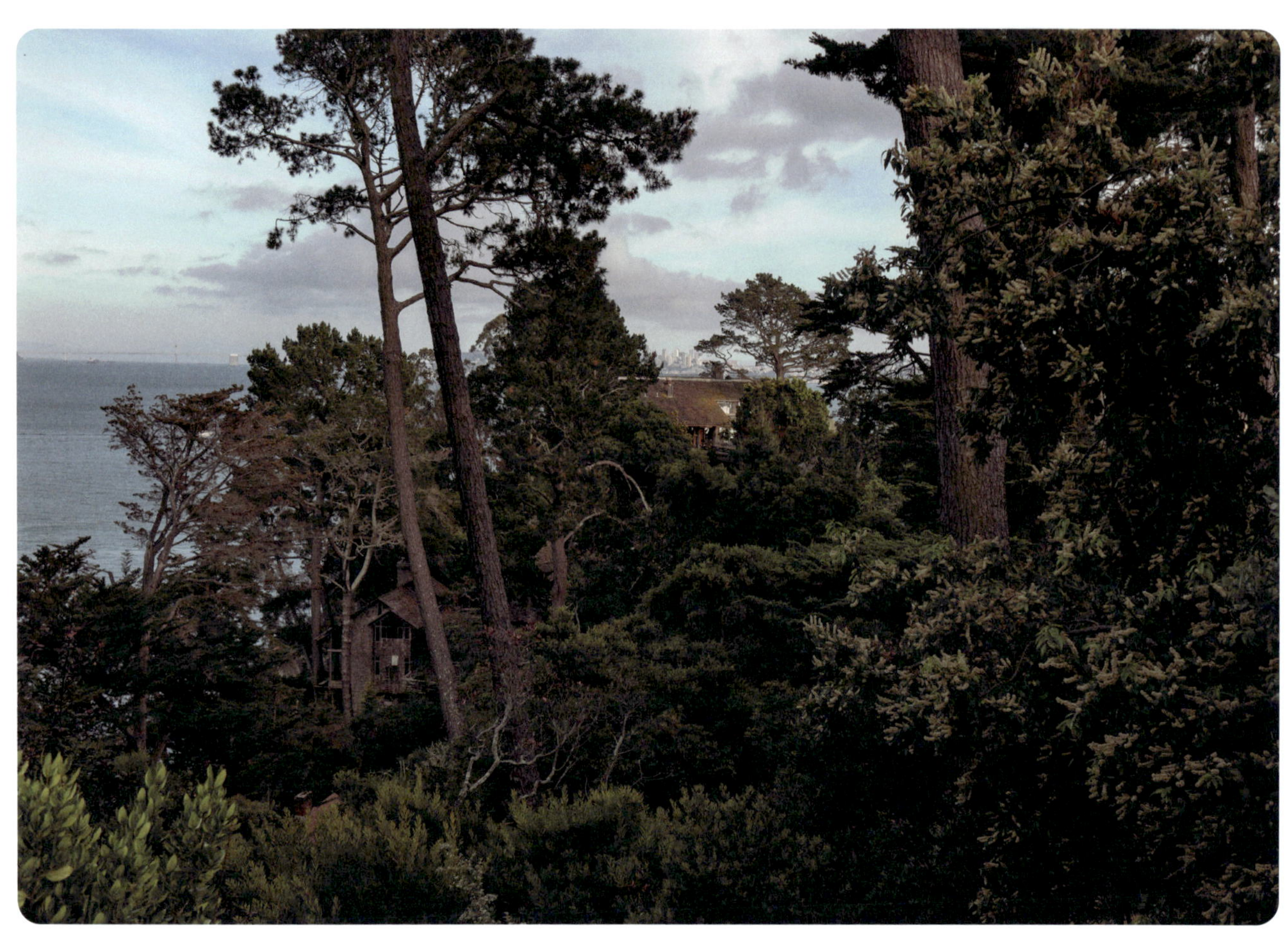

I want the fucking distance to be shorter. Not the literal distance between life in Queens or Brooklyn, or this place in Cali or Mexico or any other gorgeous place I've been, but the distance between what I grew up thinking the world was like and then learning what it could actually be—or really what it is, without me even needing to realize it. I surmised it was maybe about this feeling of care and attention. This neighborhood with the perfect architecture maybe simply registered to me as something people put a lot of care and attention into. What a concept. The artist Chloe Bass asks, "How much of love is attention?" I was thinking maybe all of it.

I listen to these small feelings, where pangs ring off somewhere in my body. The random, quick drive it took for us to get to this place I felt was so cared for and so considered didn't match with how devastatingly easy it would've been for me to have never seen it at all. Can you imagine all the things you never get to see so you never know exist? I need it to feel like a shorter distance a kid has to go to get to this place. I want the younger me to know what I was made to believe was "impossible" didn't have to be, or at least should've felt way less so. So I need to live that. I need NORE to host SNL. We need to get together to find ways. I'm not talking shortcuts. I want every part of it. I don't want the "easy" way, but fuck doing the hard-for-no-reason, racist, sexist, classist, capitalist-driven fucking gross way. There needs to be new ways.

It felt impossible that I could have a fulfilling life and respected career. It feels impossible to become some respected artist who makes work that is taken seriously, or that we could get to a place where people's ideas and intelligence are what is valued over any other thing. "Get to a place" invokes this distance for me again. A place where corporations fill up board seats with the same people they sell to, and support the minds of kids instead of just photographing their faces. Don't talk to me about "talent"! Society would have you believe that only in wild dreams could you write raps and make art for a living, that only in wild dreams could putting ideas out afford you what they call "financial stability"—a nice car, a home I own, good clothes, what they call "vacations." I haven't felt yet like I could take a "vacation." We pit living a fulfilling, creative life, doing and making things because we love them and feel called to them, up against living purportedly "safe" and taking conventional routes. Like any routes are ever truly safe or conventional, especially when Black and Brown people walk and run them. Make a route.

This name I go by, Shirt, started making me think about the ubiquity of a shirt. It was my rap name for years and then I grew to understand it differently. I was painting on T-shirts years ago and people would tell me the name was easy to remember. Now it makes me think about people who get forgotten. Not the people they make the documentary about, but the people in the background of the shot, or just off camera, out of frame. I think about people who didn't make it a lot. All the ways it could look like not making it. The people nameless and faceless in the crowd. People working, hopefully laughing a lot, and dying in obscurity. The way we just say "people" and don't think about the billions of actual lives lived. There's a lot of us here, but not a lot of distance between us. So I find another distance.

I remember reading some years ago that when sonar became widely used during the Second World War, operators detected what they thought was the sea floor. Later it was discovered that this surface was actually millions of organisms all huddled up close to one another. This phenomenon of the false sea floor became known as the "deep scattering layer," because it scattered the sonar signal.

In 2013, an executive at Def Jam told me I look like every Spanish kid from Queens that ever lived. I think she was right, though she said it like it was a bad thing.●

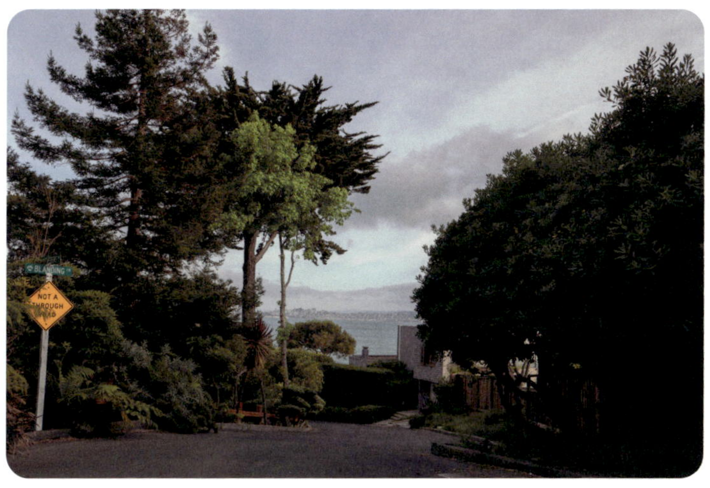

Shirt is a rapper and conceptual artist working in New York City. A forthcoming new album, I Turned Myself Into Myself *(2022), will be released on all major streaming platforms. Currently completing a two-month residency at OMITTED in Italy, Shirt lives in a 15th-century castle and is working on a series of vocal recordings. Select works are available for online viewing at rapartist.org*

NO WHERE BUT HERE

Femi Adeyemi on the possibilities for placemaking over the airwaves

Interview by Nu Goteh

Femi Adeyemi photographed by Sara Pooley in Los Angeles, 2022

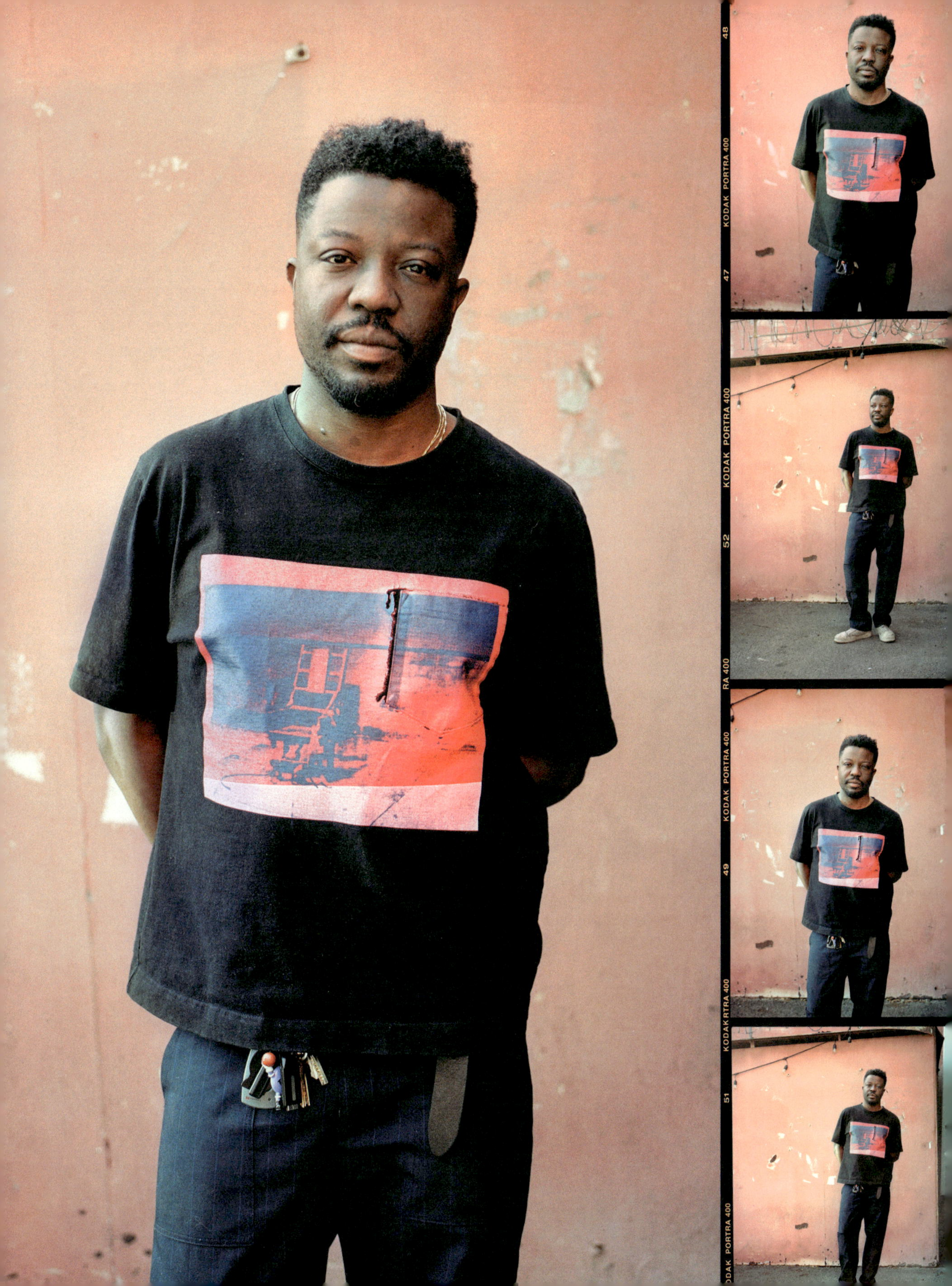

KODAK PORTRA 400
KODAK PORTRA 400
KODAK RA 400
KODAK RTRA 400
KODAK PORTRA 400
48
47
52
49
51

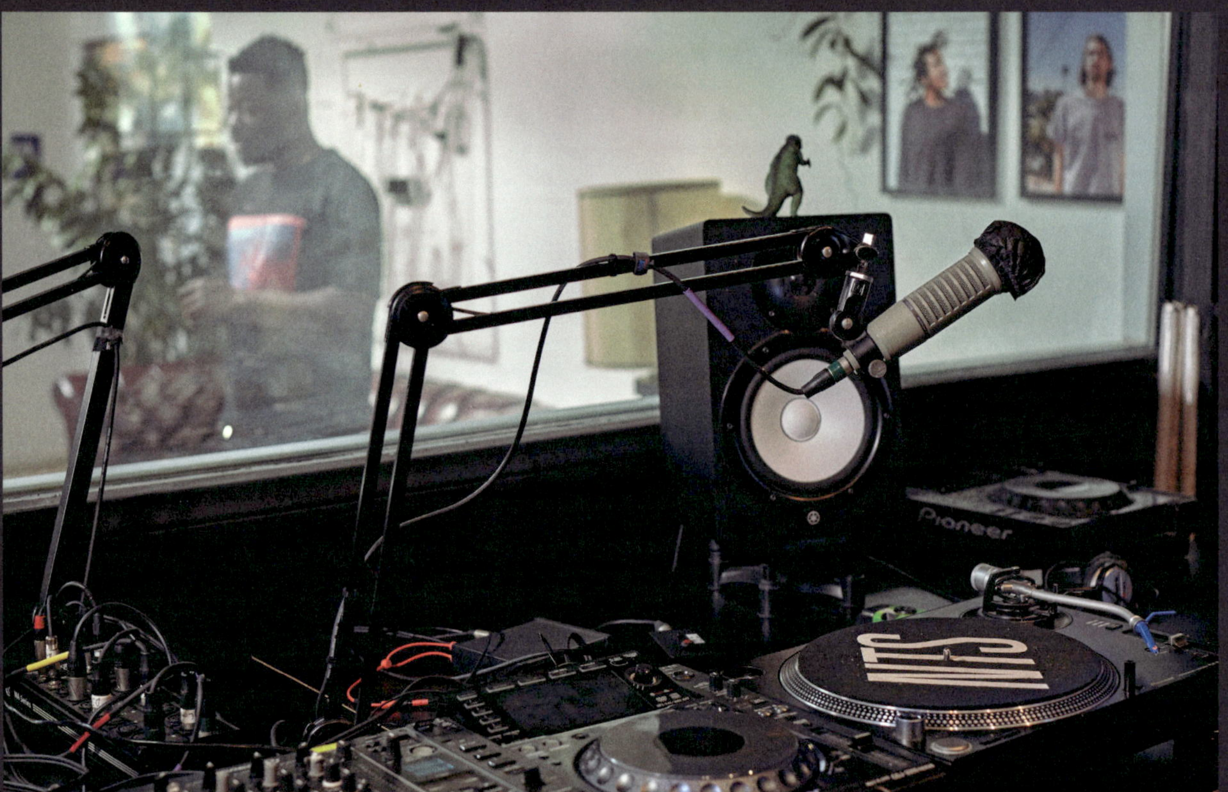

The Los Angeles NTS Studio photographed by Sara Pooley, 2022.

NU GOTEH Why did you decide to start a radio station?

FEMI ADEYEMI Music has always been a part of my life. This is thanks to my family. I was also lucky to be exposed to a wide range of music because I had access to cable from a young age. I watched a lot of music television, like MTV, and it opened my eyes to a whole world of music that I didn't know I liked. Growing up in a very diverse city like London, I was also exposed to a wide range of tastes. Radio was something that became relevant to me a little bit later because when I was at university, I couldn't afford a TV. It was the early days of the internet, so I started streaming radio on-line, such as American college stations, which were much less formulaic than commercial stations in the UK. Their freeform attitude and less-structured approach to programming really inspired me.

I started to think I might want to do some-thing in music, but I didn't know what. After I graduated, I had a few jobs—one was managing the online department at American Apparel and the other was doing marketing for a fair trade fashion company, but those didn't last long. At the time, I was also doing some DJing and connecting with

various people who were involved in music in London. I got to a point where I felt like I didn't have much to lose. Why not just *try* this radio thing I've had at the back of my mind all this time? Then there was the consideration of whether to take the pirate radio route, which would have involved avoiding the police and moving antennas around the city, or to use the internet. But the core question I kept returning to was: Why hasn't anyone created a place where you can have all sorts of sounds together? NTS came from the desire to have that alternative.

NG How do you describe your job to your parents?

FA That's a very interesting question. I don't really see it as a job. Sean, my partner who runs NTS with me, is the CEO. I told my mom I'm the founder, but the easiest way to explain it is to say I'm a music programmer—I bring people together through music.

In the beginning I used to tell her I was a DJ, and she was like, "A DJ? Is that how you want to live!? Is that what you want to do for the rest of your life?" I'd be like, "Yeah, but I'm a different kind of DJ. I'm not out in the club." She would still go around telling her sisters, "Femi's a DJ!" and they would keep bringing it up, telling me that I needed to get a proper job. I think the idea of programming made it easier for her to reckon with.

NG   As you mentioned, pirate radio has a long history, but NTS created a shift within this world that sparked many other community-driven radio stations. What about NTS's approach do you think made it that catalyst?

FA   Before I started NTS, I looked at a lot of online and pirate radio stations, such as East Village Radio, WFMU, and Dublab. There were plenty of examples to draw from, but I think that prior to NTS, most people who were running online radio stations were doing it from their homes.

It was very important to me that NTS have a physical space that is open to anyone. The energy of people coming together there would, I felt, translate to the airwaves. I think that's what made us stand out, as well as that we didn't have a "gatekeeper" attitude towards anything we did. If you love music, or you have an interest in music in any regard, come do your thing. Come play whatever you want. We will never tell you what to play. We still operate that way; if you have a show on NTS, you have absolute freedom to do what you want with that time.

We also work with a mixture of people, from more recognized DJs to someone who's maybe an architect by day and just loves listening to music in their spare time. Bringing these people together in London created a dynamic that resonated with our listeners, because everyone is a bit of a DJ in their own mind. Music is that thing that people are always proud to share.

I think that, taken together, those are the elements that set us apart. We were touching music that no one else was touching. We were taking risks no one else was taking. We were creating juxtapositions that weren't happening elsewhere. Someone might play a rap show and right after someone else might do a noise show. After all, no one likes just one thing.

NG   This issue of *Deem* is centered around the idea of place. What does place mean to you, both in regard to NTS and in general? What makes place different from space?

FA   I always say that NTS couldn't have been created in any other city except London. NTS is based specifically in Gillett Square. Hackney is such a unique part of the city with such a wide range of people. I can't imagine NTS existing anywhere else. There are a limited number of places in general that have such rich microcosms of different people, interests, and ideas. In Gillett Square, you might have an Ethiopian coffee shop, a Somali bookstore, a Nigerian barber, and a Vietnamese restaurant,

"I THINK COMMUNITY IS WHAT GIVES VALUE TO A SPACE, AND BRINGING COMMUNITY TOGETHER IS WHAT MAKES PLACE. PLACE AND SPACE WORK IN SYNC WITH EACH OTHER."

all on the same block. This range of tastes and needs is exactly what NTS represents, and that is embodied in this place. I think community is what gives value to a space, and bringing community together is what makes place. Place and space work in sync with each other. I don't know if that space would've been offered to me if I wasn't already present in the neighborhood and creating my own community there. And then bringing people together to express themselves is what created the value within that space.

NG   Though I've been to London a couple of times, I've never been to Hackney or to Gillett Square, yet I have a vivid idea of what Gillett Square is because of NTS. How do you think being in that specific location started to translate globally, translate virtually, translate to the studio, translate to the vibe?

FA   When we started out, we wanted to visualize what we were doing and leverage that people were interacting with us through the internet. This

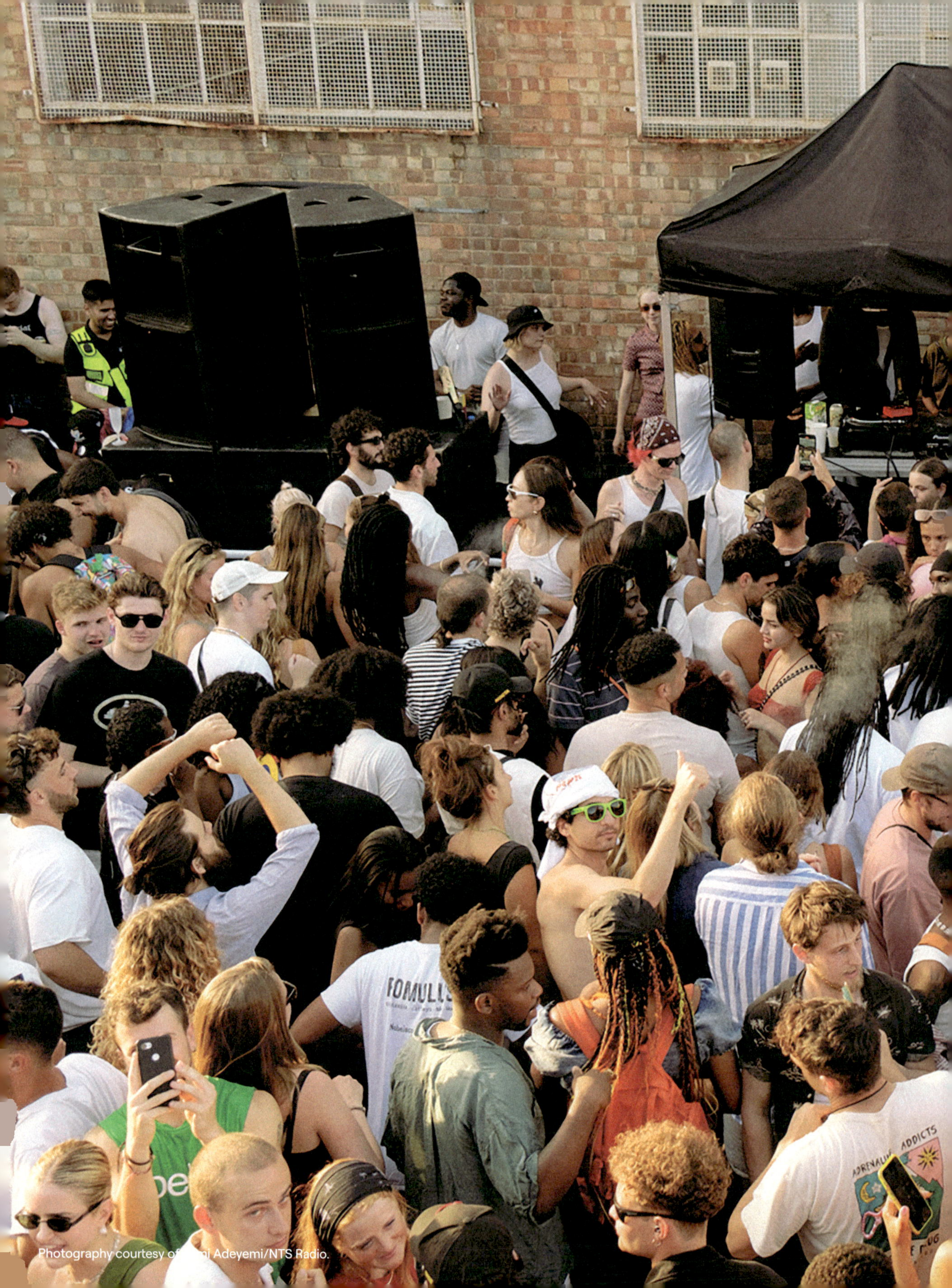

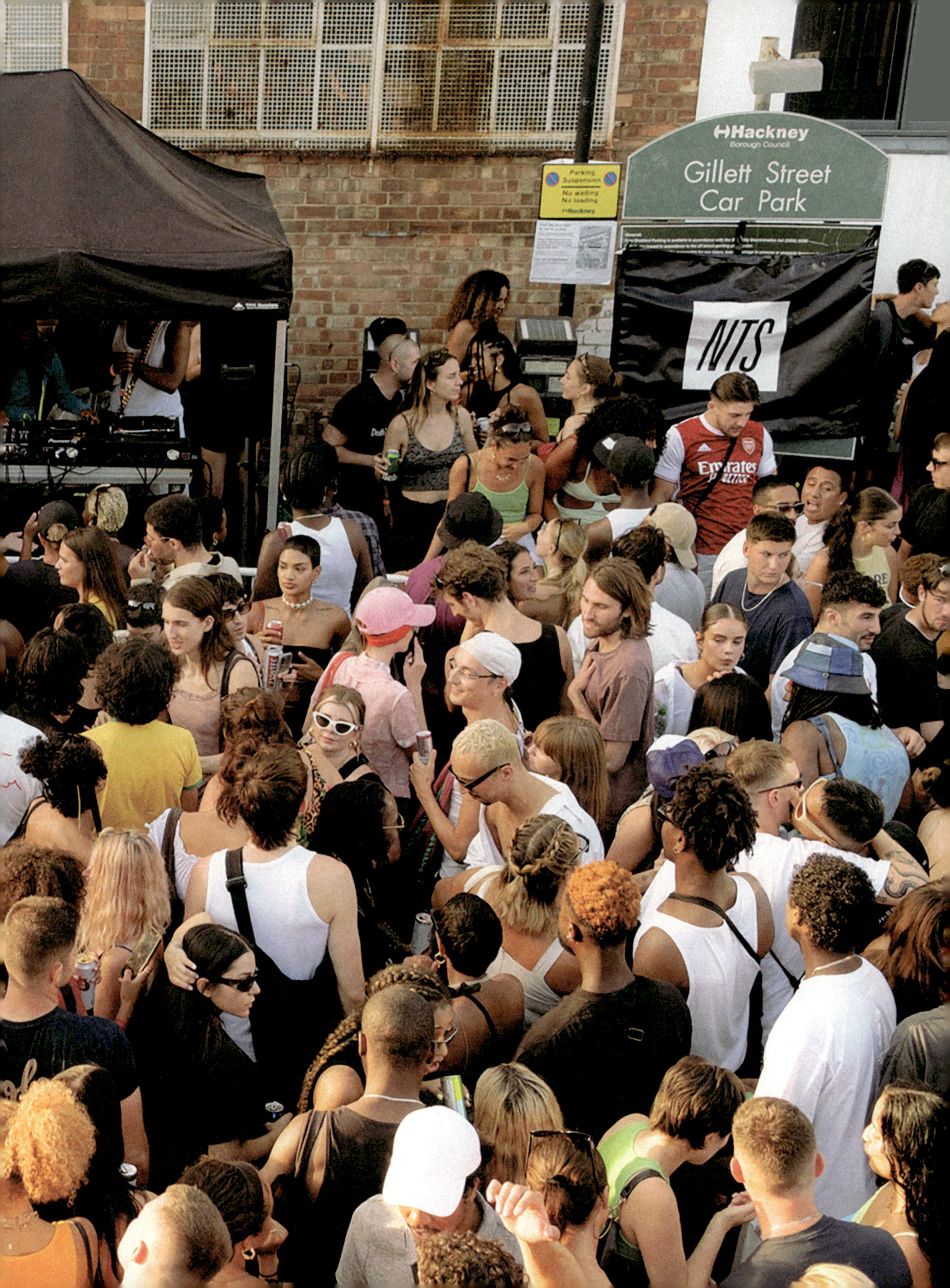

Parking
Suspension
No waiting
No loading
Hackney
Hackney
Borough Council
Gillett Street
Car Park
NTS
Emirates
FLY BETTER

was when Facebook was still popular and around the beginning of Instagram. We put a camera in the studio. We wanted people to connect with the music, of course, but there also needed to be a story around the music as well—something that could give context to the place itself, why we chose it, what that lesser-known part of the city is about, and why people were coming together there. Our approach was always bigger than just the sound.

That's also why we've never moved from Gillett Square. We've had many opportunities to leave, especially as we've grown over the years, but there is an energy in that place that makes me feel quite certain, like I said before, that NTS couldn't have come out of anywhere else, and that there is nowhere else in London like Gillett Square.

In the last two years that our studio was closed due to COVID, that energy has been tangibly lacking. Even though we have grown as a community and a company in that time, something was missing. As soon as the studio reopened and people

even necessarily know what was going on, but they could still join in. It's hard to recreate that anywhere else, but we are doing our best to cultivate the sense of place it produced.

NG What do you think it is about music that creates such a powerful sense of connection for people?

FA This is a conversation we have often within NTS, and one that I'm still torn about, because when I was growing up, people tended to identify with one thing—maybe that was rap, or UK garage, or jungle music, or it was East Coast, or it was West Coast. But I think this is less and less true for our listeners, also because of how music is consumed. If you're truly a music lover, you're generally interested in digging deeper. When I first got into music, I realized rap music was sampled. That's how I found out about jazz and, from there, electronic music, new wave, and punk.

Internally, we call ourselves a music discovery platform. We don't necessarily say it publicly, but that's how we see ourselves. In ways, technol-

"AN ALGORITHM CAN'T REPLACE THE HUMAN EMOTIONAL REACTION TO SOUND, OR THE HUMAN INTENT IN PLAYING MUSIC IN A WAY THAT CREATES A RELATABLE FEELING."

started coming back to the square, you could feel the energy return. We've also realized that even as we establish additional locations, we can never replicate what we have in London, for reasons that are physical as well as cultural. Every place that NTS creates will be different in its own way.

NG With that said, are there foundational elements of NTS that you feel you've successfully transferred from London to LA, where you now live, even while navigating this change of place?

FA I think that our sense of community is something that we managed to bring with us. It's still early days for us in LA. Though we've been here for four years, a few issues have prevented us from being able to fully activate the space, starting with the pandemic. LA is a very different kind of place than London. London is a walking city; LA is a driving city. One of the upsides of this location is that the space is significantly bigger than what we have in London. We wanted somewhere people could come and feel that this is their office, their studio, their date spot, whatever they want or need it to be. In London, the studio was more public-facing because it was literally on the street. Passersby would come sit outside and listen to the music. They didn't

ogy has enabled a crossover era that is blending genres and also creating more exposure for the underground. But despite this utility, the algorithm serves you what you continue to listen to. Of course, there are elements of exploration and suggestion, but DSPs (Direct Streaming Platforms) and algorithms don't always get it right. We do use algorithms loosely at NTS, but that methodology is not at the forefront of what we do. An algorithm can't replace the human emotional reaction to sound, or the human intent in playing music in a way that creates a relatable feeling. I personally think that's what makes the connection truly satisfying.

NG What elements of NTS started to sprout and develop in a way that surprised you?

FA In the beginning, the vision was to create a collective of people from around the world who come together to play the music they love. The plan was always to start in London and expand from there. Even though I believed this would resonate with people, I didn't realize how quickly that would happen, or how perfect the timing would be.

These days I kind of hate to use the word "culture," but I do believe we've had a significant cultural impact. We weren't the first online radio sta-

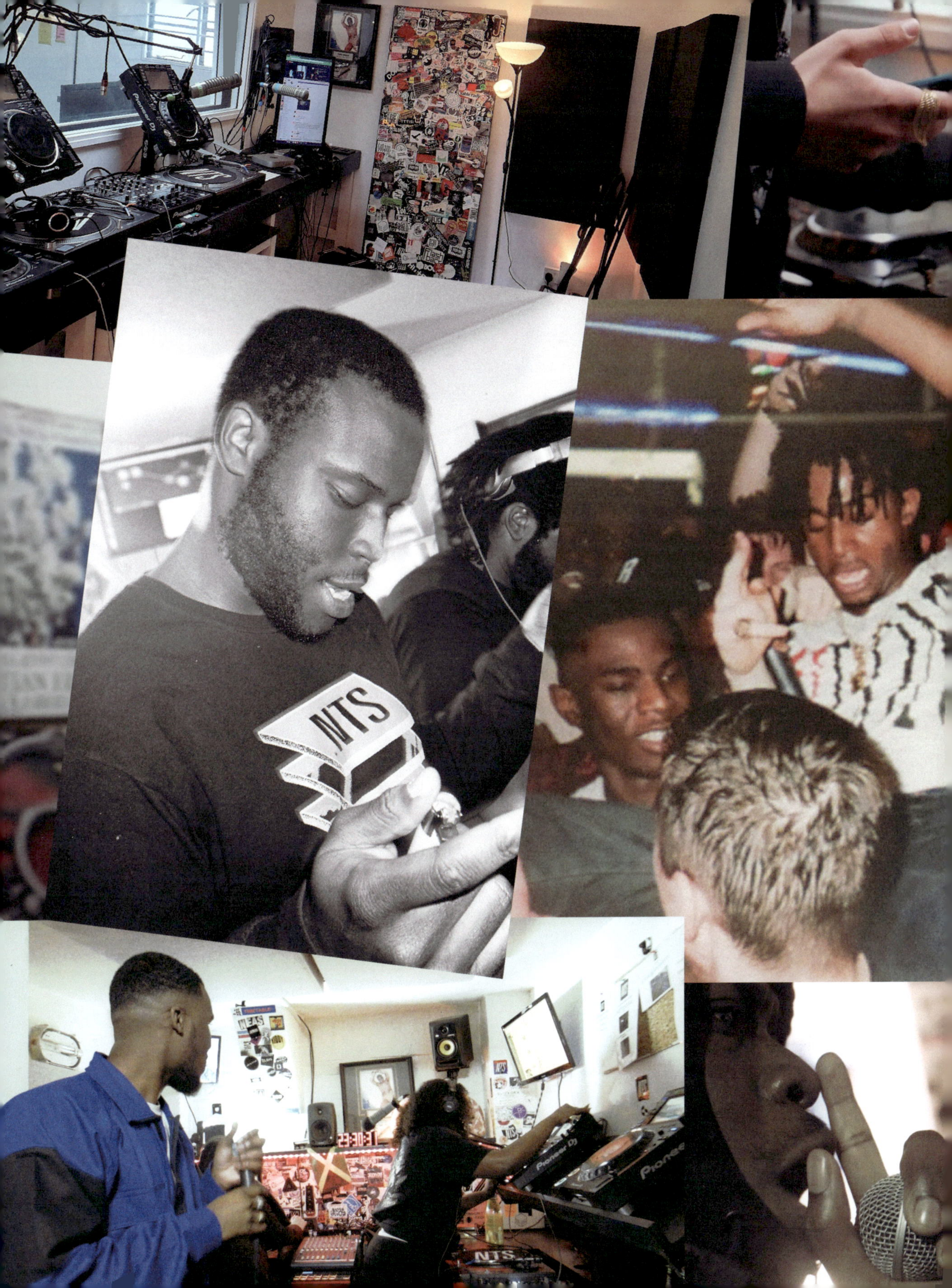

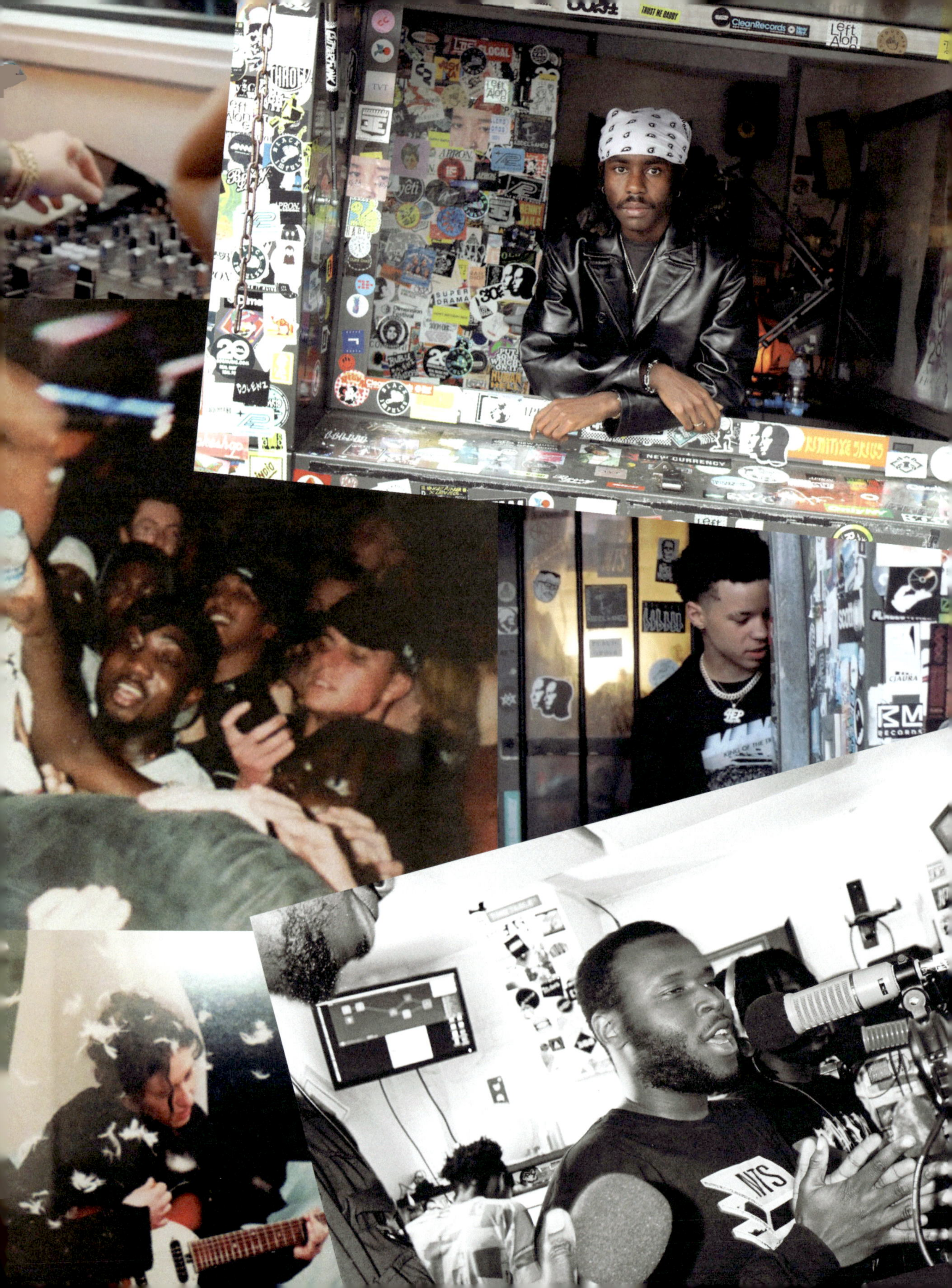

tion, but I do think we were the first to show people that a certain kind of DIY production is possible, and that anyone can grab a group of people in their local area and create a community place around a common interest or the desire for a shared experience. That's something I wasn't really expecting, especially because NTS has never done much marketing. We've always relied more on word of mouth. As we work with so many DJs and curators, the spread of information about us was always organic as well; for that reason the ripple effect felt pure, like everyone who showed up for us was genuinely interested.

NG This last question is a bit more personal. You're an elusive man. You don't give many interviews, and you tend to stay behind the scenes. But lately you have started to step forward a bit more. What prompted that for you?

FA I'm not very good at talking about myself, nor do I enjoy it. I think what has prompted a shift is the fact that when I meet other Black people, they often tell me that they would never have thought a Black person started NTS. I realized that I wanted to show younger Black creators that there are people like them out there who are doing these things, because I remember when I first started NTS and there weren't many other Black people in this space who I could reference or talk to.

I think that there are loads of us out there, but are we visible? I understand now that maybe I need to be more visible to help others see that they are not alone. Ultimately, NTS is very much a collection of people—it's an embodiment—but there are still certain aspects of my culture or my upbringing that I do think come across through the way the company is run. It's so important to me that Black people see others who look like us in whatever space we are interested in. Young people are moving so fast now, especially young people of color. It's beautiful.●

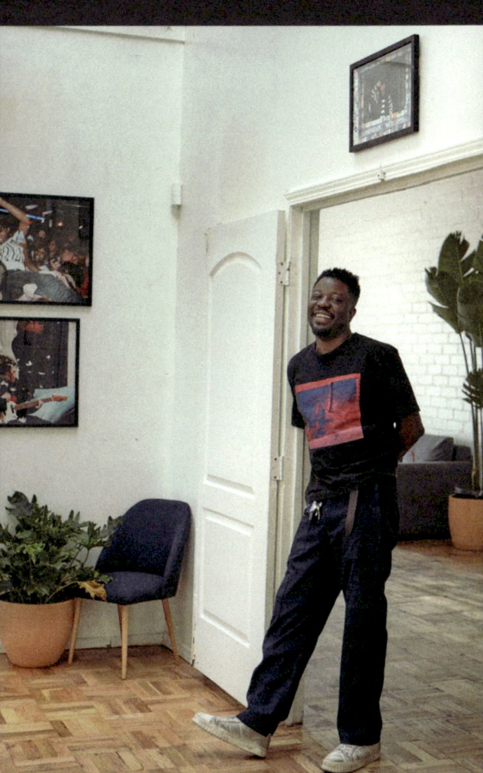

you are somebody's ancestor.
what do you have to say?

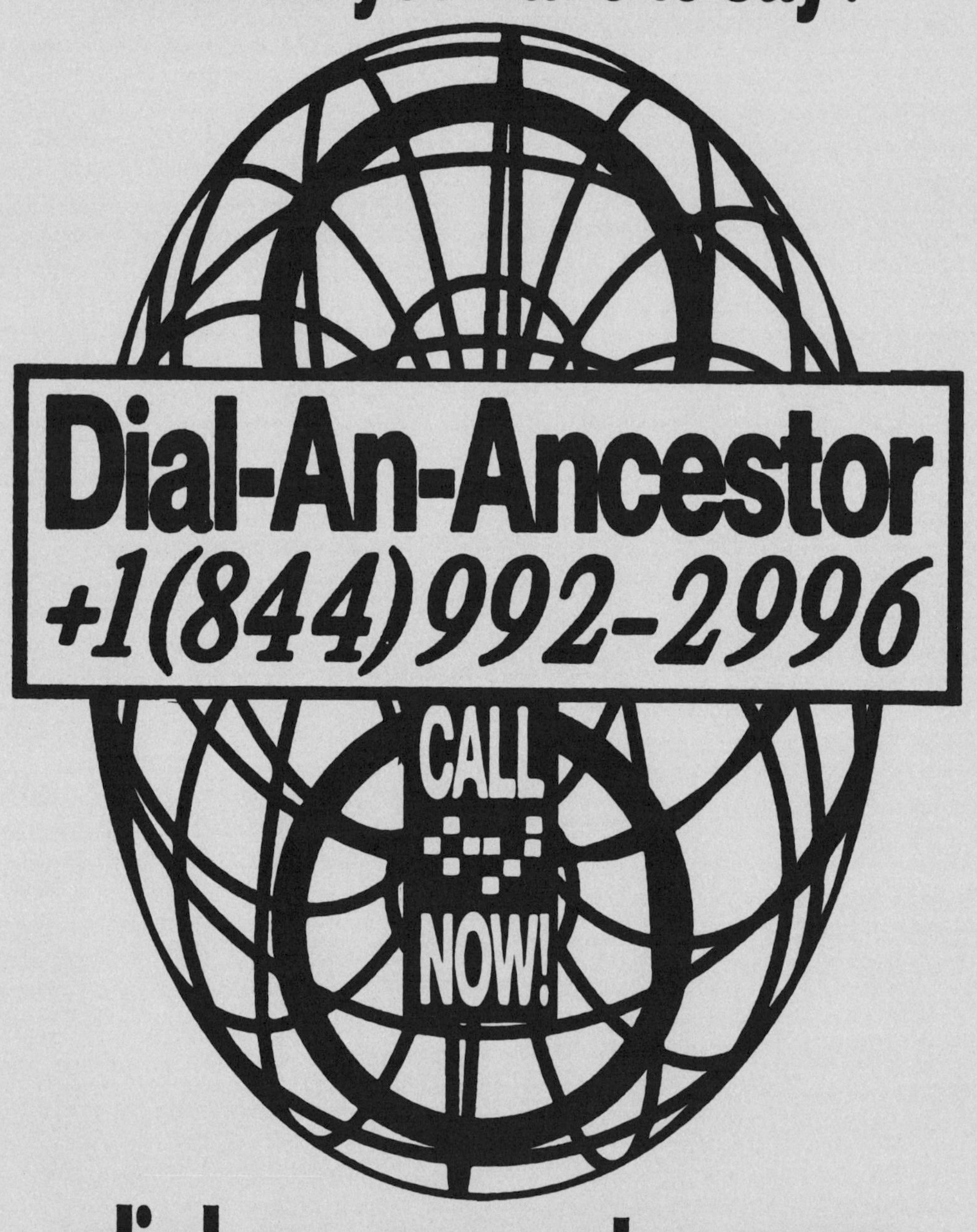

dial-an-ancestor.com

A long term participatory audio installation. Activated by us. Archiving for the future in real time.

WHY PARTICIPATE?

1. Archive and share knowledge, wisdom, and stories. We're all world-builders.

2. Cultivate deep time-humility. We're each somebody's ancestor. The hotline gets more generational as time passes. The aim is to keep it alive for 100 years.

3. Create links across space and time. We are connected in more ways than we recognize.

4. Explore connectedness and ancestry beyond DNA. We can be kinfolk beyond inherited lineage.

5. Say and hear what needs to be said. We can explore the many ways to be good ancestors, together in our many different voices. And then we can move accordingly.

BY TAMIKA ABAKA-WOOD

PRESS 1
TO LISTEN TO AN ANCESTOR

PRESS 2
TO SPEAK AS AN ANCESTOR

Tending to our
collective multiplicity

By Annika
Hansteen-Izora

Illustrations
by Jun Lin

ON DIGITAL GARDENS

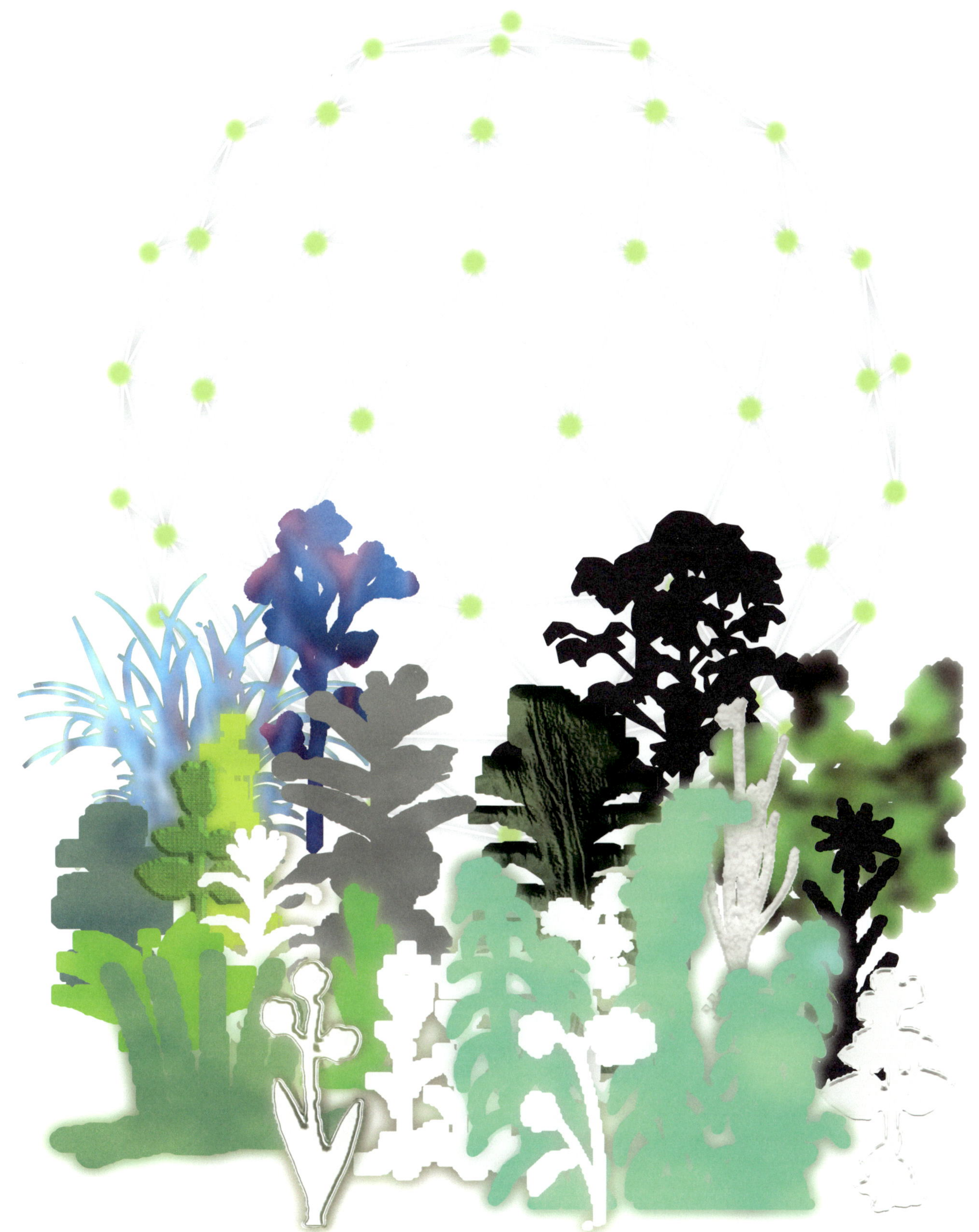

ANNIKA HANSTEEN-IZORA

"Guided by my heritage of a love of beauty and a respect
for strength—in search of my mother's garden, I found my own."
—Alice Walker, *In Search of our Mothers' Gardens*, 1967

"How do you take a walk with someone on the internet?"
—*Internet Walks*

I grew up in two locations: gardens and the internet. In both spaces, I'm learning what it means to tend to my individual and our collective dreams. My family has a lineage of gardening and techno-exploration, going as far back (in cataloged archive at least) as the garden my great-great-grandmother rooted in her 1920s Oakland home. I grew up tending both the tomato plants in our backyard and my digital art pieces in Kid Pix, later turning to online worlds like Neopets and my on-keyboard safe space of Tumblr. As a kid, gardens and the internet both offered a place to dream, create, and play.

But that was then. Today, the internet is an omnipresent force that organizes the ways we learn, connect, and love—often in ways that are more nefarious than virtuous. The internet is a place, and that place has largely been led by those who value the accumulation of capital over its users' access to safety, connection, or care.

Nature and technology are often only associated as the other's antithesis. Nature is alive, fluid, complex. Technology is machine, predictable, streamlined. The social media idiom "go touch some grass" encourages users to leave the internet for nature, the former supplying illusion and the latter providing truth. I don't disagree with this spectrum. Today, the imagination behind the internet is dominantly shaped by militarization, consumerism, and surveillance. Given the options, I understand the desire to log off and dream in greener places.

But perhaps the separtism between technology and the principles of nature is part of what led us towards this techno-doom reality. I'd offer that the space between digital worlds and nature is one we should linger in. Brand and product designer Frank Chimero noted in a 2018 talk at the Substans Conference in Bergen, Norway, that "if we're setting out to change the character of technology in our lives, we'd be wise to learn from the character of places."

What can the design of online worlds learn from the location of nature? What possibilities are lingering in the seeds of the digital garden?

Digital gardens have largely been understood as websites that allow users to explore and publish thoughts in more fluid and unpolished ways. The term "digital garden" is not new. It's been shaped by almost two decades of pondering, from early tinkerings in Mark Bernstein's 1998 essay "Hypertext Gardens" to Mike Caulfield's 2015 talk "The Garden and the Stream," which is credited with the term's first solid definition. Where so many of our feeds are designed around linear time, all major social networks and blogs follow a reverse chronological order, and everything we post is under pressure to be a perfected piece, digital gardens embrace the weird. Many have explored creating digital gardens through sections on personal websites that are dedicated to in-progress and non-linear ideas. My own blog has a digital garden: a page that is specifically for concepts I'm slowly mulling over without alignment to a particular goal or timeline. This behavior is succinctly described in Paul Ford's 2016 article "Reboot the World": "Everyone tends [their] own little epistemological garden, growing ideas from seed and sharing them with anyone who comes by."

These explorations have been critical for maintaining online spaces that embrace cyclical and ever-shifting thinking. In a techno-social world that is dominantly organized by the pressures of linear feeds, we need digital spaces and frameworks that celebrate the ideas that are seeds just as much as the fully formed blooms.

At the same time, as I wander the internet, I wonder where the digital gardens are that will connect me to fellow gardeners more deeply. More often than not, the digital gardens of today are botanic—privately owned online spaces made for visitors to fawn over while a "do not touch" sign looms in view. These private gardens are generative for our personal learning, but they are far from the communal gardens I grew up in that valued collective work and knowledge. Where are the digital gardens that lead us towards collective learning, play, and dreaming?

To that end, alongside many in the design sphere who are imagining digital worlds rooted in deeper learning, justice, and care, I offer my own fluid, ever-shifting definition of digital gardens.

A digital garden is a framework for speculation around how online space can be designed from the imagination of gardens. Here, the values of gardens, pluralism, interdependence, sustainability, adaptation, and discovery are centered in the design process of technosocial spaces. A garden is made up of the following parts:

Seeds: the content contributed by gardeners, such as text, photos, video, audio, or other digital media.

Gardeners: the users that invest in tending to and growing the garden.

Soil: the framework, meaning the design system and processes the garden is rooted in.

Elements for growth (such as water, sunlight, and the wellbeing of the gardeners): the design values that guide that garden.

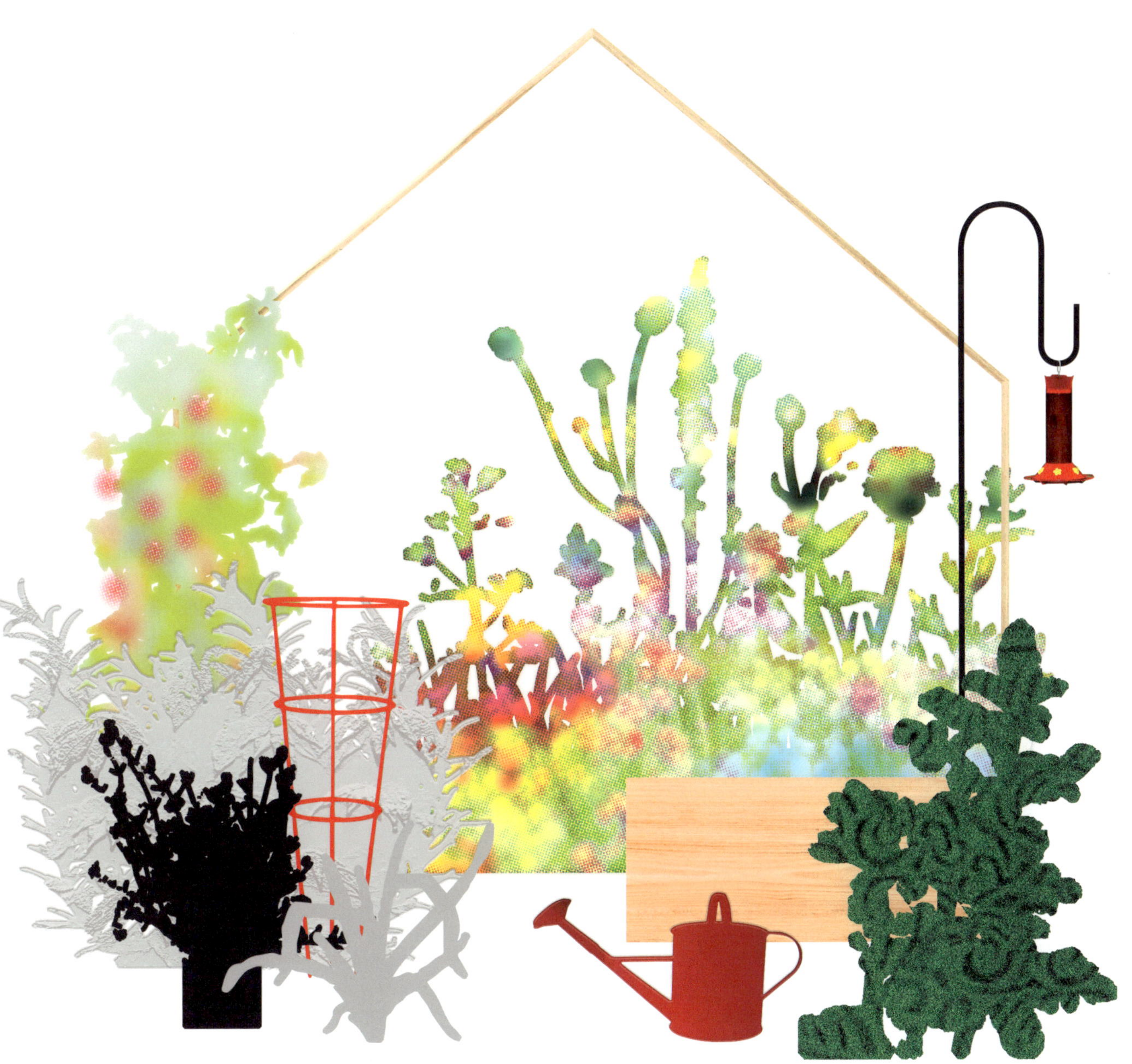

"TODAY, THE IMAGINATION BEHIND THE INTERNET IS DOMINANTLY SHAPED BY MILITARIZATION, CONSUMERISM, AND SURVEILLANCE. GIVEN THE OPTIONS, I UNDERSTAND THE DESIRE TO LOG OFF AND DREAM IN GREENER PLACES."

ANNIKA HANSTEEN-IZORA

Below are eight values that have guided my own understanding. (Note: this is by no means a complete list; any gardener knows that the lessons gardens offer are endless. Look at this as a collection of beginning seedlings, and an offering to tend to some of your own.)

Digital gardens are ecosystems that:

1

Dream past the colonial imaginings of gardens

Across time, gardens have been locations of colonization, classism, anti-Blackness, and racism, from the history of botany as a tool for colonization to the structural lack of access low-income Black neighborhoods have to public green spaces. Digital gardens take time to understand the complex ways systematic oppression appears in the material technoreality of digital spaces. Rather than design in opposition, digital gardens look towards frameworks outside the confines of supremacy, or to decolonized models of thought that have long existed.

2

Value pluralism and interdependence

Digital gardens are designed to value the contributions of multiple gardeners. Their design does not reward hierarchy. They strategize around design systems that allow interdependent care to be possible, consensually applied, and mutually given and received.

3

Invest in cyclical growth and sustainability

Digital gardens believe slow time is beautiful. They are designed to support us in reclaiming our time rather than being organized by it. Digital gardens reject the information highway for the clock where minutes are the lengths of easeful breath.

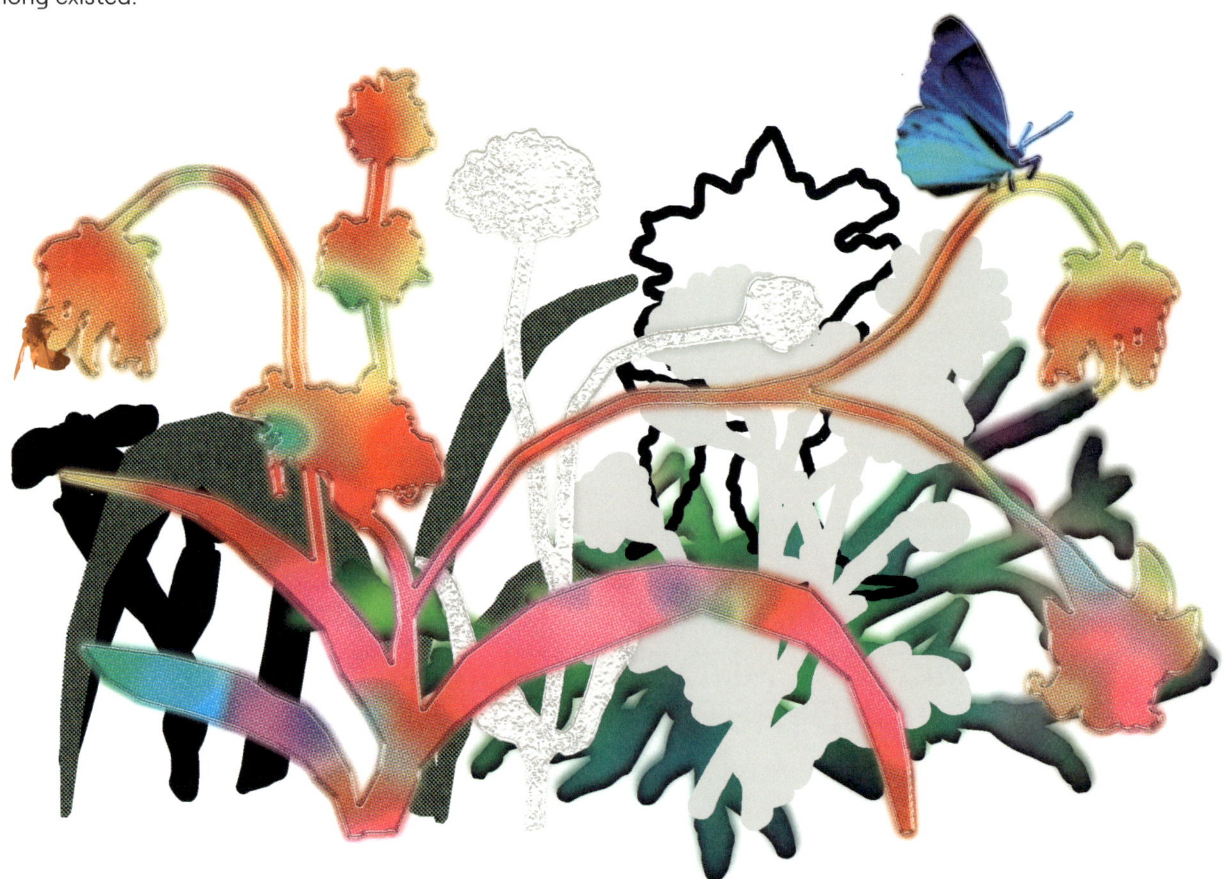

4
Reject linear time

Digital gardens believe time moves cyclically. They are bored of the reverse chronological feed that is the norm for the majority of social networks. They value iterative learning and adjust from conclusion as needed. They believe we should have easy access to our archives.

5
Embrace weeds

Digital gardens do not believe in nor aspire to Garden of Eden-style utopias. Digital gardens reject utopias, as they both ignore the realities of our intersecting positions of power and deny the cyclical existence of harm. We all will harm and be harmed. Instead, digital gardens recognize that periods of rot, weeds, and even death are natural parts of the ecosystem cycle. They value practice over perfection.

6
Stay adaptable

Digital gardens embrace that gardens and their gardeners are ever-shifting and complex. The design of digital gardens evolves to adapt to and value complexity. They embrace the design challenge of clarity that is not at the expense of its users' dynamicism.

7
Hold safety at the fore-front, not after-front

A garden is not without tools to ensure its safety. Boundaries, defined by Kamra Sadia Hakim in their work *Care Manual*, are containers housing needs and the distance at which mutual love exists. Boundaries are necessary for communal safety to be possible. Digital gardens create such protocols and give their users access to boundaries that enable transformation rather than carcerality and avoidance.

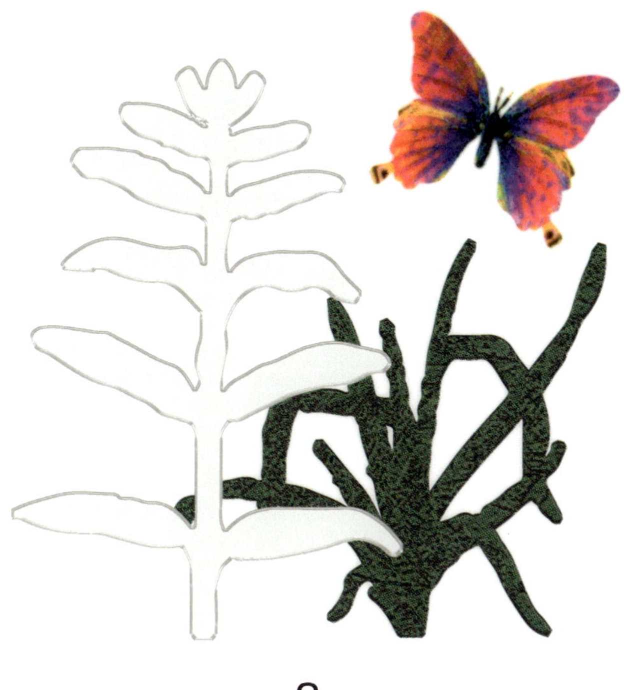

8
Look towards wonder

Digital gardens hold a component of discovery where gardeners may be delighted or surprised by what they find. They are designed to embrace a culture of learning, where one may be open to be changed by ideas.

Digital gardens are not about creating utopias. Rather, they design towards the small and slow progress of protopias, defined by futurist Kevin Kelly as "a state that is better today than yesterday." We need protopias, alternatives, and the seeds of gardens. We need space to dream, and for that dreaming to connect to concrete action.

The roots of digital gardens have long been growing, and many have arrived. We see their leaves in places like Somewhere Good, a social audio app for community conversations; are.na, a social network designed for slow learning and archiving; virtual care lab, a series of creative experiments in remote togetherness; and endless other seeds. Alongside one another, we believe in each other's collective smallness, and pull in digital gardens rooted in care, imagination, and joy.●

Annika Hansteen-Izora (they/she/he) is a multidisciplinary designer and artist. They explore the intersections of design, radical Black imagination, art, and technology to create ecosystems rooted in care.

On behalf of *Deem*, we would like to thank you for all the feedback, encouragement, and support. We value our community and look forward to connecting with you as we grow. Find more stories and stay up-to-date on future issues at deemjournal.com and on Instagram: @deemjournal

DISTRIBUTION
Deem is available through independent bookshops, specialty stores, and online. For our full distribution list, bulk orders, or to become a stockist, please contact: sales@deemjournal.com

PARTNERSHIPS
Deem seeks to align with like-minded organizations, brands, and communities that are driven by developing, fostering, and enabling solutions. For partnerships or special projects, please contact: partner@deemjournal.com

CONTACT
hello@deemjournal.com
www.deemjournal.com
Instagram: @deemjournal